DISCARDED

D1478942

THE ST. LOUIS
VEILED
PROPHET
CELEBRATION

THE ST. LOUIS

VEILED

PROPHET

CELEBRATION

 Power on
Parade,
1877–1995

THOMAS M. SPENCER

UNIVERSITY OF MISSOURI PRESS

COLUMBIA AND LONDON

Copyright © 2000 by
The Curators of the University of Missouri
University of Missouri Press, Columbia, Missouri 65201
Printed and bound in the United States of America

All rights reserved

5 4 3 2 1   04 03 02 01 00

Library of Congress Cataloging-in-Publication Data
Spencer, Thomas M. (Thomas Morris), 1967–
    The St. Louis veiled prophet celebration : power on parade,
1877–1995 / Thomas M. Spencer.
        p. cm.
    Includes bibliographical references and index.
    ISBN 0-8262-1267-0 (alk. paper)
    1. Veiled Prophet Parade, Saint Louis, (Mo.)—History. 2. Parades—
Missouri—Saint Louis—History. 3. Saint Louis, (Mo.)—History.
4. Saint Louis, (Mo.)—Social life and customs. I. Title: Saint Louis
veiled prophet celebration. II. Title.
GT4011.S2 S64 2000
394'.5'0977866—dc21
                                                                        99-057095

∞ ™ This paper meets the requirements of the
American National Standard for Permanence of Paper
for Printed Library Materials, Z39.48, 1984.

Text design: Elizabeth K. Young
Jacket design: Vickie Kersey DuBois
Typesetter: Crane Compostion, Inc.
Printer and binder: Thomson-Shore, Inc.
Typefaces: Usherwood

Frontispiece: *The Veiled Prophets Sixth Annual Autumnal Festival.*
Program cover chromolithograph by Compton Litho. Company, 1883.
Missouri Historical Society, St Louis.

To Melissa,

Michael, and Julia

Contents

Illustrations

Tables

Acknowledgments

There is probably nothing more difficult for an author than writing his acknowledgements, because it is a challenge to remember each person who helped along the way with research tips, advice, and simple but essential moral support. I hope that taking a chronological approach will help me to recall everyone. This monograph began at the University of Missouri in 1991 as my master's thesis, which formed the basis for the first two chapters. Therefore, I must first thank David R. Roediger, now at the University of Minnesota. Dave was my thesis adviser and helped me in my first baby steps towards becoming a professional historian. Additionally, I must thank Susan Porter Benson, now at the University of Connecticut, who also helped me a great deal in writing the thesis and served on my thesis committee as well. There were numerous graduate student colleagues at Missouri who pondered ideas about the Veiled Prophet celebration with me, including Steve McIntyre, Beth Ruffin, Kelly Hays, Kristine Stilwell, Randy McBee, Rebecca Thomas, Tony Carmona, and Tom Gubbels. Having this manuscript published by the University of Missouri Press is like bringing this project "back home" to Columbia where it first started.

In 1992, I moved to Bloomington and entered the doctoral program in the department of history at Indiana University. During my four years at IU, I received a great deal of assistance from numerous members of the history department, especially Peter Guardino, Jeff Gould, James Madison, and Irving Katz. However, the three who deserve the most thanks are my dissertation adviser, George Juergens, and my dissertation committee, John Bodnar and Bob Ivie. They read my manuscript carefully and made numerous helpful editorial suggestions. I also had many helpful grad student colleagues I need to thank for their informal assistance as well: Paul Murphy, John Chappell, Paul Schadewald, Andrew Denson, Michael Schreiner, Liz Osborn, Steve Sullivan, Patrick Ettinger, J. D. Bowers, Julie Berman of St. Louis University, Kelly Robison of the Center for U.S. Studies at Martin Luther King University (Germany), and Rose Feuer of Northern Illinois University.

At Northwest Missouri State University, I would like to thank the Faculty Research Committee for assisting me with a faculty research grant for the summer of 1998. This grant helped me to complete the final bits of research for the project. My colleagues in the History, Humanities, and Philosophy Department also deserve acknowledgment. They read partial drafts and helped me with final revisions to the manuscript you are now reading. In particular, I should mention Richard Frucht, Joel Benson, Tom Carneal, Janice Falcone, Jim Eiswert, and Michael Steiner. Other scholars who read the manuscript and helped me out with revisions include Lucy Ferris of Hamilton College, Gregg Andrews of Southwest Texas State University, Steve McIntyre of Southwest Missouri State University, and Roger Abrahams of the University of Pennsylvania. Their supportive words and helpful suggestions also helped me to fine-tune this manuscript.

I also need to thank those in St. Louis who helped me in my research. My greatest thanks go to Bill Olbrich and his wife, Lindy. Without their hospitality (they provided me with a bed to sleep in) and frequent productive bull sessions with them about the VP at Ted Drewe's Frozen Custard during the summer of 1995, the research for this book would not have been completed. I also would like to thank those at the Missouri Historical Society who over the years have aided my research as well, especially Kathy Corbett, Martha Clavenger, Joe Porter, and Martha Kohl. My oral interview subjects in St. Louis were also very helpful to me in writing this book, particularly Percy Green, Judge Johnson, Rusty Hager, Harold Wuertenbaecher, Ron Henges, Gena Scott, Jane Sauer, Margaret Phillips, Robert Tooley, Rusty Hager, Tom K. Smith, and Barbara Torrence. Without their insight, the story of the VP celebration during the last thirty years could not have been written. I also must thank Beverly Jarrett, the director of the University of Missouri Press, for her support through the review process and for doing such an excellent job preparing this manuscript for publication.

Finally, I must thank my family members. My parents, Tom and Gloria Spencer, helped pay for my first year of grad school at Missouri and later closely read versions of the manuscript. The week we all spent in May of 1996 proofreading the rough draft of the dissertation is not one we will soon forget. However, the biggest thanks go to my wife, Melissa Bradley Spencer, who has been along for the entire graduate school and dissertation-writing ride. I cannot adequately express in words my thanks to Melissa. She has been incredibly supportive, reading drafts and working at awful jobs in order to give me the time and the financial resources to research and write this book. To say that she has sacrificed for this book would be an understatement. Last but not least, I would like to thank my son, Michael, who was born the winter before I began my dissertation research. Michael provided important diversions from the stress of writing and made me occasionally rethink just what is truly important about life in general. It is to Melissa and Michael that I dedicate this book. Without their faith, support, and love, there would never have been a book on the Veiled Prophet celebration at all. I love them dearly.

THE ST. LOUIS
VEILED
PROPHET
CELEBRATION

# Introduction

THE SOCIAL MEANING OF PUBLIC
SPECTACLES IN THE NINETEENTH- AND
TWENTIETH-CENTURY UNITED STATES

Those of us who live at the turn of the millennium find it hard to imagine that a parade could be viewed as anything more significant than a few hours of innocent and trivial diversion. Some of us get up early on Thanksgiving to watch Macy's Thanksgiving Day Parade or, on New Year's Day, the beautiful Tournament of Roses Parade. Today, most Americans feel that parades are exclusively for the entertainment of children. It often seems like the floats are meant to be beautiful, inoffensive, and, most importantly, meaningless.

However, a century or so ago this was not the case. In recent years, scholars have become increasingly interested in the social meaning of urban public spectacles in nineteenth- and twentieth-century America. Scholars contend that these spectacles—whether strike parades, militia parades, or even celebrations of the Fourth of July—conveyed particular messages to designated audiences. The founders of the Veiled Prophet celebration in St. Louis had particular messages and audiences in mind as well when they designed their celebration.

In *Parades and Power,* Susan Davis argues that parades—the most prevalent sort of public spectacle—were "not only patterned by social forces" but were "a part of the very building and challenging of social relations" in the first half of the nineteenth century.[1] In other words, parades were part of a public discourse that reinforced the social order in some ways and challenged it in others. For example, strikers in Philadelphia used parades as both a show of collective working-class power and as a way to demonstrate to spectators that the strikers were led by "respectable men" for reasonable goals.

While Davis argues that social elites had a great deal of control over the street in the first half of the nineteenth century, opportunities also existed for members of the working class to make their concerns known to the public at large. The street was a fairly democratic arena for civic instruction and demonstration during the nineteenth century. Social groups in urban America could freely use the street for their own performances.

But by the turn of the century, the multivocal nature of the street had virtually disappeared. As industrialization changed the nature of American urban society, elites took control of the street as an arena for civic instruction and demonstration. By requiring parade and demonstration permits, elites tried to make it much more difficult to stage public spectacles or even to have parades at all. When "unregulated" assemblies took place, they were often forcibly suppressed by urban militia forces.[2] By 1900, the street had become the domain of political, industrial, and mercantile elites, as well as a growing class of upper-middle-class professionals.

In this study, the term *elite* refers to the wealthy businessmen, professionals, and government officials who took part in the Veiled Prophet organization. They certainly were elites in the political, social, and economic sense in nineteenth- and twentieth-century St. Louis. These men came from two rapidly emerging social groups that were gaining power in late-nineteenth-century St. Louis and elsewhere: the wealthy business class and the upper middle class. Whether working as insurance agents, lawyers, or managers, members of the upper middle class were now largely beholden to the business class for their livelihood. Therefore, the interests of these two classes had dovetailed by the late nineteenth century.

The elite class of St. Louisans were part of a growing national phenomenon of the period. These "genteel intellectuals," as some scholars refer to them, considered themselves "guardians of tradition" and viewed public celebrations as a means of educating their fellow citizens, especially members of the ethnic working class. According to David Glassberg, these elites "stood apart from the mass of their fellow citizens not only because of their wealth, educational attainment, and family status but also because they held positions of leadership in local and national cultural organizations" like the St. Louis Veiled Prophet organization.[3] They hoped to use popular culture for their own ends.

As Glassberg argues in *American Historical Pageantry,* during the first two decades of the twentieth century, elites tried to replace parades and official celebrations with allegorical public pageants. Through their use of allegory and selection of historical events, elites used these spectacles to convey the genteel values of social control, temperance, and industry to mostly working-class spectators. They believed these spectacles—modeled on Elizabethan pageants—were more suited than public parades for educating immigrants and the poor about American history, citizenship, and middle-class norms of proper behavior. Furthermore, elites used pageants for booster purposes, to create a form of community solidarity and collective progressive vision among the citizens of their cities. These pageants are clear examples of elites creating an element of popular culture—the pageant—for specific "educational" purposes. More than thirty years earlier, members of the Veiled Prophet organization had similar goals in mind for their celebration.

This study examines the social and cultural functions of the Veiled Prophet celebration in St. Louis, Missouri. These functions have changed greatly over the last century. What began in 1878 as a symbolic attempt to assert business-class control over the streets of St. Louis became by the 1990s a rather innocuous civic celebration. In the intervening century, the celebration went through several distinct stages—each having its own set of characteristics. This work will attempt to trace the shifts in the celebration's cultural meaning and importance over more than a century.

The Veiled Prophet organization has been a St. Louis institution since 1878. A group of prominent St. Louis businessmen modeled the organization on the New Orleans Carnival society of the Mystick Krewe of Comus. They formed the organization largely in response to a general strike by workers the summer before, when workers had both symbolically and physically gained control of the streets. A Veiled Prophet, who was to "preside and be recognized as infallible," led the organization. It is not publicly known how the Veiled Prophet was (or is) chosen, only that he has always been a successful local businessman.

The organization annually puts on the Veiled Prophet celebration, which consists of the Veiled Prophet parade and ball. In the nineteenth and early twentieth century the parade was a group of related tableaux, each representing a scene that fit in with that year's theme. For example, the first parade's theme, the "Festival of Ceres," included floats depicting various Greek and Roman gods advocating capitalist values. However, the parade's primary function from the beginning was to be a show of physical power. Parading by on the tops of floats, the members laid claim to the streets. Portraying themselves as royalty set above their social inferiors, the members tried to reinforce the social hierarchy. This theme would continue to be important throughout the celebration's history. Whether they in fact controlled St. Louis economically or politically, the elites used the celebration as a yearly chance to claim symbolically that they were in control.

The Veiled Prophet ball began and continued as a courtship ritual for the daughters of St. Louis's wealthiest families. Attending the ball is still an important symbol of social status among upper-class St. Louisans.

Throughout the past fifty years, many different ideas have been advanced about the origins of the Veiled Prophet organization. Most theories have not involved close research and have been written in many cases—especially the annual October newspaper stories—for entertainment purposes. Thus, Chapter 1 probes the murky origins of the organization, examining the alleged ties between the Veiled Prophet celebration and the Railroad Strike of 1877. The chapter argues that the Veiled Prophet parade represented an effort by members of the St. Louis business class to reclaim the streets of St. Louis from the working class and to substitute its own version of "street theater" for that which workers had formerly provided.

Chapter 2 examines the detailed newspaper accounts of the Veiled Prophet organization's annual autumn parades and debutante balls in St. Louis from their founding in 1878 to 1899. These parades presented St. Louis history and American history as the story of the triumphs of great men—who happened to be the Veiled Prophet members' ancestors. Veiled Prophet members portrayed themselves as the hereditary aristocracy of St. Louis. They wished to inculcate a civic patriotism that encouraged loyalty to the nation-state, the community, and to the elites themselves. These parades also provided spectators with advice on morals and social issues.

Chapter 3 examines the celebration as it evolved between 1900 and 1942. The celebrations continued to include educational and historical elements but began to reflect the commercialized leisure that was increasingly becoming a part of everyday life. Strangely enough, the most significant attempts to teach history through the parade occurred in the celebrations that took place between 1929 and 1933. In these parades the Veiled Prophet organization continued to teach spectators about St. Louis history, American history, and the life of George Washington. Due to the rapid changes in American culture at the time, this was the last time the organization used the parade for educational purposes. The chapter ends at the beginning of the Second World War, when elites used the parade to sell war bonds, thus more strongly linking the Veiled Prophet celebration and national patriotism. Parades ceased thereafter to be the large-scale civic events they once had been. Veiled Prophet parade floats became the whimsical creations we see in parades today.

Chapter 4 explores the celebration from 1946 to 1965. During this period members of the organization continued to control St. Louis both economically and politically. The celebration still drew large crowds and was closely covered by the news media. The ball was even televised nationally during the late 1940s. On the other hand, interest in the celebration among its own members began to wane. It became less important for elites to have the parade yearly to symbolize their control of St. Louis.

Chapter 5 studies the celebration between 1965 and 1980. The protests of civil rights groups like Percy Green's ACTION made many St. Louisans view the parade and ball as wasteful conspicuous consumption—often subsidized with taxpayers' money. The African American community became fed up with the elitism of the Veiled Prophet celebration. Membership in the organization dropped, the parade was covered less by the news media, and the organization withered.

Chapter 6 probes the celebration in its post-1981 form. In the early 1980s the leadership of the Veiled Prophet organization came up with the idea of having a VP Fair over each Fourth of July weekend. Once again the members tried to link the celebration to patriotism. Nevertheless, the phrase *Veiled Prophet* is seldom used by the organization anymore. The favored term now is *VP,* apparently to distance the organization from its past. In its latest incarnation, the Veiled Prophet parade is merely part of the larger spectacle, and the ball has been moved to a later date. In 1995, the annual celebration was renamed Fair St. Louis. By changing the name, the organization was for the first time admitting that the name *Veiled Prophet* was offensive to African American St. Louisans. The name change was an attempt to jettison the baggage of the ACTION protests of the 1960s.

This monograph studies the elites' use of public space and public commemoration over more than a century. While much recent historical work has analyzed the more democratic parades of the eighteenth and mid-nineteenth centuries, very little has been done to examine the less inclusive, elite-dominated parades of the late nineteenth and twentieth centuries. This work shows why such pluralistic parades ceased to exist and why elites felt it was so important to end them.

1. *The Veiled Prophet.* Woodcut from the *Missouri Republican,* October 6, 1878. Missouri Historical Society, St. Louis.

# Power on Parade

THE ORIGINS OF THE VEILED PROPHET CELEBRATION

The above steel engraving represents the original Veiled Prophet himself. The artist has caught very cleverly the expression of benignant firmness on his countenance, and shown with rare fidelity the dignity of his attitude. . . . It will be readily observed from the accoutrements of the Prophet that the procession is not likely to be stopped by street cars or anything else.

MISSOURI REPUBLICAN, OCTOBER 6, 1878

Newspaper articles in St. Louis today tout the Veiled Prophet as a mysterious, beneficent prince who receives St. Louis debutantes at the Veiled Prophet ball. The first Veiled Prophet had a very different image. A newspaper sketch pictured him in white robes, mask, and pointed hat, carrying a pistol and a shotgun, with a second shotgun well within reach. In the accompanying description, published alongside the picture in the *Missouri Republican,* the writer pointed to the prophet's ample "accoutrements" (weapons) as a sign that he would not be stopped "by street cars"—whose workers had recently participated in a general strike—or "anything else." Probably written by a founding member of the Veiled Prophet organization, the description underlined the image's message that the Veiled Prophet parade was intended as an expression of class and racial control.[1]

One of the more common theories to explain the origins of the St. Louis Veiled Prophet parade ties it to the general strike of 1877. A response to cuts in wages by several railroad companies for the third time in four years, the St. Louis general strike was the first of its kind in the United States and probably the most successful general strike in the nation's history. Newspaper feature stories since the 1950s have described the "first Veiled Prophet parade" as "a way of healing the wounds of a bitter labor-management fight," the strike of 1877. However, the first Veiled Prophet parade was more a show of power than a gesture of healing.[2]

The October scheduling of the Veiled Prophet celebration placed it right after the harvest, one of the pivotal events of the year for the mercantile business class. This was a time when St. Louis needed to make its best impression because farmers, their major work done, flocked to the city to sell their crops and attend the St. Louis Agricultural and Mechanical Fair. With many of the Veiled Prophet's founding members in businesses that depended upon St. Louis's position as an agricultural trading center, economic self-interest played a large part in the organization's creation. Hoping to engage the rowdy members of the working class long enough for St. Louis to make a good impression on the visiting farmers, the Veiled Prophet's organizers decided to produce a grand spectacle. They also hoped the parade would boost farmers' attendance at the fair, the popularity of which had waned after the Civil War.

Thus motivated by their own ambitions and concerns, members of the St. Louis elite founded the Veiled Prophet organization for several reasons: to assert control over the city streets after a serious challenge by St. Louis labor; to woo farmers into selling their crops to St. Louis merchants and attending the St. Louis Agricultural and Mechanical Fair; and to provide an elite organization through which businessmen could make contacts that would advance their careers. This complex collection of goals, only some of which were explicitly expressed, become clear after looking at the history and context of the Veiled Prophet organization and parade.

The Veiled Prophet organization was founded in March 1878 when a short letter arrived at the doors of approximately twenty St. Louis businessmen. It invited them to "attend a meeting of prominent gentlemen" with the object of promoting "the interests of St. Louis."[3] At the private meeting, whose minutes were leaked to the press, they discussed substituting a New Orleans–style pageant for the trade procession usually held in association with the week-long annual St. Louis Agricultural and Mechanical Association Fair. According to Charles Slayback, one of the founding members, as a result of "this meeting the Veiled Prophet started." At a second meeting a week later, the Originals—as the first fourteen members were later called—

established rules and a structure for their fledgling organization. The exclusivity of the Veiled Prophet organization was reflected in this structure: they limited its membership to two hundred, and, although originally the initiation fee was twenty-five dollars, by December 1878 the organization raised it to one hundred dollars, or one sixth of the average workingman's yearly wages.[4]

The organization set up a minimal—but clearly delineated—hierarchy for itself. The officers of the organization included the Veiled Prophet (or Grand Oracle) and two high priests. The Veiled Prophet was to "be recognized as infallible."[5] This policy certainly reflected the views of the Veiled Prophet organization members, who believed that hierarchy and absolute control of subordinates—especially their own workers—was a natural and altogether good thing.

Much of the inspiration for the actual form of the Veiled Prophet parade came from two brothers, Charles and Alonzo Slayback. Charles Slayback, who has been called "the VP's Patron Saint," had recently moved his business as a commercial merchant to St. Louis from New Orleans, where he had been a member of the New Orleans Carnival society, the Mysticke Krewe of Comus.[6] With the support of the fourteen Originals, he arranged to purchase twenty thousand dollars' worth of float paraphernalia from his "brothers" in Comus for eight thousand dollars. Several of the Originals—and a few new members recruited for this purpose—owned barges and tows; they volunteered to transport the equipment upriver free of charge.[7] Once the paraphernalia arrived, Charles's brother Alonzo Slayback stepped in. Inspired by Thomas Moore's popular poem *Lalla Rookh*—and possibly by Comus's 1868 Mardi Gras float interpretation of the poem—Alonzo Slayback wrote "The First Panorama of Progress of the Veiled Prophets."[8] From this point onward, preparation for the first Veiled Prophet celebration—and the creation of the organization through the induction of the first two hundred members—began in earnest.

Who were these founders of the Veiled Prophet—as the first two hundred members were called—and why did they join the organization? Of the two hundred founders, only the names of seventy-three are known.[9] These seventy-three were a diverse lot. Their ages ranged from twenty-seven to sixty-eight. While the few native St. Louisans in the group were from "old money," including two members of the Chouteau family and eight other wealthy and well-connected families, most of the members came from elsewhere (see Table 1).

2. *Alonzo Slayback.* Steel engraving by Western Engraving Company, 1883. Missouri Historical Society, St. Louis.

Table 1   BIRTHPLACES OF FOUNDING MEMBERS

Birthplace	Number (total members: 63)
St. Louis	10
Out-state Missouri	5
Total born in Missouri:	**15 (24%)**
Illinois	2
Michigan	2
Ohio	5
Total born in Midwest/Old Northwest:	**9 (14%)**
Connecticut	1
Massachusetts	4
New Hampshire	1
New Jersey	2
New York	5
Pennsylvania	2
Rhode Island	1
Vermont	1
Total born in Northeast:	**17 (27%)**
Delaware	1
Kentucky	4
Louisiana	1
Maryland	4
Virginia	4
Total born in South:	**14 (22%)**
Cuba	1
Germany	3
Ireland	2
Scotland	1
West Indies	1
Total foreign born:	**8 (13%)**

Table 2 FOUNDING MEMBERS' ARRIVAL IN ST. LOUIS

Time Span	Number (total members: 56)
St. Louis natives	10 (18)%
1830s	1
1840s	10
1850s	9
1860	2
Total arrivals before Civil War:	22 (39%)
1861–1865	10
Total arrivals during Civil War:	10 (18%)
1865–1869	6
1870s	8
Total arrivals after the Civil War:	14 (25%)

Approximately 39 percent arrived before the Civil War, 18 percent arrived during the conflict, and 25 percent arrived after (see Table 2). The founding members had served on both sides of the conflict; nine had fought for the Union and seven for the Confederacy. Founded within a year of the official end of Reconstruction, the Veiled Prophet organization may very well have provided a place where sectional disagreements were finally put to rest between these elites. However, most of the members had not been known for their fervent partisanship during the war. In 1861 at least thirty-nine of the founding members were between the ages of twenty and thirty-five, which placed them in the prime age group for participation in the war. Yet of this thirty-nine, only sixteen had fought on either side. The founders' political affiliations—which are known for only eleven of the seventy-three men—seem equally mixed: six were Democrats and five were Republicans.

Only their ambition and class background united these men. Most of the founding members came from upper-class or upper-middle-class families. There were no "rags-to-riches" stories among them. Several of their fathers, for example, owned major commercial firms, publishing houses, or large Southern plantations. The remaining members had solid upper-middle-class backgrounds, raised by fathers who managed large farms, owned and ran mills, or worked as commercial merchants.[10]

Whatever their fathers' occupation, all of the founding members had come to St. Louis to make money. Most had arrived in St. Louis as young men, hoping to cash in on the business opportunities created by the small economic boom of the war years and the more extensive postwar boom. Striving to become successful businessmen at a time when boosters called St. Louis the "Future Great City of the World," they saw their destinies as linked to the city's growth.[11]

This concern for growth provides another primary explanation for the founders' participation in the Veiled Prophet organization. Contrary to the claims of some historians, St. Louis's businessmen during the postbellum nineteenth century did not wait "complacently for an inevitable process to make them rich and powerful."[12] Rather, the creation of the Veiled Prophet pageant was part of an energetic effort by St. Louis's business class to expand the city's hinterland. By providing a spectacle to lure farmers to St. Louis at the end of the harvest, the organizers believed that they could increase St. Louis's share in the agricultural trade, since the farmers would bring their crops with them to the city rather than selling them to agents elsewhere in Missouri or, worse, selling them to agents in Chicago.

Although definitely too little too late, the Veiled Prophet celebration was the St. Louis business class's most innovative—and possibly most effective—attempt to do battle with Chicago economically during the last two decades of the nineteenth century. However laudable the effort, most historians agree that the competition with Chicago was already decided by the late 1870s.[13] Nonetheless, while St. Louis may have lost the economic battle for the upper Mississippi valley, the city would expand its economic influence southward during the Gilded Age via railroad construction. St. Louis would become a regional center for the shipping of raw materials from the midsouth and southwest during this period. Unfortunately, St. Louis would not become the "Future Great City of the World" that its boosters in the Veiled Prophet organization had hoped it would.[14]

Many of the Veiled Prophet's members stood to benefit directly from the expected increase in agricultural trade brought by a revitalized agricultural and mechanical fair (see Table 3). Merchants of various types dominated the Veiled Prophet organization; 34 percent of the founding members either traded or processed agricultural and in-

Table 3 OCCUPATIONS OF FOUNDING MEMBERS, 1878

Occupational Category	Number (total members: 73)
Commercial Merchant	13
Cotton Merchant	5
Tobacco	3
Milling	3
Malting	1
Total Agricultural Commerce	25 (34%)
Railroad Freight Agent	3
Railroad Management/Supplies	4
River Transportation	4
Total Commercial Transportation	11 (15%)
Dry Goods	4
Hardware	3
Grocery	2
Wholesale Ice	1
Total Merchants	10 (14%)
Lawyer	10
Total Professionals	10 (14%)
Newspapers	3
Gould's Directory	1
Telegraph Company	1
Total Public Communication	5 (7%)
Iron Manufacture	3
Castor Oil Manufacture	1
Lead and Oil	1
Total Industry	5 (7%)
Insurance	3
Banking	1
Carpentry	1
Merchants Exchange	1
Real Estate	1
Total Other Occupations	7 (10%)

Note: Unless otherwise stated, it can be assumed that individuals either are proprietors or hold upper-level management positions.

dustrial products, or depended on selling commercial products to farmers. Agricultural trade also weighed heavily for the 15 percent in commercial transportation and for the individuals whose insurance businesses competed to insure the barges transporting the crops downriver.

The founders stood to benefit from any increase in business-class prosperity. Lawyers, the second largest single occupational group in the sample (14 percent), had good reason to join with their clients in creating this organization. So did the publishers, who were dependent on advertising revenue, and the commercial bankers and real estate agents, who specialized in business properties. In all, approximately three-fourths of the founders had reasons of economic self-interest for joining the Veiled Prophet organization.

Joining the organization also provided members with a large number of potential business contacts. In fact, the business influence of the founding members was astounding. For example, nine of the founders served as president of the St. Louis Merchants Exchange during the fifteen-year period from 1872 to 1887, and twenty-four of these men were listed as members of the Merchants Exchange in 1878. Many of the founders were also politically powerful. George Bain was a longtime Republican city alderman who had been instrumental in passing and enforcing the St. Louis Social Evil Ordinance during the city's experiment with regulating prostitutes in the early 1870s.[15] Three of the other founders were intimately involved on both sides of the political and judicial battle over the St. Louis Home Rule Charter of 1876. In other words, the organization's founding members were good men to know for those who needed to negotiate their way through the intricacies of Gilded Age business and politics.

But if the founders were concerned with their own business opportunities, they also saw those opportunities as connected to the growth of the city as a whole. Like others of their age, they charted their city's progress—and their own opportunities—through statistical measurements, registered in the government census and the eagerly awaited annual Merchants Exchange reports, which listed all of the trade that had passed through St. Louis. Believing that growth of any kind was good, the Veiled Prophet's founders were committed to anything that would encourage the city's development and the expansion of its market share. As a "shot in the arm" for the St. Louis Agricultural and Mechanical Fair, the Veiled Prophet parade promised to do just that.[16] Like the New Orleans Carnival societies on which it was modeled—and which had their roots in the same sort of boosterism—the Veiled Prophet organization was designed to advance the economic standing of the city while its members advanced their own fortunes.[17]

If boosting trade was one of the main goals of the Veiled Prophet organization, class control was a second, equally important objective. As did its counterpart in New Orleans, the Veiled Prophet organization produced spectacles carefully constructed to reify the social order, with the organization's members at the pinnacle. Like Comus's Mardi Gras flotilla, the Veiled Prophet parade was intended to awe the "masses toward passivity" with its symbolic show of power.[18] Distracting workers from less desirable behavior—drinking, carousing, or parading through the streets creating their own rowdy spectacle—the organizers of the Veiled Prophet parade hoped to present St. Louis's best face to incoming farmers at a crucial time.

When the Veiled Prophet parade was conceived in 1878, the fear of working-class and racial disruption was justified. Just the year before St. Louis had experienced a week-long general strike, the first and most successful such strike in the nation's history. The strike paralyzed the city from Sunday, July 22, to Thursday, July 26, 1877. Although St. Louis's business class ultimately won the strike, the disruption had a profound effect on those who had been required to use force against their own workers. Also, many African American workers participated in the strike, thus providing the business class with a sense that black St. Louisans did not know their "proper place."

Given this context, it is not surprising that a year later St. Louis businessmen would want to affirm the established order. Nor should the mechanism that they hit upon to do so—the Veiled Prophet parade—cause surprise, for in the nineteenth century parades were a commonly used form of communication. They allowed marchers to transmit images, assert demands, and either reinforce or challenge the social order.[19] Whether held by strikers or by those organized to put down a strike, parades spoke to observers, who filtered the marchers' visual message through their own views, and sometimes responded with parades of their own. Thus the Veiled Prophet parade became the final statement in a heated debate that had begun with the workers' parades during the general strike a year before.

On Tuesday morning, July 24, 1877, members of the Coopers' Union issued the opening sally in this debate with a march on the downtown business district. Asserting their courage by marching through their employers' turf, the orderliness of their parade sent the message that respectable men with reasonable goals were leading the strike. It was this sort of orderly parade that most effectively served working-class interests, since the business class was quick to point to more rowdy displays as a justification to use force in suppressing a strike. The leaders of the strike clearly had this sort of respectable image in mind when they planned the Tuesday morning parade.

A Tuesday afternoon parade of mostly moulders and mechanics appeared more threatening and elicited concern from business leaders and their allies. Marching four abreast and led by a single torch and a fife and drum, many of the approximately fifteen hundred marchers carried lathes or clubs on their shoulders. Periodically a wave of sound would sweep through the march as a shout rose in front, "gaining volume as it rolled back to the rear." As one newspaper reported, it was "an awfully suggestive spectacle."[20] Responding to the perceived threat, business leaders met Tuesday night to form the Committee of Public Safety.

Strike leaders, attempting to regain control over the image of the strike, planned an impressive and orderly parade on Wednesday afternoon. Forbidding the participation of boys under sixteen, they made the right to march in the parade a token of manhood and simultaneously assured a calmer group of marchers, since young boys often proved to be troublemakers. Before the parade the workmen were instructed to "keep sober and orderly," and parade marshals (probably union officials) "passed along the line, cautioning against all acts of violence, and even taking clubs from a number of men." Led by a marching band, the strikers, probably numbering three to five thousand, then proceeded four abreast.[21] Yet the parade failed in its intent to assert both power and respectability through an orderly, well-organized presentation.[22] The participation of black workers led pro-business newspapermen to describe the Wednesday parade as a "riot" led by "negro roustabouts." The newspaper editors were careful to point out that black workers had public roles in the strike, therefore allowing them to discredit the motives of the strikers. In addition, a few marchers broke into stores and looted small amounts of bread and soap during the parade, causing the *St. Louis Dispatch* to characterize the strikers as "tramps and loafers" who were "anxious to pillage and plunder."[23]

The strikers had no more parades, perhaps because strike leaders felt that the looting on Wednesday afternoon had undermined their reputation for maintaining order and lessened their chance of being deputized by Mayor Henry Overstolz to keep the peace if that should become necessary.[24] Being deputized by Overstolz would show that the mayor believed the workers to be responsible and that the strike's goals were reasonable. However, by refusing to have more parades, strike leaders essentially gave up control of the streets. The elite-controlled citizen's militia acted swiftly the next day, storming Schuler Hall, the union meeting place, and ending the strike.

Having won the strike, business leaders seized the chance to regain the streets with a citizen's militia parade on the Tuesday following strike week. Marching along an irregular route through working-class neighborhoods, the citizen's militia parade was a simple show of armed power. As Lucien Eaton, a member of the Tenth Ward Guards, put it in a letter to his wife, "The show was very impressive. The mob was quite a sight and if here and there an angry face was seen it was sullen. . . . We marched so as to show that we were no myth but flesh and blood, bullets and bayonets."[25]

The Veiled Prophet celebration of 1878 represented a much more complex statement of class control. It was organized by the same men who had joined forces to restore order a year earlier; five of the Original Fourteen had large and very public roles in putting down the strike. They included city police commissioner John G. Priest, George Bain, John A. Scudder, and Leigh O. Knapp. Bain and Scudder acted as recruiters for the official city force, which was organized separately from the privately funded citizen's militia. Knapp, selected as adjutant-general of the citizen's militia, personally commanded the militia in the raid on Schuler Hall that broke the strike.[26]

When the Veiled Prophet parade was conceived, the immediate crisis had passed. With the strike suppressed, the business class felt it necessary to instruct St. Louisans on respect for hierarchy. The Veiled Prophet parade satisfied this need. By having a parade every year that showed a make-believe Middle Eastern king and his court, the St. Louis elite asserted the value of social hierarchy both in the mythical kingdom of Khorassan and in the real world of St. Louis. The fact that it was organized by the same people who had organized the citizen's militia, and that only the elite were invited to join, made clear the outlines of that hierarchy. Working-class St. Louisans who watched the spectacle may have felt wonder, as many of the newspapers of the time reported. This feeling was likely coupled with a more basic understanding of their position: Their social betters were riding in the floats; they were watching from the street.

Although the Veiled Prophet did not appear as earlier pictured in the *Missouri Republican* (carrying pistols and shotguns and wearing a white robe and pointed hat), the parade-day "accoutrements" of the first Veiled Prophet in the 1878 parade lend further credence to the most basic class-control interpretation. He was accompanied on his float by a "villainous looking executioner and a blood curdling butcher's block." Combined with the newspaper's written warning, this simple symbol effectively conveyed to working-class and black spectators what could happen to them if they went against the "natural" class order.[27]

The choice of Police Commissioner John G. Priest as the first Veiled Prophet also supports the class-control interpretation. The only prophet whose name has ever been released to the public, Priest was well known throughout the city for his active role in suppressing the strike.[28] He was also instrumental in forming police reserve groups whose role was to put down strikes in the year since the general strike. By March 1878, five hundred reservists drilled regularly in nine companies.[29] Workers obviously knew Priest as one of the people who had compelled their surrender. The man who had helped to take the streets by force during the strike now continued to rule over them during the Veiled Prophet celebration a year later, acclaimed as the king of St. Louis through his selection as Veiled Prophet.

St. Louis's business leaders hoped that the symbolic crowning of Priest as Veiled Prophet would help bolster the social order. Thousands of St. Louisans of all classes watched Priest's coronation; for the Veiled Prophet's founders, the crowd's presence at the ceremony signified St. Louis's acceptance of the social hierarchy. The members of the audience were expected to accord proper deference to their new king, just as it was hoped that they would continue to defer to their social betters after the conclusion of the pageant.

Whether the members of the audience accepted their assigned role is unclear. It can be argued that they did, at least to an extent, because otherwise, they would not have participated in the ritual. On the other hand, since parades were a major source of entertainment in the late nineteenth century, a case can also be made that parade spectators were not necessarily showing deference to their social betters simply by looking on.

The Veiled Prophet organization gave those who viewed themselves as the social and economic rulers of St. Louis a way to celebrate their status in a public way. Through their celebration, they greeted one another as members of an elite and reminded the less privileged of their place as well. The Veiled Prophet parade enabled St. Louis's city fathers to reward peace with a flamboyant spectacle, while at the same time asserting their absolute control over the city and conveying a readiness to meet all challengers.

What sort of men could come up with this kind of public spectacle? Recent scholarship by Sam Kinser that presents New Orleans Carnival societies as having their roots in "city father" boosterism helps us to analyze the Veiled Prophet organization.

Kinser sees the postbellum nineteenth century as a transition period "between the two eras of local and national concentration of socioeconomic power," calling it "the period of civism." During this time, "the largest population centers became more than large towns and overgrown villages." As Kinser argues, this era was typified by "city fathers, gravely black-frocked, bearded gentleman whose portraits line the walls of city halls and libraries across the country. . . . Cities had become indispensable points of passage toward whatever was more local or more national than they seemed to be, and at the same time they thought of themselves . . . as the very embodiment of local peculiarities and national goals." Although Kinser used this analysis to set up his discussion of the development of New Orleans Carnival societies, he could not have more accurately described the founding members of the Veiled Prophet organization, especially the "Originals." All one has to do is pick up any of the contemporary history "encyclopedias" and see the way these men's biographies are presented to understand that they were seen as "city fathers" by the booster-minded historians of the day. Most of these men have their own entries and are listed as "contributing to the development of the trade of the Mississippi and its tributaries," or as helping St. Louis to progress economically in one way or another.[30]

The city fathers of St. Louis believed they knew what was best for the city and did not appreciate challenges of any kind, no matter how trivial, from "lesser" men. The "city father" personality tended to consist of three major traits: self-confidence; pride (some would say arrogance); and a belief, strongly reinforced by booster propaganda, of their own personal infallibility. In fact, the closest that one of these encyclopedias came to admitting human imperfection on the part of one of these men was the statement that he "seldom made mistakes."[31]

However, the most pervasive personality trait among the "city fathers" was their need to have "lesser" men, whom they saw as being their economic dependents, defer to them. Both Colonel J. C. Normile and Alonzo Slayback, two of the three on the committee in charge of naming the organization, met violent ends resulting from quarrels over alleged libelous comments in the *Post-Dispatch*. It is in their stories that the personality traits most clearly manifested themselves. As a group they viewed journalists as dependents because much of a newspaper's profits came from the advertisements they placed. They were also used to dealing with the editors of a rabidly pro-business publication like the *Missouri Republican*. The middle-of-the-road and more journalistic approach of the recently founded *Post-Dispatch* came as a shock to them. In fact, the *Post-Dispatch*'s attitude seemed like a betrayal of a close (but subordinate) family relationship.

Shortly after the Veiled Prophet's fifth "visit" in 1882, Alonzo Slayback got into a political quarrel with John Cockerill, editor of the *Post-Dispatch*. Cockerill had printed an editorial that insulted Slayback's law partner, Colonel James Broadhead, who was at that time running for a seat in the U.S. Congress. On October 13, 1882, Slayback entered the *Post-Dispatch* building, according to a *Missouri Republican* headline, "to vindicate his manhood." Although accounts differed depending on who the witnesses supported, a friend of Slayback's claimed that Slayback "intended only to slap Cockerill. He carried no weapon, following in this his usual custom." This was the standard course of action for social betters who felt their honor had been impugned by a "lesser" man. Along with this code of paternalistic honor went the need for "lesser men" to defer to the judgement of their betters or, in this case, that of the "city fathers."[32] Cockerill, who was purposefully berating Broadhead in order to bait Slayback, failed to give "proper deference." For whatever reason, shortly after Slayback entered Cockerill's office, Cockerill shot him. Slayback died shortly thereafter.[33]

Colonel J. C. Normile, another member of the committee that named the organization, met an even stranger end. Normile began serving as a judge in the criminal court in the mid-1880s. In 1892, Normile felt that a *Post-Dispatch* editorial written by Orrick Johns that called him a "bump on a log" was libelous and brought a $400,000 lawsuit against the newspaper. At this point, "Instead of placating him, Johns wrote a series of paragraphs making sport of his (Normile's) vanity. These paragraphs got under Normile's skin and the libel suit went on to the courts."[34] One sees in the episode the ultimate expression of the "city father's" belief in "proper deference." Normile, who believed he was due a great deal more respect and deference because of his identity as a "city father," called this rather mild reference "libelous."

Truth-telling was part of the honor code of these city fathers. To be caught in a lie was quite a blow to a man's honor and ego. On the first day of the trial, Normile was called to the stand. The *Post-Dispatch*'s attorney, instead of asking any questions about the case itself, first asked a seemingly innocent question: "Where were you born?" According to Johns, Normile had always "represented himself as being born in New Orleans, of an 'old' family, and there was an official record of this under oath. He was actually the able and ambitious son of humble Irish immigrants. He couldn't answer without breaking his story about himself, or committing perjury. He became panicky. . . . He excused himself from the witness stand, went home and committed suicide."[35] Of course, Normile's "humble Irish immigrant" parents—in Johns's words—did send him to both Georgetown University and Columbia Law School.

Normile, while certainly not wanting to reveal his family's ethnic roots, seems to have been more concerned about having to admit before his friends who were in attendance at the trial that he did not come from an "old" family. Although his lack of gentility was clearly an embarrassment to him, Normile was probably more concerned about the fact that he had been discovered in a lie. The fact that he had been untruthful about his family heritage went directly against his belief that as a "city father" he was to be infallible and therefore incapable of lying. Also, Normile was unable to admit that Johns, clearly a "lesser" man, had successfully challenged his word in public. Once home, Normile decided to commit suicide to avoid the public humiliation of being proven an unworthy and all-too-human city father.

In many ways, the Veiled Prophet organization was similar to other fraternal organizations in late-nineteenth-century America. But the members of the Veiled Prophet organization sought their "feeling of fraternity" in a different way than through the Masons or the Knights of Pythias. According to the historian Mary Ann Clawson, mainstream nineteenth-century fraternal organizations provided for their members both a gendered and a racial "rite of unification" and a corresponding "process of exclusion." The Veiled Prophet did not fit the common definition of a gendered racial "rite of unification" because, while it did exclude women and blacks like most fraternal organizations of the period, it also excluded most classes of white men as well. Most fraternal organizations of the period, through their internal hierarchy, tended to reaffirm society's class order, but the Veiled Prophet organization refused to admit any middle-class or skilled working-class members.[36]

Like most fraternal organizations of the period, however, it did admit a few members from ethnic minorities. Among the founding members, six clearly were foreign-born immigrants and one was Jewish. The Veiled Prophet organization was also like most nineteenth-century fraternal orders in that it was mainly composed of Protestants. Of the twenty-six members for which such information is known, only four were non-Protestants.[37]

The great difference between the Veiled Prophet organization and most nineteenth-century fraternal organizations was that while it showed some degree of cultural and religious pluralism, it did not create bonds between white males of the upper, middle, and skilled working classes.[38] The Veiled Prophet organization was an elitist organization that was important to its members because it demonstrated they were at the very top of St. Louis's white male aristocracy.

It is unclear whether the founding members had to undergo any sort of initiation process. They probably did. Shortly after this first group was inducted, the organization's members seem to have developed a formal initiation ritual. One of the sources to suggest this is a satirical work by *Post-Dispatch* writer John J. Jennings entitled "The Veiled Prophets Unveiled." In this story, the protagonist, a newspaperman named Peter Pencilstubs, goes through an incredibly severe hazing ritual that it would be impossible for any human to survive.[39] For example, Pencilstubs is beaten severely with clubs until unconscious, run over by a wagon, put under water until nearly drowned, and, finally, fired from a cannon. Yet it seems likely that Jennings used a true story as the basis for his fiction. All the basic trappings of a fraternity initiation ritual are present: the members use secret passwords, make the initiate do various humiliating things, and attempt to frighten him with various threats.

The only other reference to Veiled Prophet organization initiations during this period is in the 1916 letter of Charles Slayback, which states that the initiations "were varied, but very interesting and so amusing that we always had a full attendance at our meetings."[40] Whatever happened during the initiation of new members would fit easily into the normal pattern of fraternal initiation rites. According to Mary Ann Clawson, fraternal rituals "served as a source of entertainment" for members of these organizations. Slayback's letter supports this idea, showing that the initiation rite was a fairly popular form of entertainment among the organization's members. To use Clawson's words, the Veiled Prophet organization, like other nineteenth-century fraternal organizations, "was an organizational vehicle through which its members made their own entertainment, through their active engagement in the dramatic events that were the center of the meeting." Clawson sees these forms of collective entertainment serving "as a precursor to the commercialized and mechanically reproduced mass media entertainment of the twentieth century."[41] Of course, the Veiled Prophet organization's parades also served as a major source of collective entertainment for the community at large.

The Veiled Prophet organization, like many fraternal organizations of the late nineteenth century, was founded on very basic materialistic principles. Its members joined the organization in part for economic gain through the business contacts they would make. But much recent scholarship on other fraternal organizations downplays the importance of materialistic motivations for members.[42] To Veiled Prophet members, personal economic gain was a primary goal, next to which any real desire for fraternity was clearly secondary. Just the fact that most of these men belonged to other "full-time" fraternal organizations leads one to believe that they were looking for their "feeling of fraternity" elsewhere.

Yet the Veiled Prophet organization did offer its members something on a higher level: a sense of paternity. The organization, through the parade and ball it sponsored, made the members feel like good fathers both to the city and to their own daughters as well. The increased trade during the St. Louis Fair helped the city, thus making these men feel they were being good city fathers. The success of the Veiled Prophet ball in giving their daughters a "night to remember," as well as helping the daughters find good marriage prospects, made them feel they were being good fathers in the usual sense. In their paternal role, the Veiled Prophet organizers helped St. Louis to grow and mature as a city just as they hoped to play an integral role in the same process for their daughters.

A "Panorama of Progress"

THE VEILED PROPHET CELEBRATION, 1878–1899

Alonzo Slayback, one of the Original Fourteen who founded the Veiled Prophet organization, wrote in his diary on October 5, 1878: "Today I gave to the printer the descriptive manuscript whereby I have woven a classical story, and brought into order and coherency the 'Floats' for the Parade, or Illuminated nocturnal pageant of the secret society known as the 'Veiled Prophets.' I think it is the nearest thing to a 'stroke of genius' that I ever produced." Slayback went on to say that he believed his story, "a prose poem," had "brought order, and identity out of some very gorgeous, but very meaningless representations." Slayback decided to call the parade the "First Panorama of Progress of the Veiled Prophets." Slayback was proud of his achievement and thought that he was building for the future: "the thing I like about it is that for next year, and the year after, and so on for a hundred years, the strangers who visit our October fairs can be entertained by the 2nd, 3rd or 100th Panorama of Progress by the same mysterious brotherhood, the foundations of them all being laid in this—my work—the first."[1] Slayback believed, like most of the founders, that he had helped create an organization that would endure and, to use a stock phrase of nineteenth-century boosterism, would lead to a "bigger and better St. Louis." Slayback was obviously correct in his belief that his organization would be longstanding; the Veiled Prophet celebration still takes place today, over one hundred and fifteen years later. Furthermore, his conception of what "progress" is and what it entailed also lives on in the minds of many St. Louis elites.

The Veiled Prophet parades between 1878 and 1899 provide a rare opportunity to reconstruct the worldview of St. Louis's ruling elites of the late nineteenth century. In these parades the organization's members presented St. Louis history and American history as being the story of the triumphs of great men—many of whom were their ancestors. The Veiled Prophet celebration was a physical show of power that allowed them to claim historical legitimacy as well. Organization members wished to present themselves as the hereditary aristocracy of St. Louis. They strived to inculcate a civic patriotism that encouraged loyalty to the nation, the community, and, not least, to the elites of the city themselves. (Some would argue that this aristocratic outlook still exists today.) In addition, the parades provided their working-class spectators with advice about morals and the importance of social order. The debutante balls also were important to these men, allowing them to make important business contacts and fulfill their role as fathers.

In short, Veiled Prophet members tried to use an element of nineteenth-century popular culture—the parade—for their own purposes of shaping the values of their working-class audience. These elites used the parades as part of their attempt to establish a cultural hegemony for themselves in the last two decades of the nineteenth century. Through the Veiled Prophet parades, these cultural leaders were attempting to link, in T. J. Jackson Lears's words, "the interests of [their] particular class with the 'natural' common sense of society (and indeed of humanity) at large."[2]

These St. Louis elites attempted to shape common people's values and beliefs in a way that was profitable to themselves both economically and psychologically. Given the fact that the Gilded Age was a time of great economic, political, and social upheaval, particularly among workers and farmers (who would compose the majority of the Veiled Prophet parades' spectators), these elites certainly may have felt the need to control the values of two potentially dissident groups. The Veiled Prophet parades show one of the many vehicles elites used to shape cultural reality in the late nineteenth century. These value-shaping vehicles would help to establish the cultural hegemony that the elites would enjoy into the early years of the twentieth century.

While some scholars have studied the fairly democratic parades of the eighteenth and mid-nineteenth centuries, little has been done to examine the less pluralistic and elite-dominated parades of the late nineteenth and twentieth centuries. The Veiled Prophet parades are some of the more typical of these elite-dominated parades. Unlike Bakhtin's Renaissance celebrations and other more contemporary celebrations like Mardi Gras, the street carnivals of the Veiled Prophet celebration did not involve any sort of social leveling or role reversal.

On the contrary, they mirrored the social order. Like elites in other parts of the world, St. Louis's city fathers in the late nineteenth century wanted to create "modern antiseptic urban spaces" that would eliminate the multivocal "culture of the street." The celebrations they sponsored, according to Mexican cultural historian William H. Beezley, allowed spectators "to dream, to recall their childhoods and escape their daily drudgery, and thereby diverted them from more politically disruptive behavior."[3]

The Veiled Prophet parades during the last two decades of the nineteenth century were amazing night spectacles. By the 1880s, they probably equalled the magnificence of those presented by the New Orleans Carnival societies during the same period. Most of the spectators, when interviewed years later, recalled how the parades were astounding shows of almost regal splendor.[4]

Although other papers covered the early parades, the primary public voice of the Veiled Prophet organization from 1878 into the middle 1880s was the *Missouri Republican*. Neither of the other two papers in town—the *Evening Post* and *Globe-Democrat*—printed the official parade descriptions or press releases of the organization as faithfully as the *Republican*. It is no surprise that the *Republican* served as the primary publicity outlet of the "Mysterious Conclave of Veiled Prophets of the Mississippi Valley," since two of the Original Fourteen were proprietors and editors of the newspaper. In late September and early October of 1878, the newspaper's stories indicated that it had "a reliable source" inside the organization. The source supposedly sent his information by "a mysterious messenger." Throughout this period, the newspaper's editors claimed that "the *Republican* can say nothing" with regard to specifics about the organization or the coming carnival.[5] Of course, the inside source was none other than the editors themselves.

In 1878 the organization did a nice job of pacing the release of news about the organization to build public interest. Although the coming celebration was mentioned in the *Republican, Post,* and *Globe-Democrat* during the seven months preceding the event (mostly in September), little was released to the press by the organization until late September. The first press release by the organization appeared in the *Republican* on September 29. One can see in the story an attempt by the *Republican* (and presumably the Veiled Prophet organization itself) to use the "mystery" and secrecy of the organization as titillation.

The brief account mentioned that "never a Veiled Prophet has been discovered yet" and described the organization as "bewildering."[6]

The organization's skillful manipulation of the media continued throughout the next several days. The next press release appeared in the *Republican*'s October 1 issue. A brief item, which the paper said came from "what seems to be a reliable source," simply listed the route of the parade. On October 4 the *Republican* listed eight reasons why the people should take advantage of the cheap rates offered for railroad excursions to St. Louis. Not surprisingly, two of the reasons were "to see the largest fair in the United States" and to "see the grand pageant and unique tableaux of the Veiled Prophets."[7] The fact that the railroad companies, most of whose upper management were members of the organization, were willing to drop railroad rates on the day of the Veiled Prophet celebration showed the desire on the part of the business class to provide additional incentives for out-of-town farmers to see the Veiled Prophet parade and, hopefully, the St. Louis Agricultural and Mechanical Fair as well.

The October 6 issue of the *Republican* featured an editorial, "The St. Louis Carnival," which emphasizes the connection between the Veiled Prophet's carnival and the New Orleans Carnival societies:

> The St. Louis carnival season, which began four weeks ago, will reach a brilliant climax this week if the weather treats us more favorably than it has for two weeks past. Tuesday night we shall have the most distinctively carnival feature of the season in the street process and succeeding entertainment in the Chamber of Commerce hall, by the mystic association of Veiled Prophets. It is well known that St. Louis borrows this feature from the Southern cities, in several of which it has been successfully repeated every year for many years past. Outside of New Orleans these pageants of the mystic societies are practically all there is of a carnival, although in some others there is some faint effort to reproduce the day carnival of New Orleans.

The organization's members wanted to make clear, however, that the Veiled Prophet celebration would be different and, because of its lack of class-leveling elements, superior to the efforts of the New Orleans Carnival societies:

> In St. Louis there is no intention to imitate the day procession, the general masking and the accompanying riot and license, which are an essential part of the Mardi Gras carnival in New Orleans. There has been chosen the pageant of a mystic society, as the best feature of the Creole carnivals and the one most likely to take root in St. Louis, to fill

out a list of attractions in connection with our Exposition, races and Fair, which no doubt, it is meant to repeat every year.

Another editorial on the same page, "Mystic Progenitors of the Veiled Prophets," briefly chronicled the history of other secret societies, most notably the Mystick Krewe of Comus, the Twelfth Night Revelers, and Knights of Momus. Another article on the same page gave the theme and briefly described the seventeen tableaux for the parade. The article's opening paragraph again used the "mystery" of the organization as a form of "advertising" and public titillation:

> St. Louis has not in years, if ever, endured such a painful and lengthy suspense as that which has attended the unsatisfactory contemplation of the great Veiled Prophet mystery. The Prophets are responsible for much loss of sleep, nervousness and hobgoblin dreams, and this experience is not limited to any class of citizens, but extends to the mansion and the hovel. . . . People within a radius of a hundred miles have caught the mysterious infection, and thousands will satisfy their curiosity at all hazards.

The article closed with a short letter dated October 5 from the "Temple—Veiled Prophets" to those attending the ball, telling them where to enter the Chamber of Commerce building, where the ladies' dressing rooms would be, and where men and ladies who were spectators would be allowed to sit. In this issue of the *Republican* the reader also finds the first shocking visual representation of the Veiled Prophet and the accompanying description discussed.[8]

By eight o'clock on the evening of October 8, 1878, the streets were jammed with people. The total number of people watching the first parade was estimated to have been around one hundred thousand. The spectacle they witnessed was, without a doubt, amazing for those times. One thousand torchlights were used along the parade route, as well as hundreds of "candle-lit Japanese lanterns." There was also a fireworks display along the parade route. Writers for the *Post, Republican,* and *Globe-Democrat* commented on the large number of gas lights used in the parade and the *Republican* even filled two columns describing the lighted decorations found at each address along the parade route.[9] The first Veiled Prophet parade was a captivating spectacle whose lighted opulence proved to be spellbinding for those who witnessed it.

The large crowds created several problems. In one incident an overcrowded porch gave away; fifty people fell to the sidewalk below, one of whom died two days later.[10] According to the *Post,* the great throngs of people created problems in moving the parade through the streets: "At the head of the procession came a squad of policemen, mounted and fully equipped, breaking away the great surging crowd. At times it appeared as though the dense mass of humanity would triumph, and that the procession had run against an insurmountable barrier, but the sharp points of the sabre would eventually make an opening."[11] Despite the warnings accompanying the October 6 woodcut—that the procession would not be hindered "by street cars or anything else"—the Veiled Prophet did not appear to execute his own crowd control.

Alonzo Slayback's account in the *Republican* on the day following the parade is a revealing historical document. The parade theme, "A Festival of Ceres," featured seventeen tableaux.[12] In his lengthy report, which took up more than four full columns, Slayback characterized the floats as representing the three stages of progress the world had experienced. He weaved Greek mythology and the genteel ideal of "progress" together in an ingenious manner. To Slayback, progress was the inexorable move of history from a desolate world of ice—the glacial period in Earth's history—to the development of agriculture through "human genius," to the modern world of "wealth" and "industry" in which "a thrifty, prosperous population . . . dwell[s] in happy homes surrounded by all the luxuries that enhance the enjoyment of life," luxuries that were themselves "the natural sequence of the pursuit of these industries." Progress was largely technological and was the result of unrestrained capitalism.

By adding Greek mythological figures at the right times, Slayback gave his story a sense of fantasy as well. Man has succeeded by his own genius, but the gods have helped him at crucial times. The Veiled Prophet organization, according to the story, was founded "unnumbered ages before" Demeter or any of the other mythological gods on the floats in the parade existed. The story presented the Grand Oracle as the most powerful of all the gods who were in the parade. In fact, Slayback went so far as to say that the Veiled Prophet parade was the tableaux representation of Demeter herself humbly visiting the Veiled Prophet. Unlike later years, secrecy was not paramount in this first year of the celebration. The *Globe-Democrat* even identified the Veiled Prophet (John G. Priest) and several of the others on the floats.[13] This would not happen again in the next 120 years.

Three individual tableaux in the 1878 parade warrant further examination: the fifteenth, sixteenth, and seventeenth—"Industry,"
"Wealth," and "The Grand Oracle." The "Industry" float had five god-
desses, the "Daughters of Industry," engaged in the "Arts of Industry"—
Drawing, Painting, Sculpture, and Architecture. Regarding the "Wealth"
tableau, the *Republican* writer maintained that

> Wealth in natural order follows industry, and so came the float repre-
> senting wealth in the pageant. The story of the world's progress has in
> the allegory been brought already to the present. . . . Most prominent of
> any object stood on edge a huge silver dollar of 1878, so vast in its di-
> mensions that in a circle cut from its centre stood a chair of state in
> which sat Minerva, goddess of wisdom and protectress of industrial arts
> from which in their pursuit wealth is developed.[14]

The description here is quite self-serving for the wealthy members of
the Veiled Prophet—industry is equated with wealth, and wealth is
equated with wisdom. Genteel values about the pursuit of wealth are
thereby reaffirmed. According to the Veiled Prophet organization's
members, success in industry—and life for that matter—only went to
those who were both wise and worthy. To be worthy, one must be industrious. Consequently, their workers or subordinates who lacked
wealth must have been neither wise nor worthy.

The seventeenth tableau in the 1878 parade was that of "The
Grand Oracle"—the Veiled Prophet himself. The *Republican* writer described the float in the following manner:

> Last and greatest in the procession came the mysterious personage in
> whose honor was given the grand parade in which he participated as a
> benignant observer. The present Grand Oracle of the Veiled Prophets of
> the World . . . sat upon a resplendent throne of gold, in attitude graceful
> and dignified. . . . He was clad in a close-fitting garb of dark green and
> upon his great arms were bracelets of antique workmanship. . . .
> Through the veil of gauzy white which fell over his head and shoulders
> could be discerned a countenance majestic, but thoughtful rather than
> stern.[15]

This description of the Veiled Prophet is very different from that represented in the *Republican* woodcut of two days before. The Veiled
Prophet in 1878 had a costume that used a gauzy substance for its
veil and he carried no weapons. The Veiled Prophet never wore a
pointed white Ku Klux Klan–like cap and robe in the parade. While
the earlier representation was clearly intended to send a racial con-

trol message, the first parade focused more on class control as its message. Instead of weapons, the Prophet carried a "magic mirror" and "written scroll" that proclaimed him "the prophet." However, the Veiled Prophet was accompanied on his float by "his servitors brought with him in his journey around the world." One of these was the "villainous looking executioner" mentioned earlier. The *Republican* saw things differently, describing him as "a high priest of the order, in an attitude as if about to prepare a sacrifice."[16] This symbolism was probably effective in conveying to working-class spectators what could happen to them if they went against the "natural" class order.

The first Veiled Prophet celebration apparently went exactly according to the members' plan and easily fulfilled the goals set for it. Both the *Republican* and the *Post* described how St. Louis was crowded with visitors who had come to see the parade. The total number of people who arrived by train on October 8 was estimated to have been between thirty thousand and fifty thousand. Although one cannot tell how many of them visited the fair, the goal of the organization to bring large numbers of people to St. Louis appeared to have been realized. The *Republican*'s editor on October 9 could not help but take a swipe at regional rival Chicago: "Illinois was the chief contributor (of people coming into the city for the parade) and it is safe to say that she never poured such a flood of people into her own metropolis as that which made heavy work for the road engines yesterday on all lines radiating here."[17] The organization's plan involved two steps: First, get people to come see the parade; second, get the same people to attend the St. Louis Agricultural and Mechanical Fair. The cheap rail rates obviously helped to bring farmers to St. Louis. The founders hoped that the farmers would make the trip to St. Louis in October a yearly pilgrimage. The organization's goals for the first celebration were met. Tens of thousands came from outside St. Louis to see the parade and, although it is impossible to be sure, a good number probably went to the St. Louis Fair as well.

The *Republican*'s editorial on October 10, more than likely written by members of the organization, proudly boasted that "Rarely, if ever, has so extensive an undertaking as this proved to be, been conducted with so much secrecy, and while the impenetrable veil still shrouds the organization, the extent and manifest cost of the display give assurance that those who control the organization are not only public

3. *Missouri.—Celebration of the Festival of Ceres at St. Louis, October 8th—the Vailed [sic] Prophet Chief with His Retinue Passing the Court House.—From Sketches By R. Jump.* Wood engraving from *Frank Leslie's Illustrated Newspaper,* 1878. Missouri Historical Society, St. Louis.

spirited citizens, but men of means and varied resources." The editorial gave a clue as to the members of the organization, stating that "when unmasked" the actors on the floats "are heads of large commercial firms or perhaps grave and dignified judges of the law." It contended that "the grand pageant has proved a grand success. The highest expectations about it have been more than satisfied, and the gentlemen who conceived and carried out the magnificent spectacle are entitled to the thanks, not of St. Louisans alone, but of the many thousands from abroad who witnessed it with delight." The editorial closed with a statement deeply steeped in the language of late-nineteenth-century St. Louis boosterism: "It [the Veiled Prophet celebration] is another evidence of the metropolitan character of our city. It serves to unite and consolidate a public spirit which, combined with her natural advantages, will keep St. Louis first among the cities of the West."[18] Members of the organization apparently saw the success of the first Veiled Prophet parade as a momentous first step toward St. Louis's becoming the "Future Great City of the World." Of course, unbeknownst to the elites of the Veiled Prophet organization, the regional battle with Chicago was already lost, and had been since the end of the Civil War.

One can sum up the remaining seventeen parades of the nineteenth century with some generalized observations. For example, like other parades of the late nineteenth century, the Veiled Prophet parades employed female symbols to stand for ideals. Mary Ryan has argued that female symbols "as the quintessential 'other' within a male-defined cultural universe made them perfect vehicles for representing the remote notions of national unity and local harmony."[19] In the 1878 parade, female figures represented "industry" and "wealth" on the tableaux. They were used in a similar manner in the remaining parades of the nineteenth century. However, unlike other parades in America during this period, women themselves did not actually appear in the Veiled Prophet parades. The women characters on the floats were played by members of the organization. This makes sense given the innate conservatism of St. Louis's ruling elites; they obviously felt it was improper for women to take part in such civic celebrations. Amazingly, this public taboo would remain in place until the middle of the twentieth century—well after most civic celebrations in America had begun incorporating women.

The Veiled Prophet organization continued to use local publicity in the same effective manner throughout the remainder of the nineteenth century. However, a noticeable decline in the quality and quantity of the parade float descriptions is evident in the two years following Slayback's death in 1882. In the middle 1880s newspapers began to print illustrations and descriptions—obviously written in advance—of the floats on the day after the parade. In 1884, all three papers printed descriptions and illustrations of the floats on the day before the parade, thus allowing spectators to have a clear idea of the parade's theme and to "follow along" with the floats in the parade.[20] While the *Republican* was the primary voice in the parade's early years, by the middle 1880s all three newspapers were covering the parade and ball extensively. By the late 1880s, both the *Post-Dispatch* and *Globe-Democrat* were printing official illustrations and descriptions from the Veiled Prophet organization as well. This free publicity demonstrated the enormous public interest in the Veiled Prophet celebration.

One could argue that the Veiled Prophet celebration was the largest civic event in St. Louis at the time. Between pre-parade and ball promotion and wrap-up, the three newspapers each averaged five to six entire pages devoted to the celebration annually. No other civic celebration received an equivalent level of coverage. Attendance was estimated in most years to be at least three hundred thousand, a significant portion of these spectators coming from out of town. The 1880 *Republican* estimated that "a hundred thousand strangers" witnessed the parade that year. Whether or not these visitors went to the fair as well, the numbers certainly meant that the parade was performing up to members' expectations. By 1884 the Veiled Prophet parade had become a major civic event. In that year, the *Republican* informed the public that in case of rain, they would be "notified of postponement by 9 taps on the fire bells in the city."[21] Clearly, the parade had taken its place in the life of the city.

Business and government elites certainly regarded the celebration as a major civic occasion. In 1887 President Cleveland visited St. Louis to see the parade and attend the ball.[22] In 1893, at the urging of civic leaders, several commissioners of the Chicago World's Fair came to St. Louis to view the parade. The commissioners were reportedly quite impressed.[23] However, the fact that its rival had received the exposition instead of St. Louis rankled St. Louis's leaders. The Veiled Prophet organization took direct aim at Chicago's upcoming "Columbian Exposition" when it claimed in 1892 that the St. Louis Agricultural and Mechanical Fair was "the only Successful Annual Exposition in the World."[24]

However, there was no consistent Veiled Prophet "mythology" during this period. It was Walter B. Stevens and others who developed a consistent mythology during the first two decades of the twentieth century. For all their rhetorical flourishes, neither Slayback nor the others who composed the earliest parade descriptions ever used mythology to explain the Veiled Prophet's appearance in St. Louis. In fact, at times during this period it was not clear whether there was a single Veiled Prophet or whether the organization's members considered themselves all "Veiled Prophets." For example, at times throughout this period the Veiled Prophet organization was referred to as the "Temple of the Veiled Prophets" and the "Veiled Prophets Association." The formal name of the parade was not even clear. The first three celebrations were called the "Panorama of Progress of the Veiled Prophets," while the remainder were referred to as the "Carnival of the Veiled Prophet" or the "Pageant of the Veiled Prophets." In fact, a Veiled Prophet float did not even appear in the parade in 1879 and 1880. In the remainder of the parades, the Veiled Prophet appeared as a solitary figure dressed in oriental robes and wearing a veiled crown. However, confusion about the name of the organization continued throughout the period. The singular "benevolent monarch" that St. Louisans are familiar with today did not exist until the early twentieth century.

Adding to the confusion, Slayback attempted to rename the Veiled Prophet's character "Ukel Zam" in the parade descriptions of 1880 and 1881. Although only mentioned three times in passing, the tongue-in-cheek reference to Uncle Sam shows how much the organization's elites wanted to identify themselves as patriots and promote unity through nationalism.[25] Since most St. Louisans in the 1880s more than likely identified themselves as Americans (as opposed to the regional associations that existed before the Civil War), this symbolism at least had the potential to be effective. Unfortunately for the organization, Slayback was murdered shortly after the 1882 celebration and the idea to rename the character died with him. The character and position has remained the "Veiled Prophet," or, to organization insiders, the "Grand Oracle," until the present day.

Some of the uncertainty in the organization's official mythology may have had to do with who belonged to the organization during this time. The membership's occupational profile changed greatly during the last two decades of the nineteenth century (see Table 4).[26] Between 1878 and 1899, the percentage of members involved in agricultural commerce dropped from 34 to 22 percent, a decline that continued into the twentieth century. Conversely, the number of

4. *The St. Louis Fair—Procession of "The Veiled Prophets." —From Sketches and Photographs by John A. Scholten, St. Louis.* Wood engraving from *Harper's Weekly*, October 16, 1880. Missouri Historical Society, St. Louis.

Table 4 OCCUPATIONS OF MEMBERS, 1878, 1890, 1899

Occupational Category	Number of Members, 1878	Number of Members, 1890	Number of Members, 1899
Agricultural Commerce	25 (34%)	47 (32%)	83 (22%)
Commercial Transportation	11 (15)	15 (10)	32 (9)
Merchants	10 (14)	35 (24)	56 (15)
Professionals	10 (14)	12 (8)	32 (9)
Public Communications	5 (7)	6 (4)	13 (3)
Industry	5 (7)	14 (10)	73 (20)
Financial Services	6 (8)	14 (10)	63 (17)
Other	1 (1)	3 (2)	21 (6)
Total Members	73	146	373

members involved in industrial pursuits rose from 7 to 20 percent. This trend continued into the twentieth century as well. The professional, merchant, and public communications categories stayed fairly stable between 1878 and 1899. This period also saw the growth of financial services as an occupational category for Veiled Prophet members: About 7 percent of members were bankers, real estate agents, or insurance agents in 1878. By the turn of the century, 17 percent worked in these categories. Many of these men likely moved from one sort of primary occupation to another during this period. With so much work to do as businessmen, there may not have been much energy or inclination left for the organization's leaders to worry about creating an official mythology.[27]

In addition to being successful businessmen, the members of the Veiled Prophet organization had considerable political power as well. Included among the organization's members were several prominent local politicians, including the mayor, the city auditor, circuit judges, and city councilmen. This trend in membership would continue throughout the organization's history. The worldview of the Veiled Prophet organization's elites mirrored that of city political leaders, for they were the same people.

Even without a distinct mythology, the Veiled Prophet's members had precise goals in mind with regard to the organization's parades;

they saw them as a form of public communication and education. The members wanted their parades to do three main things: entertain, inculcate upper-middle-class cultural and social values, and teach American and St. Louis history to working-class St. Louisans. The more successful of their parades during this period accomplished all three of these goals. Most achieved two out of the three. The parade descriptions are amazing historical documents. They allow researchers to reconstruct the worldview of St. Louis's ruling elites of the late nineteenth century with regard to their view of themselves, their city's history, the appropriate social order, and what constituted "proper" civic entertainment.

The parades were also spectacles that were meant to provide mass entertainment. It is hardly surprising, in that case, that some of them had no deeper meaning than the Rose Bowl or Macy's parades of today. These played on whimsical themes designed to captivate the imaginations of their spectators and do little else. Nonetheless, of the twenty parades between 1879 and 1899, only six fall into the category of having themes that were merely escapist in nature or having such strict themes they left very little room for interpretation.[28]

The less meaningful parades did, however, advocate an escape from the cares of modern adult life. They created an imaginary world that was very different from the urban and industrial society of the late nineteenth century. For example, the 1881 parade's theme was "A Dream of Woodland Life." The organization presented the Veiled Prophet's "hasheesh dream" about the wonders of the natural world. The floats created an elaborate pastoral world in which the spectator saw the work of ants, spiders, and bees. Flowers became animated and danced. The parade closed with a tableaux featuring the Fairy Queen Mab. In the 1883 parade, the organization used "Fairyland" as its theme. The tableaux depicted Queen Mab and retold a few other fairy tales—Cinderella, Sleeping Beauty, Jack and the Bean Stalk, and Mother Goose. In the 1899 parade, "Visions of Childhood," the organization presented more fairy tales and nostalgic scenes from childhood such as the Fourth of July and the circus coming to town. It presented a similar theme in 1888, "Children's Lore." The floats depicted scenes from popular children's literature at the time, including Blue Beard, Robinson Crusoe, Baron Munchausen, and Uncle Remus's tar baby story.[29]

However, the vast majority of the parades did much more than provide escapist entertainment for those who watched. The object of several parades during this period was to teach working-class spectators about genteel middle-class culture and values. The organization's members felt that they were performing a public service by educating the immigrant working class about aspects of "proper" culture. The elites thought that if educated and imbued with an appreciation for higher culture, the members of the immigrant working class could improve themselves—thus leading to their eventual assimilation into American society. From the parade themes, it seemed that all St. Louisans should have been spending their spare time reading Shakespeare and other titans of literature and learning how to appreciate great art. Apparently, the elites believed it was far better to spend time that way than in carousing, striking, or celebrating ethnic holidays.

In 1884 the Veiled Prophet parade celebrated the plays of Shakespeare. The parade consisted of twenty scenes from sixteen different plays. The scenes tended to be climactic points in these plays or scenes that gathered most of the plays' characters together—for example, "Macbeth and the Witches" from *Macbeth,* "Petrucio Carries off Kate" from *Taming of the Shrew,* "Pompey's Galley" from *Antony and Cleopatra,* and "The Forest of the Arden" from *As You Like It.*[30] Members seem to have paid close attention to the costumes of the characters on the parade's floats. The theme of the parade would not have been easy to follow for uneducated spectators. Each float had a different scene—usually from a different play. However, the parade's goal was not to tell the story of any one of the sixteen plays. The elites merely wished to raise public interest in Shakespeare's plays, hoping to convince their working-class spectators to read Shakespeare on their own.

"Arabian Nights" was the theme of the 1885 parade. The floats depicted twenty separate Arabian tales, including "Aladdin and His Wonderful Lamp," "Sinbad the Sailor," and "Ali Baba and the Forty Thieves." Each illustrated a scene from one of the stories, and the final float depicted "The Fair Scheherezade" herself.[31] This parade clearly had the same object as the "Shakespeare's plays" parade of the year before. The parade's creators hoped to raise public interest in literature.

The 1891 parade presented the works of the "Ten Popular Authors." As the *Post-Dispatch*'s writer was careful to point out, "they are not selected as the ten greatest authors or novelists, but as the most popular. There are greater novelists . . . but are not the works of the latter more popular with the people than those of the greater writers?" However, a middle-class bias in the selection of the ten popular authors was inescapable. Included among the ten authors were Harriet Beecher Stowe, Nathaniel Hawthorne, and Charles Dickens.[32] Clearly, the Veiled Prophet's members were trying to drum up interest in what they considered to be "proper" and uplifting reading material. They wished to dissuade people from reading the dime novels that were becoming more popular with the American working class at the time.

In 1896 the organization turned to great art as a subject. Each of the twenty-one tableaux in the parade represented, according to the *Post-Dispatch,* one of the "masterpieces of art from ancient to modern times." The parade was separated into three distinct sections: ancient art, Renaissance art, and modern art.[33] By depicting seven works in each of the three categories, the elites hoped to provide a broad overview of the subject for an untutored audience.

The 1893 parade on "Storied Holidays" pursued a very different subject. The second float, the "Lord of Misrule," deserves particular attention. The *Post-Dispatch* described this tableau as representing

> a court scene, in which the "Lord of Misrule" is in the act of handing down to his subjects license to hold high carnival through the holidays. A figure with the head of an ass and body of a man is kneeling before the judicial bench with hands outstretched to receive the coveted document, while about the open space in front gambol a dancing girl in short skirts, a clown blowing a trumpet and a hobby horse fitted about the body of one of the merrymakers. The idea is taken from descriptions of the golden age when Christmas gambols and holiday festivities of all kings were presided over by a "Lord of Misrule" or "Christmas Prince."[34]

But aside from that one float, the other holidays depicted did not have this sort of "leveling" characteristic and none of the holidays were celebrated with such abandon, even Mardi Gras and Twelfth Night. Role-reversal, leveling, and popular participation were not to be part of celebrations anymore. Holidays were to be celebrated in a dignified and orderly manner—much like the Veiled Prophet celebration itself.

In addition to delineating the manner in which holidays were to be celebrated, the parade gave immigrant spectators a list of which holidays to celebrate. Included in the list of twenty-one holidays were

New Year's Day, Shrove Tuesday, Washington's Birthday, April Fool's Day, May Day, the Fourth of July, St. Louis Fair Day, Columbus Day, Thanksgiving, and Christmas. As historian Herbert Gutman has argued, factory owners believed an important part of the acculturation and industrial regimentation process was teaching their workers which holidays to celebrate in America. Employers wanted to make sure their workers did not take time off from work to celebrate their ethnic holidays from the old country. The Veiled Prophet organization's membership included many factory owners.[35]

The most effective of the Veiled Prophet parades weaved history, middle-class culture, and morality together into a single tapestry. These parades, like the 1878 one that began this chapter, established a sort of middle-class historical and cultural legitimacy through the idea of "progress." History, to these elites, was the documenting of "progress" and the deeds of great men. For them, progress meant two things. First, it meant industrial and commercial advancement and an increase in population—a concept that expressed itself in a fascination with statistics like the census and the Merchants Exchange annual report. Of course, progress for the elites also meant the onward march of "civilization" toward the future. The most successful of the Veiled Prophet parades celebrated progress and modernity, which the elites saw as essential to the development of new technology, the spread of upper middle-class genteel culture, and the emerging consumer culture. Members of the Veiled Prophet organization also believed that progress would only be achieved under the leadership of middle-class elites like themselves. History, therefore, was to document the deeds of great men like themselves—whether they were military, political, or business leaders—who had led the nation and St. Louis in the advancement of civilization. Through their portrayal of world, American, and St. Louis history in the Veiled Prophet parades, these elites took credit for making St. Louis the successful place they believed it was—the place, they hoped, that would eventually become the "Future Great City of the World."

The celebration of progress and modernity was distinctive neither to St. Louis nor to the United States. William H. Beezley maintains that late-nineteenth-century elites in Mexico wished to "create a Victorian society of consumers characterized by what Thorstein Veblen called ostentatious consumption of goods and leisure that would demonstrate their personal, if not Mexico's, wealth and reputation." In these celebrations, elites wished to prove that they were modern consumers who "possessed modern qualities." Through this conspicuous consumption, elites in late-nineteenth-century Mexico hoped to present themselves as examples for the less fortunate.[36] Through their celebrations, the members of the Veiled Prophet organization attempted to do a similar thing.

The 1879 parade, like the 1878 one, presented an ideal of "progress" in world history. According to Slayback's description in the *Republican,* the parade, the official theme of which was the "Progress of Civilization,"

> was manifestly a panorama of the world's progress in the development of industrial, or, more especially, the mechanical arts, illustrated from the first crude advances, the story of which is lost in the myths of antiquity, to the highest pinnacle of enlightened modern invention and skilled workmanship, as typified in the industrial exposition of the St. Louis Agricultural and Mechanical Association.[37]

Once again, history was the progress from savagery and a desolate world to civilization and a world of wealth and luxury. The Greek gods appeared in this parade as well, teaching many of the important skills humans needed to survive and prosper. The parade celebrated the "fertile brain of the inventor," which "has year by year developed new devices to supply the needs of a civilization constantly becoming more and more exacting." It documented the world's advance from a desolate place of volcanoes, to a world in which, because man can more easily meet his basic needs, important auxiliary arts and skills can be developed. Some of these were pottery, woodcarving, sculpture, music, architecture, wheel-making, shipbuilding, glass-making, artificial light-making, watch-making, and generating of electricity. Most of the tableaux in the parade presented workers or artists performing one of these arts or skills.[38] To these elites, progress was largely achieved through the successful implementation of advances in technology.

The 1879 parade celebrated upper-middle-class gentility as well. The twenty-first float presented the Veiled Prophet's "silver dinner service," which consisted of a sugar bowl, fruit holder, and cream pitcher. As the *Globe-Democrat*'s writer put it, the float showed how man, after having taken care of his basic comforts, was able to "indulge in some of the luxuries of life—strawberries and cream." Advancement in technology allowed man to enjoy himself and, as the

Globe-Democrat writer argued, "Nothing is a more distinguishing element in civilization than a well-ordered dinner with appropriate service. It is a mark of refinement and wealth in all countries."[39] Once again the same theme appeared: Progress and the advancement of civilization ultimately leads to "refinement and wealth" for those wise enough and capable enough to take part.

The Veiled Prophet parade's cultural themes did not always go over well with local ethnic groups. In the 1882 parade, "The Veiled Prophet Travels around the World," the organization's members originally planned floats depicting thirteen different countries: China, India, Persia, Egypt, Greece, Italy, France, Russia, Germany, England, Scotland, Ireland, and America. After reading the descriptions that appeared the day before the parade in the *Post-Dispatch,* a group of local Irish Americans wrote a letter to the editors of all three newspapers protesting the scenes depicted on the Ireland float: "as Irish-Americans we earnestly and indignantly protest against the outrageous caricature of Ireland and her people intended to be represented by float No. 16 of the Veiled Prophet's procession, and as citizens of St. Louis, having a pride in our city, we courteously request that the managers of the process remove the objectionable float, or represent Ireland in a manner more worthy of her history."[40] The float, a depiction of Donnybrook Fair with several jig-dancing and seemingly drunken Irishmen, was certainly in accordance with the usual stereotype of the Irish at the time.

The Veiled Prophet organization's Executive Committee decided to remove the float and, as George Bain said in the official statement, "thus remove the possibility even of unpleasant feeling." However, as infallible city fathers, the elites in the upper echelons of the organization did not like having their authority questioned. Alonzo Slayback, who was called upon to read this statement to the press, could not abide by the simple wording of the statement. After completing the statement, he exclaimed, "Why, the float is perfectly unobjectionable! . . . It is not a caricature, but merely a piece of pleasantry and is not calculated to hurt the feelings of any one but a fool." Slayback went on to assert that "We have not enough money to be able to supply each nationality with a thoroughly complete idealization of the beauties and historic associations of its land. We tried to do this at the first procession and found that we shot over the heads of the spectators. After that we found that a float which aimed rather to convey a pleasant bit of fun pleased the people much better, and we have carried out this idea ever since." This comment indicated that the parade makers felt that, as the years passed, they needed to simplify the parade so that it would come closer to what would later be called "pure entertainment."[41] Nonetheless, the parade's themes did not get any less complex in the following years.

However, Slayback did not stop his public comment there. He went on to issue a challenge to those who might further try to defy the organization's power: "Let them raise a finger against any part of the pageant, if they dare. I feel sure that there will be on hand a sufficiently large number of people who have St. Louis' interests at heart to prevent any sort of attack. Yes sir. Just let them try it." The following day, the Veiled Prophet for that year, E. C. Simmons, told a reporter that people in the organization felt a general sense of "indignation" about the withdrawal of the float and that "he had offers of over 100 men who expressed themselves as ready to mount the float, gun in hand, and defend it against any and all who might feel inclined to attack it. I tell you, sir, that if anybody thinks that the thing was withdrawn through the want of backbone on the part of the Veiled Prophets . . . he is very much mistaken."[42] With such statements, it seems clear that the Veiled Prophet's members wanted Irish-Americans to know that they withheld the float simply out of the goodness of their hearts. Despite the placating gesture, the 1882 parade still served as an annual show of physical power for the Veiled Prophet's members. If the spectacle itself was not enough to convince the working class of the elites' power, the additional warnings would.

But there was even more to the Veiled Prophet parade of 1882. The members arranged the countries in what they believed to be the order of the "advancement" of their civilizations. China and India were the "least civilized" countries. The four most civilized countries were, as is no surprise, England, Scotland, Ireland, and the United States. The descriptions bore this out. The early floats depicted sacrificial rites or "primitive" Asian religious festivals. The later floats portrayed ocean trade or commerce as the highest form of civilization.

It was obvious that the elites saw civilization advancing as one moved west from Asia. In fact, according to the *Republican*'s description, the United States "typified the march of civilization" and was accordingly presented in the parade description as the highest form of civilization at the time.

The final five floats in 1882 were devoted to the "march of civilization" across America. The first float, "America," showed the Indian and the buffalo "being driven into the Pacific" by civilization. Three different figures stood at the rear of the float: an American soldier, a frontiersman, and, most importantly, a female figure with a wheel on one side and a book on a pedestal marked "Education" on the other. The message was clear—civilization was sweeping the buffalo and the Indian from the continent. The "savage" Indian must assimilate or perish in the new urban, industrial, and literate world of the late nineteenth century. The buffalo, also a symbol of the old and uncivilized west, would die out as well. As far as the members of the organization were concerned, this eradication was necessary for civilization to move forward.

The next float, the "Ballot Box," showed a polling place and George Washington at the helm of "the ship of state" that was "flying the national ensign from the masthead." The description referred to the ballot box as that "glorious institution . . . keystone of our liberties, that redresser of the freeman's grievances, popularly supposed to execute his will as lightning does the will of God . . ." Showing his Democratic party affiliation, the *Republican*'s writer (again, probably Slayback) argued that these scenes were indicative of "the highest civilization under the best government, or what would be the best government, if we had such trifling changes made as a readjustment of the currency, a turning over of the tariff, an upheaval in the civil service, better labor laws and other small matters . . ."[43] This float's rather rosy depiction of the American political system reflected the bias one would expect from those who were benefitting from such a system.

The next two floats, "the Indian" and "the Plantation," presented scenes from what parade makers would probably have called America's more savage past. They did in fact seem to represent steps back from what had been a logical progression of the members' conceptions of "civilization" until that point. One float portrayed a group of Indians performing a war dance in which the tribe "celebrates the anticipated murder of an Indian agent and the scalping of a whole settlement." Other than the brightness and detail of their costumes, the Indians on this float had no other redeeming qualities—as would be expected of uncivilized "savages." The plantation scene, on the other hand, showed two distinct views of plantation life. The first scene showed field slaves hard at work. The second showed "quittin' time," in which a family of slaves was shown loafing after the day's work is done. According to the *Republican*'s account, the scene showed a "young nigger" eating a watermelon and his mother exclaiming about the large size of his bites out of the melon.[44] The stereotypical caricatures of the African Americans, especially the mother, clearly fit the loafing, loud-talking, grinning, "darky" stereotype of former slaves prevalent at the time. Just like the uncivilized Native Americans presented in the float before, they had few redeeming qualities. As in the earlier float, the suggestion is that the two groups are uncivilized and must be educated and learn upper-middle-class values in order for progress to occur.

The final two floats, "Western Waters" and "Uncle Sam," move closer to what the organization's members saw as the building of American civilization. "Western Waters" portrayed a scene of a settler family floating down the Mississippi River on a raft. These settlers, the description explained, would eventually help to civilize the West.[45]

Most Veiled Prophet organization members would likely have identified with the next tableau. The "Uncle Sam" character was meant to stand for all solid businessmen, printers, inventors, or industrial capitalists. For nineteenth-century wealthy and upper-middle-class Americans, Uncle Sam personified the average American who was trustworthy, self-reliant, industrious, and patriotic—precisely the kind of individual who belonged to the Veiled Prophet organization. The *Post-Dispatch*'s writer described the float as representing

> Uncle Sam and gives a good idea of the mechanical devices which have enabled the American people to conquer a continent in so short a time. The steam engine, the press, the telegraph, the electric light are present and over all flies the American eagle, in the shape of a flying machine and guided in its aerial career by Uncle Sam, who doffs his hat affably to those who render allegiance only to him and to his great colleague, the Veiled Prophet.[46]

On the float, Uncle Sam saluted these technological wonders that have allowed America to reach the very pinnacle of civilization. These wonders, and therefore American civilization itself, were the result of the ingenuity of America's business class.

The 1886 parade took "American History" as its theme, thereby providing the sponsors an opportunity to demonstrate the important lessons that could be learned from the nation's past. The first float, "America," showed the "Goddess of Progress" in the clouds watching a group of Indians who, according to the *Post-Dispatch,* "represented the infancy of the country and in their nude dress and primitive surroundings contrasted forcibly with the symbols of civilization just a few feet above their heads." Once again, history documented progress, and progress could only begin by removing the peoples who stood in its way. This viewpoint was consistent with the Social Darwinist beliefs of this class of Americans, who believed that the lesser "races" were backwards, inferior, and stood in the way of progress. Twisting Darwin's theories to suit their own ethnic biases, Social Darwinists believed in a hierarchy of ethnicity, with "inferior" peoples being undeserving of the same basic civil rights as those from higher "races." This provided a rationalization for wiping out other ethnicities in the name of "progress."

The remaining floats chronicled the deeds of "great men." Included in the parade were tableaux depicting the achievements of Columbus, Ponce de Leon, Cortez, DeSoto, Henry Hudson, Washington, Daniel Boone, and Andrew Jackson.[47] Pocahontas was the only female figure in the parade who was not used to represent an ideal. Her historical achievement was saving the life of John Smith, who shared space with her on the same float. In this sense, the parade taught that only white men had contributed—or perhaps even could contribute—to America's inexorable progress toward the pinnacle of western civilization.

According to the *Republican,* "Missouri," the final float of the parade (apart from the Veiled Prophet's float), was "emblematic of the wealth and prosperity of the state." On the float, the *Republican* continued, "there was an immense mountain in which there was iron, coal and lead mines." A female figure personifying "plenty" was seated at the top of the mountain. In addition, the front of the float had baskets containing Missouri's most important agricultural products. The message was that the nation, and Missouri itself, had prospered under the leadership of the elites presented earlier in the parade. They would continue to prosper if similar men—elites like those in the Veiled Prophet organization—were left in charge of the city, the state, and the nation.

Interestingly, the Civil War, one of the most important events in American history up to that time, did not play any part in this parade devoted to American history. Nor, for that matter, was it ever mentioned in any Veiled Prophet parade. Of course, the Civil War would have detracted from the elites' argument that America was a nation that had experienced uninterrupted progress. It was still a painful and somewhat embarrassing memory for many St. Louisans and therefore was left out of the Veiled Prophet parades that dealt with American history.

The 1892 parade, "The History of Louisiana," allowed parade makers to tell their story using historical leaders on a more local level. The opening float, "Missouri," set the tone for the entire parade. Despite its title, the float celebrated the recent achievements of the city more than those of the state. According to the *Globe-Democrat,* on the float was a female figure who personified "St. Louis, the Mound City, enthroned upon her hills, the pride of the West, the glory of the State." Like the float at the end of the 1886 parade, it celebrated the prosperity of recent times. "In the foreground," the *Globe-Democrat* continued, "are monster melons, fruits and flowers, typical of the fertility of Missouri and mechanical tools signifying industry. In the background, the new City Hall looms up, grand, majestic while to the right of it appear the Eads and Merchants' bridges, spanning the mighty Mississippi upon whose bosom are floating palaces. The wharves are piled high with bales of merchandise, signifying prosperity."[48] This optimistic picture of state and local prosperity was clearly written from the viewpoint of one who was doing well as an agricultural merchant—something that could be said of many of those in the Veiled Prophet organization at the time. Followed by the depictions of important local leaders, the message of this tableau was clear. As the 1886 parade had also demonstrated, St. Louis's prosperity followed directly from effective local leadership.

The remaining floats in the parade celebrated the deeds of important white male leaders throughout the history of the Louisiana Territory.[49] Float topics included such subjects as the "Death of DeSoto," "Reception of Marquette and Joliet," "LaSalle taking Possession of Louisiana Territory," "Founding the City of St. Louis," "Lieutenant Governors of Upper Louisiana," "Purchase of Territory of Louisiana," "Incorporators of St. Louis," "Governors of Louisiana," and "First Missouri State Officials." Many of these leaders were ancestors of the organization's current members, and the characterizations were, as one would expect, extremely laudatory. By linking themselves with their famous ancestors, the members of the organization showed they were worthy of the same respect as their ancestors and that the bloodlines of St. Louis's leadership remained unadulterated, thus lending themselves a sort of historical legitimacy. Not surprisingly, another message went out as well. By choosing to commemorate only the achievements of white men, the floats taught that only white men were worthy of mention in the tome of local history. As the 1886 parade also made clear, only white men had been and should be in positions of power. The prosperity in Missouri, and in the nation at large, demonstrated how well they had done.

The final float took the argument about the quality of Missouri's and St. Louis's leadership to its logical extreme, depicting the first "Native Missourian Inaugurated President." Because of the quality of Missouri's leadership, the elites felt it was only a matter of time before that happened. In fact, the *Republic*'s writer argued the "scene is supposed to be what will occur in 1942." Ironically, these leaders who in 1892 seemed so sure of themselves and felt they had led St. Louis and Missouri to prosperity, would later be considered too conservative—and even inept—by many urban historians. They would be blamed for St. Louis's failure to become a major regional power in the midwest, much less the "Future Great City of the World."[50]

Finally, the 1894 parade had the theme of "Mystic Societies and Past Veiled Prophet Highlights." In this parade the organization noted that it was the latest in a long line of mystic societies that had put on civic celebrations in the United States in the late nineteenth century. The first six floats depicted a history of mystic societies in America: "Cowbellian de Rakian" and the "Strikers' Club" from Mobile; as well as "Comus," "Rex," "Proteus," and "Felix" from New Orleans. According to the *Republic*'s writer, the next float, "The Veiled Prophet," completed the historical lineage of mystic societies in America. The point was that the celebrations the Veiled Prophet sponsored were important civic events in St. Louis and that such civic celebrations had a colorful history in America.

The remaining fourteen floats in the 1894 parade rendered selected tableaux from past parades, such as "Aurora" from the "Festival of Ceres" in 1878, "The Veiled Prophet's Land Conveyance" from the 1882 parade, and the "Arabian Nights" float from the parade of the same name in 1885.[51] By resurrecting previous floats, the Veiled Prophet organization presented the past parades as historical and cul-

5. *The Veiled Prophet and His High Priests.* From the *Veiled Prophet Magazine*, chromolithograph by Compton Litho. Company, 1883. Missouri Historical Society, St. Louis.

tural events. Furthermore, their selection of floats that were primarily from parades that attempted to inculcate culture suggested that the Veiled Prophet parade was not just a celebratory rite; it was an important cultural event for the community at large.

Therefore, these parades demonstrate one of the more interesting ways elites in the late nineteenth century attempted to shape the cultural values of ordinary people, in this case the values of working-class St. Louisans. The elites in the Veiled Prophet organization clearly hoped these parades would provide them with historical legitimacy as the hereditary aristocracy of St. Louis. At the same time, these parades were also to nurture in spectators an interest in high culture, suggest a certain prescribed view of "historical progress," and reinforce the established social order.

Unlike the parade, the second part of the annual celebration, the Veiled Prophet ball, was not meant to be seen by "the masses." Debutante balls, about which little scholarship exists, played an important role in the lives of the elites who participated in them. The Veiled Prophet balls allowed sponsors to see themselves as being "good fathers" to their daughters—and these balls enabled these men to control their daughters' courtships.

This interest in debutante balls and conspicuous consumption was not unique to St. Louis. William Beezley has argued that, like their St. Louis counterparts, the elites in late-nineteenth-century Mexico "turned to rituals associated with the life cycle—those that anthropologists identify as rites of passage—to display their prominence in society." According to Beezley, these rites were "usually staged for the community to witness, but only from a distance." The literate public could only read about the rites and aspire someday to take part in them.[52]

The rules for the Veiled Prophet ball stipulated that only those with invitations were allowed to attend and that men and women must attend in "full dress":

> Guests will bear in mind that tickets are not transferable and must be presented only by the party to whom they are issued. Should any one be found in the hall who has not been invited and whose name is not on the list furnished this Committee, he or she will be required to leave, by persons designated for that purpose.
>
> Gentlemen will be requested to attend in full dress and that there

may be no misunderstanding, we designate what may be considered full dress: Black coat, swallow-tail black vest, low cut; black pants, white tie, light gloves.

For ladies, we simply mean ("full dress" means) without hats, bonnets, or wraps.[53]

The invitation list was controlled by a small committee that allowed each member to "nominate" a small number of friends to receive invitations. Later, the member may have gotten a chance to add more names to his list, meaning that either some of his nominees were deemed undesirable or that his nominations duplicated those sent in earlier by another member.[54] As far as we know, all of these rules were followed to the letter; no exceptions were allowed.

The Veiled Prophet balls were covered closely by the press. For example, during the period from 1878 to 1880, the *Republican* devoted several columns just to describing the decorations in the ballroom. In 1879 the entire invitation list was run annually in the *Republican* (as is no surprise, it was not given to any other newspaper). Every one of the seventy-three founding members had a wife, a daughter, or both who appeared on the guest list each year. In 1880 both the *Republican* and *Post* began printing detailed descriptions of the dresses worn by ladies at the ball. Apparently the editors of both papers had begun to realize that the interest in the participants' dresses on the part of women would sell more newspapers.

At first the Veiled Prophet did not select a "Queen of Love and Beauty." The first debutante selected to dance by the Prophet in the early years was called the "belle of the ball." This was very similar to the procedures in the New Orleans Carnival societies at the time. During this same period, many newspapers in New Orleans began publishing the names of the women who danced the first quadrille with Krewe members at their masquerade balls. Later, in the mid-1880s, most Carnival societies began to have annual queens at their masquerade balls. As Samuel Kinser states, the Carnival societies' "spectacles were becoming less a place for successful men to strut than for their wives, daughters, and fiancées to display their charms."[55] However, the Veiled Prophet ball, while it did not have official queens during this period, was originally conceived as a place where the women in a prominent man's family would act as public "symbols of wealth" for him.

According to Kinser, the New Orleans Carnival societies eventually found their masquerades turning into debutante balls: "Connecting the fun and games of Carnival to the more serious business of showing off eligible young women to the right people was not the intention but the result of the gradual elaboration of the Carnival societies' rituals."[56] Nonetheless, the Veiled Prophet organization's ball was founded specifically as a debutante ball.

The Veiled Prophet ball was certainly a "rite of passage" for these young women.[57] According to southern historian Steven Stowe, the debutante ball was "an elite young woman's first occasion to display her social accomplishments and enjoy being considered a lady." The ballroom was also seen as being the woman's realm. She was in control. The feminine virtues of beauty and character required in the ballroom were basic to successful courtship. If a young woman mastered them, she "might become mistress of her own courtship." Young men were "puzzled by this female realm. Direction lay in woman's touch, as powerful as it was light."[58]

However, from a father's point of view, the Veiled Prophet ball was primarily a method of controlling courtship. By this time the idea of companionate marriage had taken hold in most social circles, especially among the upper classes. Most parents believed that their children should marry someone who would make them happy. In addition, by controlling the situations in which his daughter would meet members of the opposite sex (including, presumably, some control over the list of young men invited to the ball), the father could make sure that she met the "right kind" of man, someone from the same social class.[59] Although other elite social occasions ensued in the following months, the strict rules of the Veiled Prophet ball ensured that young women would begin their social life in the proper fashion.

It is possible the fathers who were on the fringe of the social elite hoped to gain from any advantageous contacts their son or daughter might make at the ball. After all, if one's son or daughter were to strike up an acquaintance with the son or daughter of a potential business contact, all the better. If the relationship grew closer, so could one's business relationship with the suitor's (or the suited's) father. Although one cannot be certain if such motives existed in the minds of members of the organization, the possibility cannot be dismissed. Since so many of these men joined the organization primarily for reasons of financial gain, this type of ulterior motive would not be far from their minds.

The "belle of the ball" for 1878 was Miss Susie Slayback, daughter of Alonzo Slayback. The "belle" is unknown for the years of 1879 and 1880. The selection of Slayback's daughter was no surprise considering all of the work that Alonzo had put into creating the organization. This method of using the daughter's title (as "belle of the ball" or, in later years, the "VP Queen") as a "reward" for her father's efforts has continued to the present day. One writer has gone so far as to argue that the daughter acts merely as a stand-in for her father.[60]

Susie Slayback's written account of the first ball was short, and because she only referred to herself in the third person, rather strange:

> It was indeed a thrill to those who attended the first ball given by the Veiled Prophet at the Merchant's Exchange in October 1878, and especially a girl who had never made her debut, to see many well known and interesting citizens. . . .
>
> The Exchange was beautifully adorned with southern smilax, rare plants and flowers; cages adorned the walls with birds singing. The strains of Strauss's charming music was delightful for the dancers. At each end of the hall an orchestra pealing forth favorite music of the day. And everyone enjoyed the parade around the fountain.
>
> The society women were exquisitely gowned, and the beauty of St. Louis was represented. . . . The time of crowned queens did not come for 14 years, but the belle of the ball was selected by the Prophet as his most admired partner, his selection for the first queen was Miss Susie Slayback. He descended from his lofty seat to the dance floor, found his partner and escorted her from her seat on to the floor where he presented her with a very pretty pearl necklace. Her dress was white satin made with quilted skirt studded with pearl beads and trimmed with lace.[61]

Perhaps Miss Slayback, like some later Veiled Prophet queens, was not someone who enjoyed the public limelight. Her use of the third person makes one think that, even five decades later, she did not feel comfortable remembering the public role that had been thrust upon her. In fact, she seemed to think that the honor would have been better bestowed upon another of "St. Louis' beauties" who were also in attendance at the ball. She carefully pointed out that "the beauty of St. Louis was represented" and went on to say "*but* the belle of the ball . . . was Miss Susie Slayback." This situation of the Veiled Prophet queen feeling uncomfortable and unworthy of her position would become increasingly common as the custom continued, especially in more recent decades.[62]

Of course, the belle of the ball and the Veiled Prophet queen had a very limited public role during this period. Until 1885, the names of the belles of the ball were not publicly printed because, according to Karen Goering, at the time "it was considered improper for a young woman's name to appear in print." This precedent was changed in 1885 when Virginia Joy, the belle of the ball for that year, was identified in the newspapers. As she recalled many years later, "I shudder even now as I think of it. I felt honored, of course, but at the same time disgraced for life at being made so conspicuous."[63] The precedent was broken. From this point on, the name of the belle of the ball and, later, the Veiled Prophet queen, would appear in the next morning's newspapers. This was the beginning of the semicelebrity status that in future years went with being the Veiled Prophet's Queen of Love and Beauty.

Despite its outward signs of success, in 1893, according to Walter B. Stevens, a feeling existed among the membership that "the V.P. had outlived its usefulness" and "it was semi-officially announced that the last Pageant had been given."[64] To get the celebration out of its malaise, the organization's leadership came up with the idea of crowning one of the debutantes as the "Queen of Love and Beauty." This change, it was thought, would increase interest in the ball among the membership, whose daughters would be eligible to vie for the title. Judging from the newspaper accounts of the time, the idea seems to have worked.

In 1894 the organization began officially crowning a Queen of Love and Beauty every year. The Carnival societies in New Orleans had begun selecting queens at their balls about ten years earlier. The first St. Louis queen, Hester Bates Laughlin, was crowned with a replica of the crown worn by Queen Victoria. Over the next century, the queens wore tiaras similar to those awarded at beauty pageants. Later, these crowns were often fashioned into broaches to be worn by the former queens at major social events for the rest of their lives. Together with the events of the parade (in which the newly crowned Veiled Prophet meets his subjects), the symbolic crowning of the Queen of Love and Beauty helped to reassure elites that they truly were the aristocratic upper crust of St. Louis.

At the same time, the Veiled Prophet organization began sending souvenirs along with the invitations. They included things like ink wells, napkin rings, clocks, or thermometers with a "VP" symbol somewhere on them. By placing these items in conspicuous places in their living rooms, members could claim membership in the organization without having to break their supposed "vow of secrecy."[65]

The Veiled Prophet ball was held on the same night as the parade. Those attending the ball had to wait for the parade to end before dancing could begin. Members who had participated in the parade would arrive at the ball in costume and remain in costume for the duration of the ball. These "maskers"—as the newspapers called them— would follow the Veiled Prophet out of the building when he left at the end of the evening. Starting in 1894, there would be a short break in the middle of the ball for the Veiled Prophet to crown the queen, but the ceremony was not overly elaborate at this time.

Newspapers gave considerable coverage to the Veiled Prophet ball. In the early years of the celebration, the ball received more or less equal coverage with the parade in all three newspapers—a couple of pages for each. However, by the late 1880s the three papers began to cover the ball more closely, devoting an average of two to three pages to it as against one to two pages on the parade. In the early 1890s the newspapers even began to print descriptions on the day before the ball of the dresses the debutantes and others would wear to the occasion. As the 1890s progressed, the disparity in coverage between the ball and the parade grew wider, especially after the organization began crowning queens in 1894. By the turn of the century, newspaper coverage of the parade seemed almost an afterthought. This phenomenon is especially interesting since, from all contemporary accounts, the parade was an extremely popular civic event at the time. Perhaps newspaper editors had discovered that detailed descriptions of the ball and ball gowns boosted circulation much more than similarly detailed descriptions of the parade floats. Most St. Louisans could go out and see the parade for themselves; the same was not true for the ball.

One cannot measure the success of the Veiled Prophet ball as easily as that of the parade. The balls certainly were well-attended and popular affairs with elites. They were at least marginally attractive to St. Louis middle-class and even working-class women. The fact that the newspapers printed lengthy accounts of them suggests that more than just the elite women found the descriptions of the ball enjoyable to read. However, any more substantive conclusions about the effect of the Veiled Prophet ball on St. Louis women of all classes are difficult to make.

Despite its popularity, the Veiled Prophet celebration nearly came to an abrupt end on several occasions during this period. The financial crunch of putting on a large and elaborate public spectacle—estimated at between fifteen and twenty thousand dollars annually—almost got the best of the membership. The leadership did three things to increase revenue in the first two decades of the organization's existence. First, in 1878, the organization raised its initiation fee from twenty-five to a hundred dollars. This brought in more revenue from the yearly initiation of new members and made membership more exclusive. Second, in the mid-1880s, the organization began to recruit many more members (its membership reached four hundred by 1899). Third, the organization accepted outside contributions to help put on the celebration. The understanding, according to Walter B. Stevens, was that "these contributors would be favored with ball invitations for themselves and their friends." In other words, when in need of additional funds, the organization's members simply increased the number of "exclusive" invitations to the ball rather than contributing more out of their own pockets. But considering that the majority of members joined the organization for personal gain, this should not come as a surprise. Despite the revenue-making initiatives, debts continued to pile up during the first fifteen years of the organization's existence.

The precarious situation came to a head in 1894 when, according to Walter B. Stevens, the debts grew to nearly five thousand dollars. L. D. Kingsland, the Veiled Prophet for that year, introduced a resolution to the organization's executive committee that the debt be repaid and that the practice of accepting outside contributions to help put on the celebration be abolished. Kingsland argued that by accepting contributions in exchange for ball tickets, the organization had lost control of its own invitation list. The Veiled Prophet warned that he would resign unless the organization adopted his resolution. It passed easily. The organization's financial committee gathered over ten thousand dollars in contributions, half of which was used to pay off the debts, the other half being placed in a bank account. From all indications, the organization remained financially self-supporting for the next ninety years.

The first twenty-one Veiled Prophet celebrations were successes. Both the parades and the balls met the goals of the organizers, inculcating genteel culture and values, teaching history, and encouraging loyalty to the nation and to the elites. If newspaper estimates are to be believed, the parade brought in hundreds of thousands of visitors to the city, and presumably to the fair, each year. The balls also allowed the elites, who considered themselves to be city fathers, to be good fathers to their daughters as well. As the years went by and the debts piled up, the organization raised its initiation fee substantially, initiated more members, and accepted outside contributions in exchange for Veiled Prophet ball tickets—all in an attempt to increase the organization's revenue.[66] After the crisis of the 1890s had passed, the organization's financial house appeared to be in order. The members of the Veiled Prophet organization had every reason in 1899 to believe that the outlook for the future was bright indeed.

"His Mysterious Majesty"

THE VEILED PROPHET CELEBRATION, 1900–1942

In 1928, Veiled Prophet organization members deemed their efforts a success. As a commemorative pamphlet boasted on the organization's fiftieth anniversary:

> So, the Veiled Prophet is rewarded through the years in seeing his mirage of yesterday become reality: St. Louis' population of 300,000 when first he came has grown to more than a million; the wealth of his adopted citadel has increased from several million to many billions of dollars. . . . The transition of fifty years is as magical as though the ambitious Alladins [*sic*] of St. Louis, stirred into prideful effort by the Prophet's various visits had rubbed the lamp of great desire and produced a city wonderful.[1]

Envisioning themselves as these "ambitious Aladdins," the organization's members took credit for the city's continued development during the last half-century. Like the New Orleans Carnival societies on which it was modeled, the Veiled Prophet organization was designed to advance the economic standing of the city at the same time its members advanced their own fortunes.[2] Through the parade and ball during the first half of the twentieth century, the organization's members continued to tout their achievements and demonstrate conspicuous consumption for the masses. However, this period was a time of great change for St. Louis politically, socially, and economically. These changes were reflected in how the organization and celebration evolved from 1900 to 1942.

During the first four decades of the twentieth century, the celebrations continued to include educational and historical elements, but they also began to resemble the commercialized leisure that increasingly became a part of everyday life during the period. The most significant attempts to teach history through the parade occurred in the celebrations between 1929 and 1934—the first years of the Great Depression and a time in which the members of the organization were troubled about recent social and economic trends. In these parades, the Veiled Prophet leaders followed the example of their nine-teenth-century counterparts by attempting to teach spectators about St. Louis and American history. But the parades from 1929 to 1934 were the last attempts to use the parade for such overt educational purposes. As the century progressed, parades were no longer the large-scale civic events they once had been. In the 1920s, parade floats began to more closely resemble the whimsical creations we see in parades today. This chapter will end with the onset of the Second World War, when elites used the Veiled Prophet parade to sell war bonds, linking the Veiled Prophet celebration and national patriotism in the strongest possible way.

In contrast, the ball became increasingly important for the organization's members. It developed into the primary social event for St. Louis's high society, and over the years outstripped the parade as a priority.

The decline of the Veiled Prophet parade as a civic event began early in the twentieth century and can be seen in the change of newspaper coverage. The parades of the early twentieth century were not covered in much depth by the newspapers. The detailed write-ups of the nineteenth century disappeared in the first decade of the twentieth century. While the parade themes continued to be educational in nature, the press no longer provided detailed descriptions of the floats to drive home the central theme to spectators.[3] Often only the float names were listed with little else appearing in the newspapers. As the first decade of the twentieth century advanced, even the lists of parade floats moved further back in the papers.

Therefore, members of the organization decided that the Veiled Prophet parades were no longer effective as a method of public communication and education. They had composed the earlier narratives and float descriptions but in the early twentieth century they, like most wealthy and upper-middle-class elites of the time, drew inward and wanted to participate less in public events. Furthermore, the Veiled Prophet organization was clearly identified by the public with the business class by the early twentieth century. Since public opinion of big business during the Progressive Era was decidedly negative, the elites had to work through other community organizations and stage other public spectacles to get their message out. Given that most publishers and most major advertisers were members, the press coverage of the celebration would reflect the organization's wishes to deemphasize the

Veiled Prophet celebration. So the organization's members obviously thought it was no longer worth their time to provide their audiences with a description of the parade in the newspapers. Interestingly, the Veiled Prophet parades continued to be popular and well-attended affairs—continuing to draw two to three hundred thousand spectators. The elites began searching for more meaningful public spectacles to stage.

However, the parades' floats continued to reiterate the same themes—instilling cultural values in its spectators and reminding them of the achievements of great white men in history. For example, the 1903 parade's theme was "Lyric Opera," the 1904 parade celebrated "Art and Architecture," and the 1916 parade presented Shakespeare's plays. History also continued to be a popular theme. The 1902 parade, "The Veiled Prophet's First Visit to the Land of the Louisiana Purchase Territory," included floats that celebrated the achievements of Hernando DeSoto, Daniel Boone, and James Monroe. One float showed the "raising of the American Flag in the Louisiana Territory."[4] The 1907 parade presented scenes from several historical dramas, and the 1913 parade depicted the "Seven Ages of Man."

There was one major technical advance in the Veiled Prophet parades of the early twentieth century. After visiting night pageants in Kansas City and Omaha, the Veiled Prophet committee decided to change the way the floats were illuminated. In 1903 the parade began to follow the streetcar lines and the floats were lighted by hundreds of electric bulbs rather than by gaslights or gas jets from the street. The electricity was transferred from the electric lines running above the street by use of a metal pole. In order to have enough power for the lights, the floats continued to be pulled by horses.[5] These lighted floats created a more brilliant scene than ever for the spectators.

As the twentieth century progressed, the parades began to take on a more whimsical tone. The parades of the 1920s presented such inoffensive themes as "Flowers, Fruits and Plants," "Dollyanna" (a collection of dolls from around the world), "Jewels and Talismans," and "Cartoons and Comics." These parades, like similar ones in the nineteenth century, emphasized escapism over cultural values. Unfortunately, due to the lack of parade float descriptions, additional analysis of a more meaningful nature cannot be made for the Veiled Prophet parades from the turn of the century until the late 1920s.

The decline in the amount of parade coverage is also reflective of

Table 5 Occupations of Members, 1899–1940

Occupational Category	1899	1914	1919	1930	1930	1940
Agricultural Commerce	83 (22%)	2 (4%)	0 (0%)	3 (4%)	2 (3%)	5 (7%)
Commercial Transportation	32 (9)	4 (7)	5 (8)	2 (3)	1 (1)	2 (3)
Merchants	56 (15)	9 (17)	3 (5)	2 (3)	4 (6)	3 (4)
Professionals	32 (9)	7 (13)	7 (12)	7 (9)	15 (22)	7 (10)
Public Communications	13 (3)	2 (4)	3 (5)	2 (3)	4 (6)	6 (9)
Industry	73 (20)	14 (27)	18 (30)	27 (34)	16 (24)	26 (39)
Financial Services	63 (17)	12 (23)	22 (37)	28 (35)	23 (34)	15 (22)
Other	21 (6)	2 (4)	2 (3)	8 (10)	3 (4)	3 (4)
	373	52	60	79	68	67

American culture at the time. As the twentieth century progressed, Americans spent less of their leisure time reading newspapers. With the rise of amusement parks and movie theaters, Americans had other things to do for entertainment. They certainly no longer wanted to spend time reading lengthy descriptions of an event they would see for themselves that evening. By providing less parade coverage, the members of the Veiled Prophet organization and the editors of the three newspapers were merely responding to major changes in American culture.

The greatest change in the celebration involved the demise of the St. Louis Agricultural and Mechanical Fair. The parade and ball had been a part of "Fair Week" or "Gala Week" during the last two decades of the nineteenth century. But as St. Louis's status as a agricultural center began to wane in the first decade of the twentieth century, the fair went into a period of decline. By the end of the nineteenth century, the Veiled Prophet parade overshadowed the fair itself. As with the parade, newspaper accounts of the fair's events started to become shorter and shorter. After existing for more than fifty years, the fair quietly died out in the first decade of the twentieth century.[6]

However, the popularity of the Veiled Prophet parade and ball ensured that they would continue on their own. The week of the Veiled Prophet parade and ball began to be referred to in the newspapers as "Veiled Prophet week" instead of "Fair week."[7] Most St. Louis historians would agree that the Veiled Prophet celebration was St. Louis's foremost annual public celebration for more than a half century following the demise of the fair. In fact, most St. Louisans today—including some current members of the Veiled Prophet organization—do not realize that the Veiled Prophet celebration was originally merely a facet of another larger and more inclusive celebration. Of course, the obscuring of the celebration's origins by newspapers over the last century is purposeful. It helps to mask the celebration's original capitalistic and less sincerely civic-minded origins.

Why did the fair die so easily? The membership was less interested in business opportunities provided by the fair because the proportion of members in agricultural commerce was dwindling. An examination of the occupational profile for the known Veiled Prophet members during this period (see Table 5) reveals several drastic changes in the organization's membership.[8] First, the number of members working in agricultural commerce plummeted from 22 percent in 1899 to 4 percent in 1914. By 1940, the number of those in agricultural commerce actually began to rebound slightly—rising to 8 percent. On the other hand, the number of members engaged in industry and financial services increased dramatically throughout the period. The number of members in industrial pursuits rose steadily from 20 percent in 1899 to 39 percent in 1940, dipping slightly in 1930. The number of members in financial services rose from 17 percent in 1899 to a high mark of 34 percent in 1930. It was during this period that even state- and national-level politicians began to appear as members in the organization—state and federal judges, a Missouri governor, and even a U.S. senator can be found among the organization's members. The remaining occupational categories remained remarkably constant.

What does this information reveal? For one thing, the change in the organization's occupational breakdown mirrored the decline of St. Louis as an agricultural shipping hub and its rise as an industrial manufacturing center. Many of the members who earlier were in agricultural pursuits had begun to invest in industrial ventures. Many prominent family names from the nineteenth century appeared in the lists, only now these men were middle and upper-management for industrial firms rather than the agricultural middlemen their fathers had been. The rise of members employed in financial services showed the need of prominent businessmen to maintain social contacts with those who could provide them with venture capital. Several prominent nineteenth-century family names also appeared as bankers. In fact, more of the younger members of the "old money" St. Louis elite moved into providing financial services than any other occupational field.

This information uncovers another social and economic role that the Veiled Prophet organization filled for its members: It served to preserve the economic status of the members' families. The contacts members made in the organization ensured the economic success of the members' sons. By making contacts with other prominent businessmen, Veiled Prophet members were able to find jobs for their sons in industry and banking, thus ensuring the continued economic and social success of their families. At the turn of the century, Scott McConachie insisted that "even though the larger and more impersonal corporation began to replace the family proprietorship and partnership as the dominant business form, the sons of prominent families often had easier access through their family connections than did the average young man" in St. Louis.[9] Members originally tried to use the debutante ball to control the courtship of their daughters. That goal certainly still existed during the first decades of the twentieth century. Therefore, members used the contacts made in the organization to provide for their children's futures—whether their children were male or female. As in the nineteenth century, the concerns of paternity were a leading reason why members joined the organization.

However, the collusion on the part of members had major consequences for the economic, social, and political power structure of St. Louis during this period. One could argue that many of the same powerful families controlled St. Louis in 1940 as in 1899. This continuity of power still exists in St. Louis today, if anything to an even greater extent. At least part of the reason for this is the skillful use of the Veiled Prophet organization itself by the elites. If the "Big Cinch"—St. Louis reformers' epithet for what they believed was a closed and conspiratorial business elite—existed, it would have had one of its power bases in the Veiled Prophet organization.[10]

The power and influence of the Veiled Prophet membership, as in the nineteenth century, was considerable. They played important roles in every major political and cultural event during the period. Veiled Prophet members held eleven of the twelve seats on the executive committee for the 1904 World's Fair and fifty-four of the ninety-seven seats on the World's Fair board of directors. David Francis, the chairman of the World's Fair committee, had been a member of the Veiled Prophet organization since its beginning in 1878. When St. Louis celebrated its centennial in 1909, the organization's members made sure that the Veiled Prophet parade had a prominent role in the celebrations of the week.[11]

National political figures acknowledged the Veiled Prophet organization when they visited the celebration. During the first fifty years of the celebration's existence, two major political figures who wished to curry favor with the powerful in St. Louis visited the Veiled Prophet parade and ball. As mentioned in chapter two, Grover Cleveland viewed the parade and visited the ball in 1887. While running for president, William H. Taft visited the celebration in 1908. After delivering three speeches in the city, Taft viewed the parade and attended the Veiled Prophet ball that evening. From newspaper accounts, it seems Taft spent most of the time visiting with wealthy attendees at the ball, presumably hoping to solicit their financial and political support for his campaign.[12]

Veiled Prophet members continued to be socially conservative, but at the same time they were boosters of the city and pro-growth in politics. David Thelen argues that some Missourians at the turn of the century were "inspired by a combination of vision, greed, and restlessness" to seek "a new order based on economic growth" and "unleashed entrepreneurship." Elites in the Veiled Prophet organization certainly held such beliefs. Their political ideology is most clearly seen in the constitutions of the Commercial Club and Businessmen's League. For example, Commercial Club members founded their organization "for the purpose of advancing by social intercourse and by a friendly interchange of views the commercial prosperity and growth of the city of St. Louis."[13] A large number of Veiled Prophet members belonged to one or both of those organizations. In addition to personal prosperity and preserving their families' status, this pro-growth goal was the foremost political and economic tie binding members of the Veiled Prophet organization.

Therefore, the elites in the Veiled Prophet organization were moderate progressives in the political sense. By and large they were not concerned with social justice; they only supported progressive movements when they helped to foster growth or their own personal prosperity. They wanted a centralized government that was controlled by the business class and therefore supported the various charter reform drives that took place in St. Louis during the early twentieth century. However, whenever progressive organizations began to move beyond pro-growth and pro-centralization reforms into advocating social justice reforms, the elites would withdraw their financial support and, by putting pressure on leaders, bring a swift end to such reform proposals.[14]

This generalization holds true when one examines the history of the St. Louis Civic League, St. Louis's foremost liberal progressive organization in the second decade of the century. In 1911, the Civic League and the important members of the Businessmen's League headed a drive to change the city's charter to one that provided a more centralized form of government. The charter drive failed, largely due to working-class opposition. Working-class St. Louisans wanted to continue to elect their councilmen by wards rather than moving to an at-large system of representation. After the 1911 charter reform drive, business elites abandoned the Civic League over tenement reform and other social-justice reform issues. For the business class, social justice always took a back seat to what they believed to be the more important goal of economic growth. Once the attempt to pass a new city charter had failed, business leaders no longer saw any reason to participate in the league's activities.[15]

This recalcitrance on the part of business elites in turn caused the Civic League reformers to break with them during the early part of the decade. To increase popular support, the Civic League advocated democratic reforms like recall and referendum—reforms the business elite certainly did not support. The later versions of the new City Charter (scheduled for plebiscite during 1914 and also championed by the Civic League) contained several such reforms.[16] At first, business elites rejected the new charter.

However, in 1913 business elites and Civic League leaders once again found themselves drawn together as political bedfellows. During the intervening two years, the business elites had difficulty generating popular support for their goal of centralized and efficient city government. By the middle part of the decade it had become obvious that the Veiled Prophet parade was failing to instill in spectators a sense of loyalty to the elites and their larger political goals. Despite their misgivings about the Civic League, the business elites joined with local progressive groups to present another type of public spectacle, the historical pageant. The elites hoped this pageant would ultimately help to unify St. Louisans behind the idea of centralized government. Thus, in 1914, Veiled Prophet members played an important role in designing the St. Louis *Pageant and Masque*.[17] Prominent members of the Veiled Prophet organization held nearly a third of the seats on the three main committees of the St. Louis Pageant and Drama Association (SLPDA), the organization that produced the pageant. In fact, the members of the SLPDA got the idea of creating a single unifying public spectacle from their past experiences with the Veiled Prophet celebration. Their first idea was to link the pageant with Veiled Prophet week in some way. However, this idea was eventually abandoned in favor of making the *Pageant and Masque* a separate event.

While David Glassberg has argued that the elites in the SLPDA were trying to use the St. Louis pageant to further the progressive goals of better government *and* social justice, the lack of participation by business leaders in the Civic League brings that conclusion into question. Of the 254 members of the Civic League in 1913 and 1914, only 31 were also members of the Veiled Prophet organization. The powerful business class in St. Louis supported the SLPDA but not the Civic League. They wanted the centralized government called for in the revised version of the charter but little else the Civic League wanted. Still, they swallowed their pride and returned to the progressive fold during 1913 because centralized city government was a cause too important to spurn. They supported the new charter even though it included so-called popular democratic reforms.[18]

Many important Veiled Prophet members helped to put on the St. Louis *Pageant and Masque*, written by Percy MacKaye in 1914. The mammoth production played to four hundred thousand spectators between May 28 and June 1 in Forest Park. The pageant part of the presentation, like the Veiled Prophet parades of the nineteenth century, glorified St. Louis's civic leaders through the period of the Civil War—including Pierre Laclede, Auguste Chouteau, and Thomas Hart Benton. This part of the celebration was merely a form of the Veiled Prophet parade writ large, and it nicely met the political needs of the business class, who wished to encourage the audience to be loyal to their current political leaders and vote for the charter. That goal was made abundantly clear in one of the four presentations. According to the *Post-Dispatch,* one of the actors who portrayed Thomas Hart Benton in the July 1 presentation even welcomed troops home from the Mexican War with the appeal that "Now that you all are safe at home, I hope you will work and vote for the new charter."[19]

The second half of the presentation, the masque, was less clear in its meaning. In the words of Elizabeth Schmidt, the masque was a confusing allegorical combination of "murky symbolism and bad verse." In the masque, the citizens of St. Louis, led by the symbolic figures of Cahokia and St. Louis, rose up to defeat the symbolic figure of Gold—who was in command of their city. Schmidt interprets this allegory to mean that through united effort and cooperation, St. Louisans can "hope to defeat the evil forces of greed, power and corruption that threatened civilization." While such an anticapitalistic interpretation of MacKaye's meaning for the spectacle may be accurate, business elites like those in the Veiled Prophet organization would have seen it differently. They would have felt that the spectacle showed that only if the right kind of people (symbolized by the aristocratic and divine character of "St. Louis") are looked to for leadership can St. Louisans build a more perfect society. Of course, the elaborate symbolism of the masque was more than likely lost on the audience. David Glassberg argues that at the performances "a picnic atmosphere prevailed over that of a solemn civic ritual. . . . Vendors hawked hot dogs, sandwiches, ice cream, popcorn, lemonade, and soda water."[20] Civic leaders were finding that this type of public spectacle, like the Veiled Prophet parade, had its limitations.

Despite the shortcomings of the *Pageant and Masque,* a little over a month later, the charter passed in a public plebiscite. Newspaper writers were quick to credit the performance of the *Pageant and Masque* with contributing to the victory. Labor leaders, who had worked hard to defeat the charter because of its proposal to further centralize city government, argued in *St. Louis Labor* that "whenever Big Cinch is anxious to 'put one over' on the people the old Roman Method must be applied: 'Panem et Circenses'—bread and plays! In St. Louis the Big Cinch can accomplish its purpose with pageant plays—without bread. The Railroad and Street Railway Octopus make golden harvest, the Hoteliers and Department Stores get their share of the business graft!" To the embarrassment of liberal progressives, the electorate later used the popular initiative measure in the charter to pass a segregation ordinance in 1916.[21] Most business leaders in the Veiled Prophet organization would have felt this action proved what they had been saying all along about the sagacity of such popular democratic reforms. However, despite the apparent success of the *Pageant and Masque,* very little else was done with the genre nationwide after 1914. The historical pageant did not replace the Veiled Prophet parade as St. Louis's annual civic event and the SLPDA quietly disbanded within two years.

While the business elite in the Veiled Prophet organization may have lost the battle over the political reforms in the 1914 charter, they did not lose many others. Their vision of St. Louis was the one that prevailed in the first half of the twentieth century. During this period St. Louis became a city controlled by a clique of businessmen and aldermen who, in collusion with the mayor, made most policy decisions. The city grew rapidly and became a major industrial manufacturing center. While never attaining the economic power of its old rival, Chicago, it did make great strides in industry.

Ironically, even though the elites in the Veiled Prophet organization had no interest in measures for social justice, the Veiled Prophet character was used by the *Post-Dispatch*'s editors to call for such reforms and to criticize elite rule. The editors took advantage of the fact that the Veiled Prophet was essentially an ill-defined character. For several years after the turn of the century, the *Post-Dispatch* printed an annual fictional "interview" with the Veiled Prophet. This interview could be used in a variety of ways. In 1900 the *Post-Dispatch*'s editors used the Veiled Prophet to decry the recent discovery that a group of public officials had allowed an illegal gambling racket to operate in the city. In 1902 the editors used the Veiled Prophet character as a progressive voice to attack city officials for their "boodling" ways. In 1904 the Veiled Prophet congratulated David Francis and the World's Fair for drawing St. Louis "out of its provincial self."[22]

Later, the *Post*'s editors used the Veiled Prophet figure in cartoons to make fun of or criticize elites. In 1906 the Veiled Prophet lamented the supposed decline of public interest in Veiled Prophet events. He was shown in a 1909 cartoon being ignored by the public during the city's centennial celebration. A 1911 cartoon depicted a large number of "popular" and "inspiring suggestions" for floats for the Veiled

Prophet parade like "A Pennant-Winning Ball Team," "The Common People Enthroned," "Trust Magnates in Jail," "A Model Hospital," "39 cent hats," and, last but not least, "Invitations to the [Veiled Prophet] Ball." These float suggestions indicate the problems of living in St. Louis at the time, problems the *Post*'s cartoonist blamed largely on the elites in the Veiled Prophet organization.[23] Clearly, the editors of the *Post-Dispatch,* like the members of the Veiled Prophet organization, used the Veiled Prophet symbol to serve their own political goals.

As the *Post-Dispatch*'s annual "interviews" further obscured the murky image of the Veiled Prophet, members of the organization felt they needed to regain control of the image and of the celebration itself. There had never been any attempt to present an "official" version of the Veiled Prophet's story. While attempts had been made in early parades to place the celebration within the context of St. Louis society, nothing of an "official" nature had ever been published. That changed with the appearance in 1911 of Walter B. Stevens's *History of St. Louis, the Fourth City, Volume 2.* Stevens, a former journalist for the *Globe-Democrat,* the secretary of the Louisiana Purchase Exposition Company (the group behind the 1904 World's Fair), and the man who would be the Veiled Prophet in 1916,[24] wrote an official account of the history of the organization and its role in St. Louis society.

Stevens argued that the Veiled Prophet celebration was linked with the celebrations in New Orleans and was only one in a long line of public celebrations of its type (he referred to short-lived celebrations in Memphis, Baltimore, Kansas City, and Omaha). However, only the New Orleans, Mobile, and St. Louis celebrations still existed in 1911. He suggested that "two conditions seem vital to the success" of this type of celebration: "secrecy of organization" and "charm of the spectacle." Stevens contended that the way the organization carefully selected its members had "contributed . . . to the powerful and enduring character of the organization." Stevens stressed the elitism of the organization by saying that the organization "represents all the good elements of society" and was "rigidly exclusive of those who are not in good repute." He believed that someone fortunate enough to be inducted as a member would soon find that "he is in the midst of his friends."[25] In fact, judging from the intermarriage linking some of the more prominent families and the fact that membership usually passed from father to son, members, once inducted, might have found themselves among their own family.

Stevens described the spectacle's popularity as well as the apparent deference afforded to the elites by the crowd:

> The stranger, blasé with the sights of the world, marvels at the popular hold of the Veiled Prophet. He sees the population of a great city densely massed along a route of five miles. He hears but few loud shouts of applause. The long line of floats passes through hedges of humanity almost as mute as the costumed figures in the tableaux.
>
> The multitudes come. They wait patiently. They greet decorously the Veiled Prophet at the head of his retinue. They stand absorbed until the last float has passed. They melt away. Twelve months later they are back again, with their cousins from out of town, to gaze on the mystic spectacle. No diminution of the people's interest in the Veiled Prophet is discernible. On the contrary the throngs on the streets grow with the years. The urgency of requests for invitations increases.[26]

While Stevens may have exaggerated the celebration's popularity, his description of the eerie silence of the large crowd of spectators rings true. This type of spectacle is certainly a far cry from other rowdy and all-inclusive spectacles that characterized the mid-nineteenth century. There were no brass bands or groups marching in ranks, only elites passing in front of a working-class crowd that remained strangely silent.

This silence is consistent with the findings of other scholars examining similarly quiet cultural events, who urge us not to mistake this acquiescence for deference. They argue that in societies that have a clearly delineated ruling class, such public displays of seeming deference are for the benefit of the ruling elites themselves. The political anthropologist James Scott argues that in societies there exists both a public transcript and a "hidden transcript," forged in secret away from the prying eyes of powerful elites.[27] Therefore, these scholars argue, it would be inaccurate to see the quietness and orderliness of the crowds at the Veiled Prophet parades as a sign of social deference. While the working-class crowd might have intended to give this impression (and Stevens certainly fell for the ploy), the real feelings of the event's spectators were probably quite different.

Stevens also raved about the technological advances in the celebration and the city itself. He said that in 1878, "St. Louis was a city of horse cars, of gas lamps," and "of 330,000 population." He boasted of the parade's improvements:

> The route was from Lucas Market place to the Chamber of Commerce. In 1911 the distance traversed is three or four times as

great. The floats roll along asphalt streets which had neither pavement nor sidewalks in those early days. The electric current from the trolley is the illuminant. It has taken the place of the oil lamps, the flambeaux and the Roman candles which lighted the pageant for twenty years. The Veiled Prophet has kept pace with the city's growth and improvement.

In this way, Stevens implicitly linked the Veiled Prophet celebration to the progress made by the city since the organization's founding. He later said that without such a benevolent organization there could not have been such technological progress in St. Louis.[28]

Stevens's work gives the reader a sense of what it was like to participate in the Veiled Prophet parade. For example, he described how the organization assigned each participant in the parade a number. For the rest of the evening the participant was given instructions according to that number and was referred to only by that number. In this way, the member's name was never spoken in front of the crowd. This elaborate way of maintaining anonymity is still used today.[29]

Stevens argued that the entire community enjoyed the Veiled Prophet celebration, which explained its continued success:

> The temperament of the community! Without that favoring, the organization and the preparation would be powerless to compel success. The Veiled Prophet is not more popular with one element than with another among the people of St. Louis. Wide-eyed and wondering, the ranks of faces of every hue and nation which enter into the population of the city are raised with like degree of interest when the Veiled Prophet passes. The mystic pageant temperament pervades all St. Louis. It is lacking in most other cities of approximate latitude. . . . But here, in the heart of the county, with the most thoroughly composite population, the most typical Americans, the Veiled Prophet is at home.[30]

Stevens's words contrast with those of progressives who argued that a public spectacle should unite the community behind a single goal. Stevens contended that the community unites in a very different way: The celebration allowed middle- and working-class St. Louisans to come together in paying respects to their leaders and social betters. In short, he provided an elitist view of what the celebration entailed. Like many in his social position, he believed deference and public appreciation for the work of elites were necessary for community cohesion.

Interestingly, members of the African American middle class seemed quite receptive of the Veiled Prophet celebration during the

1910s and 1920s. The *St. Louis Argus*, the leading newspaper of the black middle class, usually listed the Veiled Prophet parade route on its front page during this period. In fact, members of the black middle class wanted a bigger role in the celebration. The editors of the *Argus* complained that "men prominent in professional and business life . . . were not received as they should have been" during the 1916 celebration. The black middle class was also quite interested in creating its own elitist celebration during the period. The *Argus* of the late teens and twenties was full of advertisements for "African (or Colored) Veiled Prophet Balls" at black establishments such as Jazzland, the Classique, the Olympia Club, and the Capitol Palace during the first week of October. Furthermore, these celebrations appear to have been taken quite seriously by participants. Most of the celebrations ended with the selection of an African Veiled Prophet queen and her court, which was dutifully reported by the *Argus* the next day.[31]

However, not all St. Louisans were as deferential as Stevens had suggested. Stevens was accurate in describing the general manner of the spectators; there certainly were no major attempts by working-class spectators to interrupt or disrupt the Veiled Prophet parades. But in one not-so-subtle way the working-class crowd did try to lessen the social meaning and overdone regality of the parade: by throwing objects at the floats. In this way, by making a sort of farce out of the parade, working-class spectators could both enjoy the parade's spectacle and resist its show of social power and status. Such behavior was widespread throughout the parade's history. As Curtis Wilson wrote in a 1972 article in the *Post-Dispatch*, the members who rode on the floats had historically been "hidden under padding and eyeframes" that he said concealed their identity but, more importantly, served "to ward off rocks"[32] and other missiles hurled from the crowd.

In fact, Robert Tooley, later Den Superintendent of the Veiled Prophet organization, said such "resistance" was institutionalized and a part of the yearly parade in the 1930s. As he recalled: "every confectionery in the city I think stocked peashooters before the parade. . . . That way you'd get these peashooters and these dried peas and you could shoot them at the floats and, hell, when we tore those old trailers [the old railroad cars that served as the bases for the floats every year] apart I'll bet you we found, gee-whiz, hundreds of thousands of dried peas between the boards of the trailers." Tooley described still another way that working-class boys tried to rob the parade of its dignity. Boys would attempt to knock the metal pole loose that conducted the electricity for the float from the trolley lines above the street. When the pole was disconnected from the line, the lights on the floats would flash off and on until the operator (a man who followed each float holding the metal pole to the trolley line) could get the pole back onto the line. As Tooley remembered, "I told Ted Satterfield [Tooley's predecessor as Den Superintendent, who worked for the Veiled Prophet organization from 1933 to 1973] that one time and he said, 'Were you guys doing that?' I remember people doing that all the time."[33] While some might call such behavior boyish nonsense— Tooley certainly felt that way—its social meaning should not be overlooked. Anything that detracted from the membership's presentation of themselves as elites represented a conscious or unconscious protest against elite power. More significant types of protest were in the organization's future.

This interpretation of resistance is also consistent with the findings of other scholars. Robin Kelley contends that in such performances "one finds the hidden transcript emerging 'onstage' in spaces controlled by the powerful, though almost always in disguised forms." Kelley finds that these forms can include "open attacks on individuals, institutions, or symbols of domination."[34] Therefore, the working-class spectators' practice of throwing objects at the Veiled Prophet parade floats may have been the St. Louis working class's manner of making its true feelings known to those in power.

In fact, the Veiled Prophet organization encountered a fair amount of open opposition from the working-class press during the first three decades of the twentieth century. Writers at *St. Louis Labor,* the leading socialist and working-class newspaper, viewed the Veiled Prophet celebration very differently than their elite counterparts. While *St. Louis Labor* had presented the Veiled Prophet and the ensuing Carnival Week as positive for St. Louis in the 1890s, the newspaper turned on the celebration in the early years of the twentieth century. There was an important reason for this about-face on the part of *St. Louis Labor.* During the early 1900s, there was quite a struggle going on between social classes for public demonstration (and communication) space in St. Louis.

Beginning with the streetcar strike of 1900, the police, elites, and labor unions were increasingly at odds with one another. During the streetcar strike, a hastily formed and elite-backed "posse" fired upon strikers, killing three and wounding fourteen others. After the strike, elites in St. Louis organized more effectively to control the police and thus would never again "personally gather arms to intimidate the working class." The elites became more adept at using legal means (such as court injunctions) to quell public worker resistance. However, overt symbolic attempts at intimidation did continue. For the next twenty years the police would hold their annual "riot gun" parade. In this parade the police would display weapons originally used by the posse in the streetcar strike. In this way, according to Dina Young, calls for "law and order" were commonly "connected to anti-union-ism" in a very clear way.[35] Consequently, in the years following the streetcar strike socialists and other working-class groups found themselves being denied parade and demonstration permits. In some cases, socialist demonstrations were even attacked by city police.[36]

During the early 1900s, the writers at *St. Louis Labor* began to write negatively about the celebration and would continue to do so for the next thirty years. In 1906, the newspaper quipped that the "Carnival Week was a week of genuine rowdyism under the disguise of local business patriotism."[37] In short, workers understood what the aims of the celebration were and disregarded them. While elites may have wanted workers to behave themselves during the celebration, they would have none of it. In 1907, *Labor* was quite upset that Mrs. Moses Fraley wore a gown and diamonds worth $68,000 to the Veiled Prophet ball. "Will some poor woman figure out how many years, of three workdays each, a working man with $400 wages a year has to work in order to earn enough to support his family and buy $68,000 worth of jewels for his wife?"[38]

Bitter that the streets were no longer free for more democratic spectacles, the working-class press stepped up its attacks on the Veiled Prophet celebration in the 1910s. In 1913, *Labor*'s writer asked, "Who decides who is to be 'queen' of the Veiled Prophet's ball? Must she have qualifications in addition to that of a Dad with a strong bankroll?" The writer went on to contend: "It is marvelous to observe how barren of real worth the annual parade and ball of tinsel and glitter is. Aside from giving work to a few people, the whole thing is a sham and a humbug. The merchants find it brings Reuben to town and enables them to separate him from his cash. That is the main thing."[39] In 1914, *Labor*'s writer argued that "Veiled Profit" was actually "the correct spelling" for the name of the celebration. They went further to argue that the veil "consists of some paint, tinsel and electric light; the profits are very real and substantial however." In short, the working-class press during the 1910s believed the parade and ball to be nothing but a meaningless tinsel and glitter show for out-of-town visitors. The streets were now tightly regulated and were no longer free to be used as a means of public communication. Interestingly enough, even socialists saw the need for their own fall celebration—perhaps as counterprogramming. The Annual Socialist Fall Festival took place between 1909 and 1911.[40]

Later in the century, during the 1920s and 1930s, as the socialist and working-class press began to have trouble surviving financially, their attacks on the celebration became increasingly caustic. In 1925, *St. Louis Labor* contended that the "St. Louis Veiled Prophet celebration is getting as old as Methusalem and it is high time that our business elite think of something new and something more sensible and creditable to this community."[41]

In the closing weeks of *St. Louis Labor*'s existence as a newspaper, the editors mentioned the Veiled Prophet celebration again. One of the last gasps of the newspaper in 1930 was to attack the celebration one last time. As a workers' advocate, Martin A. Dillmon found the lure of the parade on the populace to be rather frustrating and perverse:

> I accidentally got into Washington Avenue the night of the Veiled Prophet parade, and had a helluva time getting out of the crush. Each side of the street was lined with a mass of people eager to see the aristocratic plutes promenade their finery. If once we get these same folks just as hot in an election campaign? Gosh, what a headache for reaction!
>
> Newspapers told with big gusto about the pomp of the Veiled Prophet ball, "which ushered in the social season." A flood of lights was arranged "so as to bring out the elegance of women's gowns," we are told. Printed photographs told the story further. Of course, the "social season" must be properly ushered in, oh, yes. But as I looked at those photographed vulgar displays of wealth and silks, I could not help but think of the hundreds of St. Louis mothers and children who went to bed that very night without enough supper, besides the growing number of undernourished children who are being given special care in St. Louis open-air schools in an effort to spare them from the ravages of tuberculosis![42]

The working-class press by 1930 could not help but be upset that workers (who they felt should have known better) seemed so thoroughly under the annual celebration's spell. By 1930, the once multivocal public sphere was now tightly regulated and populated by far fewer voices—and the voices heard the loudest, according to the working-class press, were those of wealthy elites.

Further frustrating the working-class press's efforts to end the annual celebration was the fact that members of the Veiled Prophet organization became increasingly adept at public relations as the century went on. When America entered the First World War the organization was careful that its image, and that of the Veiled Prophet himself, was linked with altruism and patriotism. In August 1917 the organization issued a statement to the press announcing its decision to suspend activities for the duration of the war: "When news of dead and wounded American soldiers and sailors, who have fought our fight, may come to us at any moment, it is no time for pageants, parades or balls. This organization is one of pure altruism; not one of its members derives any personal profit or benefit from any of its activities, which are solely in the interest of all the people of our city."[43] This statement asserted that its members were altruistic patriots, not the greedy war profiteers that St. Louis labor leaders were making them out to be at the time.[44] According to the release, the businessmen now made it their long-term goal to push for American victory in the war instead of making a profit. Of course, those "altruistic patriots" who owned or invested in war industries clearly stood to make profits beyond their altruistic dreams. Such patriotic rhetoric helped to bolster the image of the organization and the business class in the eyes of the community. The organization later held a "Victory and Peace" parade in 1919. The floats in the parade depicted the Allied powers in the war, and the final float was entitled "Democracy."[45]

During the 1920s, the organization was careful to safeguard the image of the organization and its mythical potentate. In 1927 the Veiled Prophet organization faced another serious decision. Because the city had been struck by a devastating tornado in late September, the organization decided to delay the celebration three weeks. According to members, spectators greeted the parade in 1927 "as a deliverance celebration, typical of the spirit of a people that in their allegiance and enthusiasm overcome the greatest obstacles."[46] While this account may have overstated the impact of the celebration, holding the celebration instead of canceling it represented a return to normality that the community needed.

The most important attempt to shape the Veiled Prophet's image occurred in 1928 when the organization published the illustrated pamphlet "His Mysterious Majesty the Veiled Prophet's Golden Jubilee: A Short History of St. Louis' Annual Civic Carnival." Because it celebrated the organization's fiftieth anniversary and had a gold cover, the pamphlet became known as the "Golden Book." It gave the Veiled Prophet a mythology and linked him with the important events in St. Louis history. The benevolent character of the Veiled Prophet that most St. Louisans are now familiar with came from the story presented in this pamphlet. The pamphlet was distributed to all organization members and to the Court of Love and Beauty at the ball. Perhaps most importantly, several copies were given to the Missouri Historical Society and the St. Louis Public Library.[47]

The Golden Book was a revealing historical document. Like the detailed parade descriptions of the late nineteenth century, it provided the reader with a rare chance to examine the worldview of the elites who made up the Veiled Prophet organization at the time. It demonstrated what they believed the role of the organization and its celebration to be (they referred to the celebration as a "great spectacle of civic unity"). It also argued that the elites would play an active role in determining St. Louis's future.

The Golden Book begins its story by describing the homeland of the Veiled Prophet in a scene reminiscent of an oriental fairy tale:

> It was late afternoon in Cathay. The greenfolds of the hills were gay with tumbling waterfalls; the fields a miraculous fusion of almonds and lilacs; the meandering rivulet blue with hyacinths—a vale of Cashmere-like fertility, opulent with golden nectarines, honey and grape-laden vines. On the distant horizon in the flush of sunset, trudged a camel pack, exquisitely outlined as though carved in jade by some Oriental artist; the far-flung fantastic music of caravan bells pleasantly filled the valley; fireflies were beginning their nocturnal wanderings among the roses and orchids, while the subtle perfume of the otra, the quintessence of eastern perfumes, filled the air.[48]

After several more paragraphs of such fluff, the opening section of the work closed by informing the reader that in this pamphlet the Veiled Prophet or "Grand Monarch" will compose "his memorabilia of a half century of beneficent reign over the farthest-flung dominion of his realm, the great Saint Louis."

The writer, in the guise of the Veiled Prophet, recounted that the Veiled Prophet, having heard Laclede's founding myth, decided to help St. Louis reach its full potential:

> Clearly now, after fifty years, came the recollection of that day in the long ago when he had gleaned from old records the early prophesy of a youthful but intrepid Frenchman, Pierre Laclede Liguest, made to Governor de Neyon in 1763:
> —"a situation where I intend establishing a settlement which in the future shall become one of the most beautiful cities in America."
> A vow too enthusiastically made by noble youth to remain unfulfilled. Here was the magic city of his dream! He would help! And so, in 1878, he visited far-off Saint Louis.
> In jubilant mood, he had come to encourage wholesome revelry at a time when the garnered crops of the golden harvest gave greatest promise for men's efforts.

By linking itself with the noblest of St. Louis's historical figures, Pierre Laclède Liguest, the organization created a founding myth for itself as well.

The pamphlet went on to chronicle the events of the past fifty years of economic growth in St. Louis; growth which, according to the Veiled Prophet, he had helped to encourage. The city of three hundred thousand and lit by gaslights had become a much larger metropolis of one million, illuminated by electric lights. The writer said that the Veiled Prophet was pleased by such progress:

> What a supreme satisfaction was his that Saint Louis has grown to leadership in education and art, as well as industry, with the first kindergarten school in America, the first electrically illuminated streets, the first great civic pageant and masque, the first municipal opera. . . . [T]he first!—the first!—the first—what a telling mark of civic pride those "firsts," how typical of the St. Louisans who can best enjoy today if it holds some promise of tomorrow. . . .

The view of history evidenced in this passage is similar to that employed in the Veiled Prophet parades. History to the elites was the chronicling of the achievements of great men—a recording of their "firsts." The Golden Book's author maintained that the Prophet inspired city leaders to achieve their "firsts."

The pamphlet contended that the Veiled Prophet required members of his retinue to have a "broader vision of citizenship," which included planning for "orderly growth" and "look[ing] out and upward." This altruistic organization, the pamphlet explained, was now "in its third generation," and the sons and grandsons of the organization's founders desired to see "their city become what Liguest prophesied for it, the best place in all the land in which to establish a business and the best place to make a home in the real sense of that word." While not necessarily calling in so many words for a "bigger and better St. Louis," economic growth was clearly the primary goal for the elites.

The Veiled Prophet, the writer argued, annually gave the organization's members "the admonition that they were knights errant for the upbuilding of their city, civically, commercially, educationally, socially, and artistically." This attempt to present themselves as "knights errant" dovetailed with the authoritarian and aristocratic perspective on the world held by the elite. They were the leaders who should be making the decisions for the city.

The Golden Book continued with a passage that tells the reader a great deal about how the members of the organization felt about themselves and the success of the celebration. In this passage the Veiled Prophet himself becomes a metaphor for the power of the business elites:

> This beloved despot, evasive but real, who rules with an iron hand encased in velvet, is as much a power in St. Louis than most of the royalties that survive on the earth. He rules by kindness, fellowship and love. He inspires by precept and encouragement.
>
> So, the Veiled Prophet is rewarded through the years in seeing his mirage of yesterday become reality: St. Louis' population of 300,000 when first he came has grown to more than a million; the wealth of his adopted citadel has increased from several million to many billions of dollars; its palaces and workshops of commerce have spread from a few blocks to many square miles in extent, and its commerce and fame encircle the globe.

The concept of the Veiled Prophet as a benevolent but firm monarch was a metaphor for how the business elites wanted to rule the city—with an iron hand in a velvet glove. If challenged, they believed it was perfectly within their rights to "take the gloves off" when skirmishing with political or economic opponents. After all, they thought it was only through their leadership that St. Louis had been able to prosper. Without such leadership the city might still be mired in the economic mediocrity of the late nineteenth century.

The pamphlet closed by briefly chronicling the events of the first several celebrations. The back of the pamphlet provided lists of the themes of all the Veiled Prophet parades and of all the Veiled Prophet ball's known queens, information made available for the first time to the organization's members.

The final page of the Golden Book contained a poem, "The Beloved Despot," that conveyed the supposed grandeur of the Veiled Prophet:

> The Veiled Prophet is always young;
>   always inviolate; always superb!
>
> He brings with him a freshness, an
>   urgency, a noble impulse!
>
> The white haired patriot's throne
>   is raised in the hearts of his
>   subjects, for the seeds of the Divine
>   which he sows in the minds of men.
>
> The Veiled Prophet never knows
>   the weight of human hours—
>   nor the sweet shadows of twilight.
>
> He is a morning whose uprisen sun
>   no setting ere shall see;
>
> A day that comes without a moon—
>   The spirit everlasting!

It was not important whether the mythical Veiled Prophet actually existed. The important point was the inspiration he provided for St. Louis's business elites to make the city a better place to live.

Combined with Stevens's earlier writings and the 1917 proclamation, the public relations campaign by the Veiled Prophet organization proved successful. It gained control of the Veiled Prophet symbol. After 1928, the myth presented in the Golden Book continued to be reiterated year after year in all St. Louis newspapers. Leaders of the Veiled Prophet organization established that their group would be presented in a positive light for the next forty years. Under pressure from the business elites in the Veiled Prophet organization (a group that usually included their publishers), newspaper editors made sure their writers described the Veiled Prophet celebration using the rhetoric presented in the Golden Book. Like the writer of the Golden Book, journalists described the celebration as a vital part of St. Louis history and, until the late 1960s, continued to link the organization to most of the positive developments of the twentieth century.

In stark contrast to the parade, the Veiled Prophet ball became more important to the city's elite during the first half of the twentieth century. Newspaper coverage of the party throughout this period was incredibly detailed. This became the premier social event in St. Louis high society, being a recognition of business success as well as a debutante ball.

The changing of the ball's venue signified the changing membership in the organization and the event's growing importance as a civic event. The ball was held at the Merchants Exchange from 1878 to 1908; the building was very important to the mercantile elite, for it was where most agricultural trading took place in St. Louis at the time.[49] The location attested to the power of mercantile elites in the early years of the organization. However, in 1909 the ball was moved to the St. Louis Coliseum and in 1935 to Kiel Auditorium.[50] Both of these venues were publicly owned and could accommodate a much larger crowd of eight to ten thousand spectators. These changes of location for the ball acknowledged the popularity of the event with members of the middle and upper classes. Since both of these later venues were publicly owned, it also meant that public tax monies were used to provide the members of the Veiled Prophet organization with the necessary services for the event, such as security and electricity. Because it often took two to three weeks to decorate the Coliseum or Kiel Auditorium, these public auditoriums were out of public service for several weeks during the year.

In 1915 some members of the organization came up with the idea of holding an even more exclusive gathering on the night of the ball—the Queen's Supper. The supper was held after the ball and was paid for by the Veiled Prophet queen's father. Invitations to the Queen's Supper were coveted more than invitations to the ball. After all, only a few hundred would be invited to the Queen's Supper while several thousand could view the ball. By having the Queen's Supper on the same night as the ball, the organization's members could have two social events on the same night that performed two important social functions. The ball made participants (those on the stage) feel like social superiors to those in the audience. In contrast, the Queen's Supper allowed the truly elite to gather together socially on the same night in camaraderie. The Queen's Supper made the members of the Veiled Prophet organization feel they were members of a coherent ruling class.

As the years passed, the crowning of the Queen of Love and Beauty became increasingly important to members of the organization. Prior to 1922 the crowning was a secondary part of the ball's program. Programs from the earlier era listed the order of dances for the ball with a space for the dance partner's name to be written in. In 1922 the crowning ceremony was listed in the Veiled Prophet ball's official program as a part of the evening's events. After 1922 dance programs for the ball consisted of four major parts: a concert program, the "Grand entry" of the Veiled Prophet Krewe in their costumes, the crowning of the queen, and a shorter dance program that included eight to ten dance numbers rather than fourteen to sixteen as in the past.[51]

Another addition to the ball in 1922 was the Veiled Prophet's Bengal Lancers. This group of twenty-six men, World War I (and, later, World War II) veterans, performed drills at the ball. Until 1937, the Bengal Lancers dressed in "swashbuckling" costumes with plumed hats. In 1937 the Lancers adopted the British Army's Bengal Lancer uniforms. According to the *St. Louis Globe-Democrat,* the uniform included a "red tunic, white trousers, black boots, blue-and-gold turban, blue cummerbund and white gauntlets." The Lancers carried bamboo lances with red-and-white pennants. The Lancers formed in two rows on each side of the Veiled Prophet's dais and gave a distinctive salute as the Veiled Prophet, the maids of honor, and the queen entered.[52] The Bengal Lancers added military pomp to the ball and provided the organization a way to recognize war veterans. Serving in the Lancers was a desired accolade for veterans in the organization. Because the Lancer Guard had only twenty-six members, most applicants for membership were turned down. Only a select few could become members of the guard.

In 1924 the organization acknowledged the growing importance of the ball, which had thus far been held on the same night as the parade, by moving the ball to the night after the parade.[53] This way the parade participants did not have to change after the parade and the ball could start at a more reasonable hour. Before 1924 the ball had started an hour or so after the parade was over, often around 10 or 11 P.M. Thereafter, the ball was no longer auxiliary to the presumably more important event, the parade; the ball became its own separate event.

The pomp and circumstance of the Veiled Prophet ball became increasingly important to the organization's members. Those who participated in costume in the ball began to enjoy the social facets of

the event more than they had in the past—such as being clearly recognized as social superiors to the ten thousand spectators in the audience. After all, the parade had lost its appeal for them as a show of
social status or power. The ball allowed them to produce this show of
social status in a much more controlled atmosphere. There would be
no peas or stones thrown at them by the thousands whom the organization had invited to see the ball.

How was the Veiled Prophet queen chosen during this period? She
was always from a family that had deep roots in St. Louis. Many of the
families of the queens had been prominent in the founding of the organization in the 1870s; family names such as Capen, Chouteau,
Shapleigh, Simmons, Walsh, and Wells were common. In fact, by the
1930s the annual newspaper articles pointed out that some of these
young women represented the second or even third successive generation in which women from their families had been crowned the
Veiled Prophet queen.[54] This generational continuity in Veiled Prophet
queens demonstrated how closed the upper social class in St. Louis
was to outsiders. It also showed how successfully the elite of St. Louis
used the organization and others like it to preserve the long-term social and economic status of their families.

The manner of selecting the queen changed little during this period. In 1915, the *Globe-Democrat* said, "the selection, like that of the
old belle of the ball, is made on the night of the ball. Now four girls
are told to go to a certain room at the Coliseum. Three are maids of
honor and the fourth, the last to be escorted to the ballroom, is the
Veiled Prophet's queen."[55] The three maids of honor or, as they were
sometimes called, "special maids," generally came from the same
high social class as the Veiled Prophet queen, but they did not have
the "pedigree" that the queen usually had. In fact, many of the Veiled
Prophet queens could trace their ancestry back to some of the original settlers of St. Louis. The historical connection was important to
members of the Veiled Prophet organization; by crowning the young
women, the organization demonstrated its historical legacy.

The remaining "Veiled Prophet maids" in the ball, daughters of
the organization's members, could number anywhere from fifty to a
hundred in any given year. These maids, although their fathers were
in good social standing, were not from families that had historically
been powerful in St. Louis. If anything, their fathers were nouveau
riche, usually middle management or proprietors of small to middle-
sized businesses or corporations.

6. *Dorothy Shapleigh, 1908 Veiled Prophet Queen.* Photograph by Strauss Studio. Missouri Historical Society, St. Louis.

The Veiled Prophet queen's role became more arduous as the years passed. They became local celebrities, spent their time giving autographs, making speeches, and serving as dignitaries at various civic functions. They were also featured in newspaper stories as what we today call "role models" for young people. In a time of rapidly changing social mores, the Veiled Prophet queen's role was somewhat anachronistic: she was required to be unmarried, wholesome, and, above all, chaste.

In 1928, the organization spared no effort for its fiftieth anniversary. It hung large and elaborate posters all over downtown St. Louis, published its Golden Book, and prepared for a larger than normal yearly celebration. The organization's fiftieth anniversary celebration was planned to be as great as any other in its history. The members believed that although the parade had lost some of its stature, the celebration was still enjoyed by St. Louisans. The 1928 parade, "Through the Centuries," presented events from biblical times and ancient history.[56] The members still believed that the crowning of the Queen of Love and Beauty was, as stated in the Golden Book, a unifying social event in which a virtuous maiden was held up as an ideal.

The Veiled Prophet queen for 1928 was Mary Ambrose Smith. The selection was a typical one. She came from a historically powerful family: Her father, J. Sheppard Smith, was the president of the Mississippi Valley Trust Company. The *Post-Dispatch*'s writer described her in the following manner:

> Celebrating the golden anniversary of his reign among us, the August Prophet this year placed the crown of love and beauty upon the head of a descendant on both sides of her house of the founder of his beloved St. Louis, Pierre Laclede. True to type of her French ancestry is Mary Ambrose Smith. She resembled not a little her cousin, a former Veiled Prophet's queen, who was Julie Cabanne, being rather tall, of deep brunette coloring with straight black hair which she wears parted smoothly over the ears and knotted low upon the neck. She had a serene but earnest air until, catching glimpses of friends and relatives around her, at last she did smile. Then deep dimples showed in her cheeks and her face became radiant.[57]

The fiftieth anniversary parade and ball were, by all accounts, very successful. Smith was a luminant queen and, presumably, she would execute her duties ably.

However, only twenty days later, the Veiled Prophet organization would issue a tersely worded official statement: "The Veiled Prophet Queen has returned the crown, thus abdicating. The throne is declared vacant." Thus ended what came to be known as the "Scandal of 1928." As it turns out, Smith had been married to Dr. Thomas C. Birdsall in August. According to the *Post-Dispatch,* the abdication was "in line with the rule, observed inflexibly in the past, which requires that the Queen shall be unmarried. This rule has usually been interpreted as requiring the Queen to remain single until after the end of her one-year reign, but the latter custom was violated at least once in the past."[58] Members of the organization were shocked. Smith, a descendant of patron saint Pierre Laclede, had betrayed them. Her conduct, they felt, had cast a pall over the entire fiftieth anniversary celebration.

Only years later in a 1979 interview with the *St. Louis Times* did Smith talk about the difficult experience. She was sent away by the Veiled Prophet, who gave her traveling money and told her to "begone, don't register at any large hotels, and don't use your real name." In fact, when she passed over the Mississippi River leaving St. Louis, Smith even reclined the seat of her car in order to avoid being seen by reporters who, she claimed, were "looking for her everywhere." "I felt like a hunted criminal," she said. "I was just shattered."[59]

Because the Veiled Prophet membership wanted to make an example of her, the social censure for Smith was purposely harsh. According to the *Times,* Smith was "made to feel she disgraced her family. None of her friends stuck by her (she was told she could not visit their houses), she never was invited to another VP ball, her picture was removed from the collection of queens' portraits at the Missouri Historical Society, and her name was deleted from the Social Register." Smith later revealed that her brothers and sisters and some friends knew she was married. They told her not to tell her father because "it would break his heart," she recalled in the interview. At the time, she said, "I didn't know what to do, so I didn't do anything." However, Smith said she was not "overly bitter at being ostracized" but that "you'd think by this time [1979] they'd let up and forget."[60]

Why was being married such a disgrace for Smith? Why was it such a major concern for members of the Veiled Prophet organization? According to Smith, when the Veiled Prophet for that year found out she was married, he responded "Why didn't you tell me, little girl. We would have thrown someone else in the breach." The membership of the Veiled Prophet was a bit behind the times for the late 1920s, for despite that decade's more liberalized sexual attitudes, sexual purity remained one of the major requirements for being the Veiled Prophet queen. The assumption, at least at the time, was that because she was a maiden, she was also a virgin.

It was important that the queen be a virgin for at least one simple reason: she was a role model for children. In the members' eyes, she played a role little different from being a child herself. That the Veiled Prophet addressed her as a "little girl" was revealing. Nevertheless, the situation revealed a huge generational gap in sexual mores. The Veiled Prophet membership felt the queen should represent their ideal of young womanhood: pure, white, and virginal. It was an ideal that they believed their daughters were quite capable of fulfilling. It never occurred to them that this ideal no longer held as much meaning for the younger generation.

There was another facet to Smith's story that the members found profoundly disturbing. She had acted on her own when she decided to marry Birdsall. She had defied the established line of parental authority. Not only did she not ask her father's permission to marry Birdsall, but she did not even inform him of the marriage. Most of the members probably found both of these transgressions upsetting to them as fathers and certainly worthy of the hasty and extreme condemnation meted out to Smith. Smith violated what the members of the organization believed were fundamental social conventions based on paternal authority, and therefore she could not serve as a role model for children. Her actions showed disrespect for the ultimate male authority figure as far as they were concerned: her father.

The Scandal of 1928 had far-reaching implications for members of the Veiled Prophet organization. The next several Veiled Prophet parades after the scandal strove to reassert male authority in history and in the world. The members used the historical topics of the next several parades to rebuild the patriarchal order that Smith's actions had so clearly violated. They depicted a world in which men were clearly in control.

It is important to place the parades from 1929 to 1934 in their proper historical context. Only twenty days after the 1929 celebration ended, "Black Tuesday" on Wall Street ushered in the Great Depression. In addition to the goal of restoring faith in male leadership, Veiled Prophet parades during the first five years of the depres-

7. *Kiel Auditorium: The Veiled Prophet with His New Queen, Lila Childress, 1935.* Photograph by Taylor Photographers. Missouri Historical Society. St. Louis.

sion also attempted to restore faith in America's traditions and in the capitalist system. James Scott asserts that during times of crisis, the hidden transcript of a subordinate class can become public. In times of major upheaval, open acts of defiance are viewed as possible and even necessary.[61] During the early years of the Great Depression, thousands of unemployed workers were marching regularly in the streets of St. Louis demanding relief. Led by the pro-Communist Unemployed Council, these workers were castigating city leaders and the business class for their inaction in tending to the needs of the unemployed. During this period, there were numerous public demonstrations that were brutally broken up by the police, sometimes with deadly consequences.[62] Therefore, the members of the Veiled Prophet organization, deeply troubled by the social, political, and economic trends of the period, used the Veiled Prophet parade between 1929 and 1934 to reinforce their ideas of patriarchal order, their belief in "legitimate" elite leadership, and their affirmation of capitalism. The organization's members were using the parade to answer the calls for cultural and political change being issued from other groups in St. Louis at the same time. They were obviously hoping to convince working-class spectators that no such change was needed. They also decided that style was as important as substance; the parade's floats needed to be more artistic. Beginning in 1929, Oscar Berninghaus, a distinguished St. Louis artist, designed the parade floats and continued to do so until 1942.

The 1929 parade, "The Traditions of St. Louis," once again was a medium of public communication and education in which the Veiled Prophet organization's members were linked to St. Louis's historical forefathers. To emphasize the educational purpose of the parade, the organization sponsored a contest for schoolchildren "to encourage advanced study of the historical features of our community." Prizes were awarded for the best four three-hundred- to five-hundred-word essays on the parade's theme. The organization produced thousands of pamphlets for schoolchildren that described the parade floats and related them to the parade's theme.[63] For the first time in several years, the newspapers printed detailed descriptions of the parade's floats.

In their description of the parade, the organization maintained that it was intended to "inspire every growing citizen—the boys and girls—to cherish, and pledge to perpetuate in their day the heritage that has been passed along to them by illustrious forefathers." The events presented on the floats emphasized the achievements and important place in St. Louis's history of white men. In a passage reminiscent of the Golden Book, the pamphlet boasted that the Veiled Prophet "has seen the city grow from an unpopulated wilderness to the great valley metropolis of today, and he knows what mighty strides of commerce, art and culture the little village which Laclede founded on that eventful February 15, in the year of 1764, has taken to reach the modern St. Louis."[64] As in parades with similar themes during the late nineteenth century, the organization used the occasion to remind St. Louisans, young and old, of their history and of the great positive changes carried out by the city's founders and early leaders—many of them ancestors of the organization's current members. In this way, St. Louis's elite once again lent themselves historical legitimacy.

The first two floats represented the leading community symbols of the time, Saint Louis and the Veiled Prophet. For the first time in the event's history, the parade was led by Saint Louis rather than the Veiled Prophet. Saint Louis, popular as a symbol since the World's Fair (and also a major character in the St. Louis *Pageant and Masque*) had been King Louis IX, the Crusader King of France, and was the city's namesake. The image on the float was familiar to most St. Louisans, for it was merely a rendering of an already existing statue, "the Apotheosis of St. Louis," in Forest Park. The second float presented the Veiled Prophet and his four courtiers, the two high priests, the Almoner and the Herald. The Prophet's chariot was drawn by buffaloes, and he was being welcomed by an Indian who, according to the pamphlet, was "signaling a mid-western welcome to the Eastern potentate." That the Veiled Prophet took a backseat to the city's namesake belied the importance the organization placed in the Veiled Prophet symbol. The Prophet would never play second fiddle in his own parade again.

The first group of floats presented important events in St. Louis's early history. "The Mound Builders" presented a group of Indians building a burial mound. The next two floats, "Early Explorers" and "Laclède and Chouteau," presented several scenes of Marquette, La Salle, Laclede and Chouteau meeting Indians who "peer inquiringly" from behind trees. The next four floats depicted the region's transition to American rule. "The Louisiana Purchase" showed James

Monroe signing the Treaty of Cession. "The Three Flags" portrayed the March 9, 1804, ceremony in St. Louis that ceded the territory to the United States. Important leaders like Amos Stoddard, Meriwether Lewis, William Clark, Auguste Chouteau, and Pierre Chouteau were portrayed. "Lewis and Clark" showed the explorers paddling up the Missouri River. "Fur Traders" depicted an ongoing negotiation between a trader and a group of Indians over several animal pelts. These floats were followed by several floats that presented idyllic, nostalgic, and light-hearted scenes from major historic eras in St. Louis's past, such as "Steamboat Days," "Early Traffic Congestion," and "The Gay Nineties."

Several other floats in 1929 presented what the Veiled Prophet organization considered some of the city's greatest achievements during the last fifty years. These floats included "Eads Bridge Construction," "Shaw's Garden" (now the Missouri Botanical Garden), and, of course, "The World's Fair." The World's Fair float included a depiction of the World's Fair Plaza, representatives of several different countries and, most importantly, statues of David R. Francis, president of the World's Fair, and Grover Cleveland and Theodore Roosevelt, who visited the fair. Several floats showed other famous men who had a connection—either directly or indirectly—with St. Louis: "Lafayette," "Grant," and Lindbergh's recent crossing of the Atlantic in the "Spirit of St. Louis." Thus, the floats continued to demonstrate the important place of white men—to the exclusion of all others—in St. Louis's history.

With the inclusion of the "Spirit of St. Louis" float, the parade makers had taken their audience through St. Louis's history and reached the present. The final float in the parade, "St. Louis of the Future," showed "the great buildings of the Memorial Plaza, in the midst of which is seated on high an allegorical figure of the new St. Louis, crowned with laurel, holding aloft the scepter while the fairies of peace and prosperity dance before her."[65] The allegorical figure, presumably a woman, represented the bright future for St. Louis. The vision of the future was the usual optimistic view for boosteristic elites during this period: lots of new tall buildings, peace, and, above all else, prosperity.

The 1930 parade, "Traditions of the United States," treated United States history in a similar manner. The organization again had an essay contest, this time for the best essay on the "History of the United States." This time the organization's pamphlet for schoolchildren urged them to be "inspired" by the parade "so that they will forever cherish and perpetuate the aims and ideals of their illustrious forerunners, exemplified in service to their country." The pamphlet stated that in the parade the Veiled Prophet's artists would take spectators "back hundreds of years—the time when America was first discovered—back to Leif Ericson and Christopher Columbus. From there on, in graphic illustrations, are unfolded episodes and exploits in the history of the United States which have contributed to its development to the point it has reached at the present. Beautiful, thrilling, and inspiring is this history." The pamphlet's writer stated that every float in the parade was designed to "stimulate in St. Louisans a greater pride in their country, to the advancement of which their city has liberally contributed."

This parade, like the previous year's, gave its spectators the same overt messages about St. Louis history: Men were the important contributors and men had always been firmly in control of this country's destiny. Some of the floats included "The Norsemen," "Columbus at the Court of Spain," "The Landing of Columbus," "Boston Tea Party," "Franklin Print Shop," "Paul Revere," "Declaration of Independence," "Washington Crossing the Delaware," "Fremont and Carson," "Lincoln and Douglas," "Thomas Edison," and "Admiral Byrd." Unlike the 1929 parade, the 1930 parade's makers allowed one woman to appear important in American history: Betsy Ross. She was the subject of one float all by herself, in which she is depicted sewing the first American flag. Ross, the embodiment of the good mother and wife, was certainly not seen by the organization's members as a threat to the patriarchal order so carefully affirmed in the rest of the parade.[66]

As the Great Depression deepened, many Americans blamed the selfish nature of capitalism for the country's problems. In 1931, the Veiled Prophet organization presented a parade that was a response to these oft-heard allegations. The 1931 parade, "The Romance of Commerce and Industry," presented a romantic history of commerce. The organization still held its essay contest and issued its descriptive pamphlet.[67] The newspapers printed descriptions of the parade's floats as well.

Despite the fact that "industry" was in its title, the parade focused entirely on a history of commercial trade in America. The parade makers avoided controversy by stressing the positive aspects of world trade in America's history. Since some members were the owners of plants whose workers were being laid off by the hundreds at this time, the parade planners decided to avoid presenting anything from America's industrial history. However, the title of the parade indicated that they must have meant to do so during the parade's planning stages. The Veiled Prophet led the parade from a float that resembled a galley that was being rowed by two African slaves. The remainder of the floats presented various idealized scenes from America's commercial history. Floats in the parade dealt with colonial commerce, whaling, street merchants, frontier fur-trading, the South's antebellum cotton trade, and America's trade with India, Arabia, the West Indies, Germany, Japan, China, South America, Holland, Ireland, Mexico, Italy, Scotland, and the Hawaiian Islands. These floats showed the goods the country traded in the international market. According to the *Post-Dispatch,* the "West Indies" float was a scene showing "An adobe hut, surrounded by stacks of bananas, pineapples and tobacco nestles at the foot of slender coconut palms on the float. Natives gather fruit. Monkeys play in the trees, and a laden mule cart stands near by."

Two other parades, in 1932 and 1934, focused on the importance of patriarchal control in American history. The 1932 parade, "The Life of George Washington," presented a detailed account of Washington's life in the bicentennial year of his birth. This parade documented Washington, who, for these elites, was the first "great man" in American history. The twenty floats in the parade included such topics as "The Cherry Tree," "Boyhood Days," "Washington the Surveyor," "Braddock's Defeat," "Spirit of '76," "Valley Forge," "Surrender at Georgetown," "Indian Wars," "Drafting the Constitution," "The Inauguration," and "Mount Vernon."[68] As in the nineteenth century, the Veiled Prophet membership admired Washington and considered him representative of the best of patriarchal authority.

The organization's last parade trumpeting the achievements of male leaders took place in 1934. The organization abandoned the essay contest and did not issue a descriptive pamphlet. However, newspapers did cover the parade in some detail. The parade's theme, "Great Adventurers," was certainly in keeping with the "great white men" view of history employed in the earlier parades. The parade documented the deeds of such "great men" as Noah, Richard the Lion-Hearted, Marco Polo, Columbus, Ponce de Leon, Cortez, Magellan, Henry Hudson, Napoleon, Sam Houston, Santa Anna, Buffalo Bill, and

William Peary.[69] The fact that women were not included among the ranks of "great adventurers" affirmed the organization's belief that only men can make history.

In the middle of the decade the parades changed drastically. Beginning in 1935, the themes of the parades reverted to their 1920s form of escapist entertainment. In the midst of the nation's deepest economic downturn, members of the Veiled Prophet organization chose to provide a few hours of pleasant diversion rather than attempt to teach history. Their retreat from historic topics was complete. The theme for a few of the Veiled Prophet parades during this period were: "Toyland" in 1935, "Childhood Memories" in 1937, "Songs We Sing" in 1938, "Arabian Nights" in 1940, and "The Circus" in 1941. Descriptions of the parade floats again disappeared from newspapers and were replaced by a list of the parade floats with little additional comment.[70]

This abandonment of the parades as a source of public communication would remain the case, with only one major exception in 1942, to the present day. The parade makers moved away from serious historical or cultural topics and moved toward providing the spectators with a few hours of diversion from their daily cares—daily cares which, during the Great Depression, were quite considerable.

In 1937 the Veiled Prophet parade was followed by a public festival complete with public dancing and an exhibition of ethnic dances. The festival was the result of public pressure put on the Veiled Prophet organization by Mayor Bernard F. Dickmann and a few prominent St. Louis businessmen. These leaders hoped the success of the festival would lead to the establishment of a permanent fall festival. Newspaper editorials endorsed the idea, claiming that this was an era in which "his mysterious majesty" would soon become "his democratic majesty" and the pretensions of the Veiled Prophet parade and ball would be pushed aside in favor of more inclusive spectacles. The *Globe-Democrat*'s editorial summarized this theme most effectively:

> The Forthcoming visit of His Mysterious Majesty, the Veiled Prophet will be a visit indeed. He will meet the people as he has never met them before and learn how St. Louis enjoys itself when not restrained by a stiff shirt and tails. He will see the people dance for pleasure undimmed by ritual. . . . Added to the usual program will be folk and public street dancing which His Majesty will view from a platform set in Memorial

8. *Veiled Prophet, 1935.* Photograph by Ruth Cunliff Russell. Missouri Historical Society, St. Louis.

Plaza. It is hoped that the democracy of the moment will appeal to the annual visitor and that it will become a feature of other fall visits. . . .

But the new program offers new opportunity. The veiled mystery will meet the people face to face, watch them in their folk and popular dances and maybe sweep his veil aside and cast a smile on the new democracy. . . .

We see the promise of permanently enlarged fall festivities if the forthcoming test proves well.[71]

From all accounts, it was a rousing success. The governor of Missouri, Lloyd C. Stark, introduced the Veiled Prophet to loud cheers from a crowd that probably numbered in the tens of thousands.

However, despite the outward signs of success, a similar public event did not occur in 1938. In fact, this sort of public event was not connected with the Veiled Prophet celebration again until the 1980s. Why was the more inclusive civic celebration abandoned after such success? Unfortunately, no answer to this question appears in the public record. No newspaper editorial or writer ever referred to such "democratic" hopes for the annual fall celebration again. It seems likely that the elites in the organization—for whatever reason—simply decided they would not lend their symbolic potentate to such a public spectacle again. Due to the power of these elites, they were more than likely able to stop newspaper editors from questioning their decision and the topic never surfaced again in public discourse. When the organization began planning a public festival in the early 1980s, newspaper writers and even members of the organization acted as if the idea of linking the Veiled Prophet celebration with a public festival was a new one whose time had come. Little did the editors and members know that newspaper editors and civic leaders had said the same things forty years earlier.

After the United States entered the war in late 1941, the Veiled Prophet organization did an abrupt about-face and used the 1942 parade as a method of public communication. The goal of the 1942 parade was to raise money for the Greater St. Louis War Chest Campaign and to teach St. Louisans about the possible sacrifices and terrors of the war ahead. The parade took place a few weeks later than normal, on October 22, 1942. The newspapers published an official description of the floats, the first such description published in eight years, which proclaimed that the Veiled Prophet organization supported the war effort and encouraged St. Louisans to give to the public-spirited campaign. In contrast to the escapist parades presented by the organization since 1934, the *Globe-Democrat* reported that "It was not intended by the Veiled Prophet that this somber visit be a time of diversion."

The floats represented many possible facets of the war ahead. The Veiled Prophet's float was followed by one that represented the St. Louis War Chest Campaign. This campaign was designed to raise at least $4,850,000 for 102 different welfare and war relief agencies. In the center of the float was "a tableau of live figures representing average Americans . . . climbing a pyramidal platform to deposit their voluntary gifts" into the St. Louis War Chest. The next three floats portrayed the three major domestic goals of War Chest agencies: protecting the family, preserving public health, and helping young people. The sixth float, "Our Allies," showed the flags of the Allied nations and depicted a group of soldiers from one of the Allied armies. The seventh float, "Conquered Nations," was a representation of those nations that had been conquered by the Germans in the early years of the war. The *Globe-Democrat* described the float this way: "Toppled walls and splintered timbers give in vivid realism the results of daring to question the whims of the so-called master races, while the masked figures, by their arrangement and postures, furnish a glimpse into the courage and tenacity of the people who have become victims of modern barbarism." Another War Chest program, the U.S.O., was the subject of the seventh float. The final float, "Giving Is Fighting," showed the fighting man who was to stand as the primary symbol for the St. Louis War Chest campaign.[72]

In order to drive the patriotic message home, the Veiled Prophet's herald spoke for him later that evening in front of a crowd of twelve thousand gathered for a War Chest benefit show. The address was met with cheers:

> He also wishes to convey his pride and satisfaction in the work that you are doing in this world at war. Twenty-five years ago, during another war, your Prophet implored you, his people, to carry forward the torch of freedom. This he entreats you to do again. He reminds you that now is no time for revelry when there is so much to be done. And, although he must, as always, return to Khorassan, his heart and interest remain here with you until his coming again at the time of victory. Signed, with his seal, this twenty-second day of October, 1942.[73]

Interestingly, there was no attempt in the statement to make the organization seem altruistic as there had been in 1917. The organization was content to link the Veiled Prophet symbol with patriotism and the good cause of raising money for war bonds. By linking itself with the patriotic cause, the organization maintained the positive image of the Veiled Prophet as a benevolent monarch. They hoped St. Louisans believed that, despite its elitist nature, the organization was truly a compassionate and patriotic institution. In accordance with the Veiled Prophet's stated wishes, the Veiled Prophet parades and balls for the years 1943–1945 were canceled. The Prophet had declared that now was not the time for merrymaking. Too much remained to be done in the war effort.

It would not be until four years later, in the fall of 1946, that His Mysterious Majesty would visit St. Louis again.

"More and More a Social Phenomenon"

THE VEILED PROPHET CELEBRATION, 1946–1965

In December 1946, Allan Y. Davis, a member of the Anthropology Department at Harvard University, conducted a brief study of the Veiled Prophet celebration. In a paper presented in January 1947, Davis argued that the celebration established "the social primacy of the influential business families of the area" and that it acted "as a form of social control by linking socially approved behavior and economic success so closely together."[1] Relying largely on Walter B. Stevens's writings and a few newspaper clippings, Davis contended that the celebration in 1946 acted as a mechanism of social stratification and that the event represented both a Rite of Intensification (marking the passage of an annual season) and a Rite of Passage (for those maids who attended the ball). Davis's conclusions seem confirmed by the findings in earlier chapters of this work.

As an outsider examining the celebration for a very brief period of time, Davis did a remarkable job of analyzing how the two halves of the celebration began diverging. Perceptively, Davis maintained that the Veiled Prophet celebration was becoming "more and more a social phenomenon" and that the parade was becoming less important to its members:

> Probably the largest factor in cutting down the importance of the night pageant was the death . . . of the Annual Fair, which the Veiled Prophet activities were designed to buttress. . . . The Veiled Prophet organization, surviving the deaths of both city expositions and the World's Fair, also survived both World Wars. A reasonable theory suggests that the effect on the Veiled Prophet's Order of these great tests was a tendency to strip it [the celebration] of its accessory elements, leaving it, in its purged state, a more frankly-avowed annual social event.[2]

Later in the paper Davis contended that for the organization's members, "the pageant [the parade portion of the celebration] ha[d] lost much of its original significance" and that the parade had come to serve a very limited public or civic purpose. Davis thought that the members of the organization would eventually abandon the parade as a part of the celebration, leaving only the ball, which he believed to be "the social function in its pure form."[3]

Davis's insight about the social change in the celebration is borne out by an examination of the celebrations during this period. From 1946 to 1965, members at the very top of the Veiled Prophet organization gained a large measure of control over St. Louis both economically and politically through semiofficial organizations such as Civic Progress, Incorporated. The period was the "golden age" of the celebration: The parade drew large crowds and the ball was closely covered by the news media. In fact, the ball was even televised nationally during this period. On the other hand, this was also the time in which interest in the celebration among its own members began to wane. Having largely gained control over St. Louis during this period, the parade was much less important to the elites as a symbolic vehicle through which to claim they were in control.

The decline of the Veiled Prophet parade as a form of public communication continued after World War II. As in the first half of the century, the parades drew large crowds in the streets but not a great deal of publicity in local newspapers. The parade makers no longer provided spectators with a narrative linking the parade's floats into a common theme. They continued to reject the idea of achieving a large social goal through the parade. The parades were certainly escapist in nature, focused more toward pleasing children. Prominent themes during this twenty-year period included "Modes of Travel," "Special Days," "Mother Goose Tales," "Once Upon a Time—Books," "Songs We Sing," "Parade of the Animals," "Delights of Childhood," and "The Joys of Toys." Occasionally, the parade makers presented a historical or cultural theme, such as "The Story of St. Louis," "The Veiled Prophet Salutes the Municipal Opera," "Folklore and Legends," or "Great Adventurers."[4] Even in these parades, there was no overt attempt, as in earlier celebrations, to teach history and link it to cultural values. By the early 1960s the decline of the parade as a means of public communication was complete. The local newspapers had even ceased listing the titles of the parade floats in the parade-day newspapers.

However, while social control and patriotism were no longer an overt part of the parade's message, another cultural value had taken

9. *Veiled Prophet Parade at Night, on Olive Street East from 11th Street, 1959.* Photograph by Lester Linck. Missouri Historical Society, St. Louis.

center stage: self-fulfillment through the joy of consumption. While many of the earlier parades had presented consumption in a positive light, some of the parades during the 1940s and 1950s focused entirely upon it. The Veiled Prophet parade was not an unusual cultural event in its emphasis on consumption. Many scholars argue that the major defining cultural value of twentieth century America has been consumption.[5] The Veiled Prophet parade's postwar themes comfortably reflect this rise of a culture of consumption during the 1940s and 1950s. This unrelenting focus on consumption continues in the organization's parade even today.

There were some major technological changes in the parades during this period as well. In 1946 the floats were pulled by large tractors rather than horses. Why the change? Robert Tooley explained the change: "Well, after the war, when the dairies went to using trucks instead of horses—you see, before then, you could get the horses from the dairies to pull the floats. But then, when the dairies went to trucks, the horses were no longer available. So they used big farm tractors and they pulled the floats with them for several years." In 1954, generators provided the power for the lighting on the floats. For the first time since 1903, the floats did not have to follow the streetcar lines.[6]

At about this time, another important St. Louis elite organization was founded: Civic Progress, Incorporated. In 1953 Mayor Joseph M. Darst established the organization to serve as a "civic conscience." The Civic Progress organization was (and still is) a group of prominent chief executive officers of the largest corporations and banking institutions in St. Louis. The group also has several ex-officio members, including the two leading political executives (the mayor of St. Louis and the St. Louis county executive), the presidents of the three largest universities (Washington University, St. Louis University, and the University of Missouri–St. Louis), and the chairman of the St. Louis Regional Commerce and Growth Association. In the beginning, the organization had twenty-one members; as of 1999, there are thirty-one.

Through Civic Progress, St. Louisans at the very top of St. Louis's social and economic structure have influenced government decision-making. The members of Civic Progress have worked closely with the city of St. Louis on city bond issues and have been instrumental in most of the city's downtown renewal projects, such as the Gateway Arch and Busch Stadium. Some have argued that this organization represents an unelected shadow government that makes policy for the city. Because of their power over loan capital in St. Louis, any large-scale civic or business project must be brought to Civic Progress first for approval.[7] Their power over these matters continues to the present day. The connections between Civic Progress and the Veiled Prophet organization were (and still are) quite strong. Of the Veiled Prophets since 1953, most were members of Civic Progress. Arguably, the Veiled Prophet organization since 1953 has been the social arm of Civic Progress.

The founding of Civic Progress certainly had an effect on the Veiled Prophet organization. During this period the organization's members began to lose interest in the celebration—at least the parade part of it. With the creation of Civic Progress there was less need for business elites to join the Veiled Prophet for business reasons: The governmental officials and business elites that they needed as contacts were now gathered in one place, Civic Progress. The membership of Veiled Prophet remained static during this period because elites outside the organization found little need to join. Having largely gained control over St. Louis through organizations like Civic Progress, the parade lost its symbolic significance for the elite.

In 1952 the Veiled Prophet organization faced the first public scrutiny of the founding members' motives. The St. Louis Emergency Defense Committee made the first public claim of ties between the Veiled Prophet celebration and the General Strike of 1877. In a leaflet produced by the committee, it suggested a conspiracy by "Big Business and the press to hide the true origins of the VP parade."[8] The committee consisted of labor and civil rights leaders opposed to the Smith Act, a 1940 antisubversion act that made it a crime to advocate or teach the forcible overthrow of the government. This law was being used to jail Communist and labor-union leaders during the McCarthy era in St. Louis. The Defense Committee's leaders claimed that the Veiled Prophet organization and the business class were using it to jail protesters against the Korean War. The leaflet gave a drastically different view of the Veiled Prophet parade and organization than any that had been expressed publicly before:

> Summer 1877: The US was in nation-wide depression. General railroad strike spreads to St. Louis and its major industries. The strike was for a living wage and an 8 hour day. Leading St. Louis business men set up a "Citizen's Committee on Public Safety." Under the Committee's

leadership 4000 armed troops, a contingent of the National Guard, artillery, and vigilantes attacked the unarmed strike headquarters at Fifth and Biddle.

Negro and white strike leaders were arrested, charged with being "foreign agents," "Communists," and sentenced to harsh prison terms.

The strike was broken. To celebrate, St. Louis business leaders held a victory march of 3000 armed troops and a battery of cannon to intimidate St. Louis working people and prevent the organization of unions.

John G. Priest, vice-president of the St. Louis Police Board, organized a regular militia of 2000 men to "protect" St. Louis from further "labor disturbances."

A year later, in 1878, St. Louis saw its first VP parade and John G. Priest was the first VP. This was the only time the VP's identity was ever revealed.[9]

William Sentner, a prominent trade-union leader in St. Louis, claimed in a later press release that the Veiled Prophet organization "started as a vigilante movement that had its beginning with the breaking of the St. Louis general strike in July, 1877 . . . the crew of 'best citizens' maintained their organization as a secret honored guard."[10] The committee's and Sentner's arguments contradicted the mythological fairy-tale-like version presented by the print media regarding the founding of the Veiled Prophet organization.

Even if the parade had declined in symbolic importance for the members of the organization and the community at large, the Veiled Prophet character was still especially powerful for children. In 1956 the organization published an illustrated children's book by Vincent Sanders and Theodore Drury Jr. entitled *The Story of the Veiled Prophet*. Reminiscent of the 1928 Golden Book, the book continued to present the Veiled Prophet as a benevolent Middle Eastern monarch who came to St. Louis because he wanted to bring happiness to a worthy city in another part of the world. However, the Prophet had trouble finding a people he believed were worthy of such a spectacle. Having found other parts of the world to be petty or "too set in their ways," the Prophet chose St. Louis because it was a city that was "built on the heritage of the Old World" but was "growing with the spirit of freedom of the New World." People in America and St. Louis "had time for play and pleasure," unlike people in other countries whom Sanders and Drury portrayed as less developed and somewhat barbaric. Sanders and Drury argued that the ability to laugh and play was a distinctly American notion; other countries just did not have this freedom or, for that matter, their people did not have the free time. This belief in the cultural superiority of America was typical of the Cold War period. Needing to feel secure in such an uncertain time, many American writers—especially of children's books—wrote forcefully about the superiority of American society and culture.

The remainder of *The Story of the Veiled Prophet* recounted the events of the first celebration from the omnipotent view of a fairy tale's narrator, describing how the Veiled Prophet celebration was a rousing success and captured the hearts of all St. Louisans. The final paragraph of the book strongly resembled the conclusion of a children's fairy tale:

> And so it came to pass that, because of his growing fondness, the veiled ruler each year selected the fairest maiden in the city and crowned her Queen of Love and Beauty, to carry on his reign of happiness until his return. This then, is the story of the Veiled Prophet of Khorassan and how he first brought his gift of carefree hours to the city of St. Louis, a gift which he has continued to bestow each year down to the present day.[11]

The Veiled Prophet organization continued to be masterful in handling publicity. The membership knew how to control the media and maintain a positive image. Of course the fact that most, if not all, of St. Louis's newspaper publishers and editors continued to be members of the organization helped in that regard. Annual stories appeared in every newspaper, recounting the history of the organization in a flattering light. In 1958 the *Globe-Democrat* even dedicated an entire section to the history of the Veiled Prophet organization and celebration.[12]

The biggest change in the celebration during this period occurred in 1963 when the entire celebration was moved to weekend nights. The ball was now held each year on a Friday night and the parade on the following Saturday night. Prior to 1963 the celebration was held on Tuesday or Wednesday evenings. The move came as organizers realized that to have the largest crowds the celebration had to be held on the weekends. After all, most middle-class St. Louisans now lived in the suburbs and had to drive some distance into the city to attend the celebration.

The ball continued to be important to the organization's members. It remained the premier social event in St. Louis high society. The ball was closely covered by the press and the queen's picture ap-

peared on the front pages of the newspapers. The queen continued to
be viewed as a semicelebrity by the press and by many St. Louisans as
well. As Davis noted in his paper, "there has been a continual increase
in the number of girls singled out as maids of honor—an increase
which has very closely followed the increasing amount of prestige attached to the purely social aspects of the annual coronation ceremony."[13] During the 1950s and 60s the number of Veiled Prophet
maids increased to an average of fifty per year.

What did one of these ceremonies look like? Helen Dudar, a free-
lance writer and former New York journalist, wrote an insightful
tongue-in-cheek article about the Veiled Prophet ball in *Focus
Midwest* magazine in 1962. Dudar's sarcastic description of the 1962
ceremony was particularly striking and perceptive. Hers was the only
detailed description of the ball from this period:

> The preliminaries may vary from year to year, but the main events
> are as fixed as the constellations. One sees first a procession of
> "matrons of honor," stylishly-gowned and magnificently corseted. They
> are followed by a promenade of "maids of honor," advertising families
> of some importance.
>
> There are trumpet flourishes, maneuvers by a company of young
> men in crepe beards and Bengal Lancer's uniforms, and heralds'
> announcements in home-made archaic language that unfailingly sug-
> gests a walk in a field of melting marshmallows. ("His mysterious
> majesty, in his great wisdom, has selected the finest maid of his beloved
> city. . . .") Finally, the Veiled Prophet appears, his face hidden behind
> silver gossamer and his figure enrobed in a Cecil B. DeMille approxima-
> tion of what any self-respecting Eastern potentate would wear. In turn,
> each of four "special maids" make entrances.
>
> At last, the curtains part to reveal the new queen, her identity, until
> then, a reasonably well-kept secret. At first a dazzling sight, she is a
> fixed smile surrounded by an 18-foot embroidered train and a gargan-
> tuan bouquet of orchids. Before the prophet's throne, she lowers herself
> to the floor in a bow that is very nearly a scrape. As she kneels, his un-
> practiced hand maims her $15 hairdo with her symbol of regality, a
> platinum headache band surmounted by a diamond and sapphire
> replica of a crown, cleverly fashioned so that it may removed later and
> worn as a pin.[14]

Dudar's sarcasm aside, it was clear that by 1962 the organization's
Veiled Prophet ball had become an annual choreographed ritual, a far
cry from the debutante balls of the late nineteenth century.

The Veiled Prophet queens continued to come from a few prominent families, usually families with long-term connections to St. Louis on both sides. The intermarriage among these prominent families was evident in the names of the queens and many of the debutantes of the era. Most of the debutantes were from families that, wishing to carry on and acknowledge both sides of the family line, used the mother's maiden name as the girl's middle name. This middle name/mother's maiden name was included prominently in newspaper publicity and in the Veiled Prophet ceremony. Veiled Prophet queens during this era included Anne Ferrar Desloge, Dorothy Claggett Danforth, Helen Dozier Conant, Eleanor Simmons Koehler, Sally Baker Shepley, Audrey Faust Wallace, Carol Lammert Culver, and Alice Busch Condie. As in the 1930s, many Veiled Prophet queens had mothers and grandmothers who had also held that coveted title.

Although many of the same family names continued to appear as queens and debutantes, these young women's fathers were now involved in entirely different occupations from their grandfathers. The three largest occupational groups among known Veiled Prophet members (see Table 6) in 1950 and 1960 were industry, financial services, and professionals. Of known Veiled Prophet members, 80 percent now made their living in these three areas. By the 1950s these elites had completed the transition from an agricultural trading economy to a modern industrial economy. The sons and grandsons of the late-nineteenth-century mercantile elite now worked as bankers and middle and upper management in St. Louis's leading industrial firms. These men's fathers and grandfathers successfully used social organizations like the Veiled Prophet to maintain their families' financial and social status. Interestingly, Veiled Prophet members no longer owned the firms they worked for; they now managed them.

Dudar argued that the Veiled Prophet queen and the maids of honor always had certain class and ethnic characteristics:

> By tradition, the queen is usually native-born and a debutante, signifying membership in that social class which formally places its girl children on the marriage market. She is likely to be an alumna of Mary Institute, the most fashionable local girl's prep school, or, if she is the occasional non-Protestant, a graduate of Villa Duchesne, the fashionable Catholic girls' institution. The daughters of Israel may aspire no higher than the second string section. The order's membership includes a scattering of Jews and, from time to time, a Semitic name, usually with an Episcopalian affiliation, will be found among the several dozen ordinary maids of honor.[15]

Table 6 OCCUPATIONS OF MEMBERS, 1940, 1950, AND 1960

Occupational Category	1940	1950	1960
Agricultural Commerce	5 (7%)	4 (4%)	0 (0%)
Commercial Transportation	2 (3)	1 (1)	0 (0)
Merchants	3 (4)	2 (2)	1 (2)
Professionals	7 (10)	19 (21)	8 (19)
Public Communications	6 (9)	4 (4)	4 (9)
Industry	26 (39)	27 (29)	17 (40)
Financial Services	15 (22)	27 (29)	11 (26)
Other	3 (4)	8 (9)	2 (5)
	67	92	43

Dudar's findings reflect the same class and ethnic markers evident since the founding of the organization. Most Veiled Prophet queens were Protestant or Catholic; there were very few Jews in the organization. Since there were no African Americans in the organization, there were no African American queens or maids of honor. These basic class and ethnic characteristics, with very little deviation, still hold true for the Veiled Prophet queens and courts of today.

As debutante balls faded as prominent events in St. Louis society during the 1950s, the Veiled Prophet ball remained an important event. Dudar called it the "Ben-Hur of the debutante parties." It was an all-too-important marker of a man's social and economic position in the community to fall by the wayside. As a former queen told Dudar: The queenship is "not so much an honor for the girl as for her father. They're choosing the father, a man who has done a lot for the city and, I guess, a lot for the order, so the girl, she's just there to stand in for her father."[16] Therefore, the Veiled Prophet ball continued to be less of a debutante ball and more of an annual social ritual that physically reified the lines of social stratification for the entire St. Louis community. It was, as Davis argued, a "mechanism of social stratification."

The Veiled Prophet queen and, to a lesser extent, the special maids, continued to be viewed as semicelebrities in St. Louis. In 1950 the ball was moved to the night before the parade so that the queen and her four special maids could appear on a float in the parade.[17] The social pressure from the organization for the queen to remain unbetrothed and sexually "pure" continued. An ever-increasing amount of public appearances was required of the queen as well. As Dudar argued in her article, the Veiled Prophet queenship made it possible "for a quite ordinary [looking] young girl to achieve celebrity. She is photographed, flattered, and sought after." If the young woman was in college, she was expected to suspend her studies for a year. However, Dudar warned, "no silver lining is without a cloud." The end of Dudar's article very strongly addressed the changes in the life of a "Queen of Love and Beauty":

> "No matter how drab-looking or charmless the girl may be," a young man observed recently, "she doesn't have to worry about a Saturday night date for the next year. For some bachelors, especially the men who are only half-way 'in,' it's important to be seen with her. I've known a couple of girls nearly destroyed by this. Because if she's a drag or not especially pretty, she'll be dropped the moment her term ends. There's a new queen and a new flock of debutantes every year."
>
> A former queen, a handsome young matron, agreed that temporary adulation offers psychic hazards. "You get a lot of attention, but you sort of begin to lose any sense of your identity," she said. "I found myself wondering if people liked me because of me or because of the title." . . .
>
> "I was shy and didn't want to do it, but I didn't want to disappoint my father. . . . It was an interesting year, though. You do all sorts of charitable work and get to see parts of the city you never saw before. . . . I've often thought the title, Love and Beauty, was unfortunate. Children expect to see a fairy princess. Sometimes the queen isn't pretty and children can be pretty cruel about their disappointment.
>
> "Looks shouldn't matter that much. It's really not so much an honor for the girl as for her father."[18]

Apparently, being Veiled Prophet queen was a time-consuming and sometimes not so rewarding position.

The Veiled Prophet ball was popular among ordinary St. Louisans as well. Beginning in 1949, the ball and the parade were televised locally by KSD-TV, and in 1950 and 1951 the ball was broadcast nationwide on television. Live local television coverage continued throughout the 1950s and 1960s. One survey by KSD-TV in 1950 revealed that 80 percent of the homes with television on that evening were watching the Veiled Prophet ball. Robert Tooley, who twenty years later would become Den Superintendent for the organization, remembers vividly his experience with the 1949 broadcast: "We went to a tavern that had a television set. My wife said, 'See if the bartender will turn on the VP ball.' And so I went up and told him. He said 'I'll turn it on but if anybody complains I'm going to turn it off.' So he turned it on and, I'll be damned, everybody in the whole bar watched the VP ball, the whole thing."[19] Why did St. Louisans find the ball so entertaining? Most St. Louisans probably enjoyed the "fairy tale" nature of it. By watching the ball they were vicariously living the experiences of the elites dancing across their television screens. Female St. Louisans probably enjoyed looking at the elaborate ball gowns of the maids and matrons and imagining what it would be like to be dancing with young wealthy gentlemen while wearing a two-thousand-dollar gown. Male St. Louisans probably imagined being the wealthy tuxedoed escort of an elegant, virginal young lady.

One can see the theme of escapism through consumption appearing in the practice of watching the ball on television as well. The popularity of the ball on local television made Veiled Prophet members feel their annual celebration of wealth and social power had widespread public support. The Veiled Prophet organization members assigned the deferential role of audience to middle-class and working-class St. Louisans. Whether spectators truly accepted their role is still an open question.

Dudar felt that "the public discussion" about the ball in the telecasts and other media was always "keyed to spasms of admiration." She was amazed that none of the television journalists covering the ball or parade seemed to want to stop and analyze the rather strange spectacle they were witnessing. "It may never have been better expressed than it was last fall by a lady TV commentator, trapped into silence during a lull in the proceedings and desperate for additional narrative. As she put it, while the camera focused on a distant back view of the new queen, 'It's all so sincere.'"[20] Few St. Louisans wanted to analyze the ceremony as Dudar had. Thus by the middle 1960s, the Veiled Prophet celebration was a part of St. Louis culture and, as evidenced by the television ratings, an increasingly important part. By the late 1960s and early '70s, many, if not most, St. Louisans would change their mind about the appropriateness of the Veiled Prophet celebration as a civic celebration.

"Whacking the Elephant Where It Hurts"

THE VEILED PROPHET ORGANIZATION, ACTION, AND ECONOMIC JUSTICE IN ST. LOUIS, 1965–1980

December 22, 1972, was a cold and snowy evening in St. Louis. Inside cavernous and warm Kiel Auditorium, the festivities at the Veiled Prophet ball were right on schedule. At about 10:30 the matrons had completed their part of the program and the last maid of honor, Beatrice Busch, was making her way around the stage. The Veiled Prophet of Khorassan, dressed in ornate robes and wearing a silky veil and gold crown, watched the proceedings from his throne. The several thousand spectators, most of whom had been in their seats for more than three hours, were growing restless. The Queen of Love and Beauty, the queen of the Midwest's oldest and most public debutante ball, was to be named next, and then it would all be over until next year.

Suddenly a woman in the balcony shouted, "Down with the VP!" and scattered leaflets, which fell on the spectators below. Quickly the auditorium's security guards carried her out. Then, to the left of the stage, there was a much more serious noise: A woman had apparently fallen from the balcony. A man went over to see whether she had been hurt, and after a few words with him, she disappeared through the right stage door. Since the woman seemed unhurt—and had fallen out of a section reserved for housekeepers and other servants anyway—all eyes returned to the stage where the Veiled Prophet was preparing to name his queen.

Next, just as Miss Busch completed her pattern around the stage, the woman who had fallen was somehow standing next to the Veiled Prophet. Before anyone could stop her, she removed the Prophet's crown and veil to reveal the face of Tom K. Smith, an executive vice president for the Monsanto Company. Surprised and angry, Smith quickly recovered the crown and veil and replaced them as if he could still hide his identity. The Bengal Lancers, the Veiled Prophet's private honor guard, roughly dragged the woman backstage by her arms, neck, and feet. For the first time this century and only the second time in the ball's ninety-five-year history, the Veiled Prophet's name became public knowledge. Despite the rather bizarre interruption, the ball went on as usual, as if nothing had happened.[1]

The unveiling of the Veiled Prophet at his ball in 1972 represented the crowning achievement of the civil rights group ACTION. From the years 1965 to 1984, ACTION protested at all events connected with the Veiled Prophet celebration. Although ACTION's targeting of the Veiled Prophet debutante ball may appear frivolous, the issues involved—economic justice in the form of jobs for minorities—were quite serious. Despite their denials, the Veiled Prophet organization clearly found it necessary to respond to the challenge by ACTION.[2] Over the next several years many major changes occurred in the Veiled Prophet organization.

ACTION, which stood for Action Committee To Improve Opportunities for Negroes, was an unusual organization in the late 1960s. The group's goals represented a sort of practical middle ground—neither accommodationist nor nationalist. The story of ACTION offers a local case study of a group that was ahead of its time in emphasizing economic opportunities and in employing "theater-of-confrontation" tactics. Moreover, ACTION was an exception to most of the generalizations that have been made about civil rights groups during this period; unlike other organizations, the St. Louis group remained integrated and viewed white members as a valuable asset. While national civil rights group such as the Congress of Racial Equality and the Student Nonviolent Coordinating Committee battled over the issues of black nationalism and separatism, ACTION advocated a more economically centered and practical set of immediate goals.[3]

Civil rights scholars describe the period between 1965 and 1975 as a sort of "middle period" that was "something completely different" from the earlier national activism of the civil rights groups of the early 1960s and the more radical activism of groups in the late 1970s. There have been few case studies of local grassroots civil rights organizations during this period and civil rights scholars have yet to study the period in much depth. During this period most civil rights groups shifted their goals. Some historians have argued that by 1965 the "classical" phase of the civil rights movement—which James Ralph has defined as "the destruction of the legal foundations of racism in America"—had ended. As Ralph put it, the "passing of one era inaugurated a troubling time of transition" in which civil rights workers "insisted that equal results, not equal treatment, become the standard of public policy." ACTION is a prime example of this ideological thrust on the part of civil rights organizations. Members of ACTION believed that the struggle for basic civil rights was more or less finished and that the important struggle for economic rights remained ahead. As Martin Luther King contemplated whether he should pursue an economically based campaign in Chicago, ACTION pursued just that in another large midwestern city, St. Louis.[4] In short, ACTION offers historians a chance to study a local civil rights group that advocated economic justice in a midwestern city during the little-studied "middle period" in the civil rights struggle.

Originally founded by Percy Green and a few members of the St. Louis chapter of CORE's employment committee in April 1965, ACTION was, in Green's words, "committed to direct-action protest," by which he meant confrontation with specific opponents with specific goals in mind.[5] The St. Louis Jefferson Bank protests in 1963 divided the St. Louis chapter of CORE. The chapter subsequently abandoned the idea of direct-action protests.[6] Green and several members of the employment committee, a growing faction inside CORE that called for more direct-action activities, felt betrayed. "CORE was apprehensive," Green told a reporter in 1970. "The members had battle fatigue or something, I guess. We needed a group that would be a spark for change in St. Louis."[7]

ACTION's primary goal, in the words of former member Jane Sauer, a white female, was "to obliterate racism through economic justice, through jobs," and "through communication with the upper echelons of St. Louis in order to promote change."[8]

Specifically, ACTION advocated more and better-paying jobs for black men. ACTION activists believed this focus on job opportunities for black males would be the most beneficial course to follow because men were the primary breadwinners for their families in the black community at that time. As Percy Green explained, the members of ACTION "thought that would cut down on the risk factor of black men running the risk of committing burglaries, you know, cut down on the criminal approach to getting money to feed their families and so forth." Members of ACTION believed that blacks had a right to equal and well-paying employment opportunities, which were central to a good quality of life. Sauer explained ACTION's economic views this way: "It's up to you whether you want to buy a house. But you have a right to have a job that will let you buy that house. It's your right to have a grocery store that has better produce . . . you have a right to own a car, shop wherever you want. And the only way to have these things is to have a job."[9] For ACTION activists, civil rights coexisted with economic rights. African Americans needed the civil rights legislation passed in the early 1960s, but this legislation meant little if they could not find jobs to sustain themselves. True freedom and economic liberation involved being able to support a family. African Americans needed jobs that would provide for a family's basic economic survival.

Unusual for the time, ACTION remained an integrated group. For many ACTION members, integration represented a tactical move. Police were less likely to brutalize whites or charge them with crimes. Jane Sauer said that ACTION

> used white people as a protection. When they arrest a white person they don't know what they've got. It's different when they pick up a black—they can be sure that he has no status. When they picked me up they didn't know what they had. I came from a highly educated professional family. They didn't know—what was her family going to do if we rough her up? It wasn't like a poor black man who couldn't afford to hire a lawyer or, worse yet: "the *Post-Dispatch* might cover it if we roughed her up."[10]

For Jacqueline Bell, a black female member, working in an integrated group reflected the real world, a world in which blacks and whites lived together and needed to work together. When asked why ACTION remained integrated, Percy Green replied that "our thinking was that the whites in our organization were very productive and what we were primarily interested in was performance."[11]

All members of ACTION had to agree to one thing: The organization would always have black leadership. Green felt that "black folks had the right to make mistakes for black people rather than to have white people make mistakes for them." Whites certainly did play integral roles in the organization, but a black leadership made the important decisions. As Green said, "One way to find out whether one was still tainted with racism was if one could accept black leadership." In fact, ACTION members believed that black leadership was therapeutic for whites.[12]

ACTION's protest tactics demonstrated that locally based groups during this middle period of the civil rights movement did not choose just one tactical approach. ACTION's goal of better-paying jobs for black men required members to use both nonviolent direct-action sit-in protests similar to those of national civil rights groups of the early 1960s and "guerilla street theater" or theater-of-confrontation protests reminiscent of radical feminist groups in the late 1960s. ACTION's location in a conservative midwestern city forced the group's members to use a combination of tactics to further its goals. ACTION's protests had to be physically unthreatening because, according to Margaret Phillips, a white female and former ACTION member, "St. Louis is a very conservative place. The far-out, fringy kinds of behavior never percolated here."[13] However, ACTION's tactics at the different Veiled Prophet events evolved over time. While the first Veiled Prophet protests in the middle 1960s were nonviolent sit-ins meant to disrupt the parade, protests in the 1970s mixed sit-in tactics with guerilla street theater, in which symbolic acts (i.e., the unveiling of the Veiled Prophet) played a central role.

In addition to protesting at the Veiled Prophet ball and parade, ACTION tried to achieve economic and social justice through protests at large corporations in St. Louis. ACTION targeted these employers because, unlike smaller businesses, their businesses would not be economically threatened by a single successful protest. Members of ACTION believed that these large employers owed a special duty to the community to promote equality in hiring practices. The businesses targeted by ACTION included McDonnell-Douglas, Wonder Bread, Southwestern Bell Telephone, Laclede Gas Company, and the Union Electric Company. These protests often involved picketing, sitting-in, pouring syrup and animal excrement on company equipment and, in the case of McDonnell-Douglas, breaching their security.[14] ACTION members generally considered these protests against corporate employers as central to their goal of increasing minority employment opportunities. For most ACTION activists, the Veiled Prophet protests remained something of a sideshow.

At the same time, ACTION picketed other organizations, most notably Roman Catholic churches and protestant churches of all denominations (both black and white), as well as Jewish synagogues. ACTION members believed the churches had failed to provide moral leadership on civil and economic rights issues. ACTION members also researched the property holdings of the Catholic church in St. Louis and found the church was one of the city's largest slumlords. Protests involved picketing, interrupting services and, on a few occasions, reading speeches to the church's members.[15]

Like radical groups of the late 1960s, ACTION often staged protests that were examples of theater-of-confrontation tactics. "Percy has a genius for guerilla street theater," said Margaret Phillips. By "guerilla street theater," ACTION activists meant that they tried to get their point across visually and vocally, without touching or harming people. "As we all know, you can send out the most beautifully worded press statement and it will fall flat," Phillips said. "But you do something theatrical and all the press are there." Street theater effectively pointed out injustice to those who may have been insulated from it by race or class. "Hey, when something hurts, you've got to scream Ouch!" Phillips contended. "You don't need a medical degree to scream ouch. We were just screaming ouch." The ultimate goal was to raise the viewers' consciousness—to alert them to the economic injustices perpetrated on minorities.

Like the New York Radical Women's Miss America Protest in 1968, in which a sheep was crowned "Miss America," many of ACTION's protests were confrontational and symbolic but not physically threatening. One notable St. Louis protest involved burning a dollar bill, which symbolized the Protestant establishment's values, in front of an Episcopal church congregation on a Sunday morning.[16] Unlike the more extreme groups, ACTION members were not advocating a radical redistribution of power; they only demanded the moderate goal of equal economic opportunity. Unfortunately, their message was sometimes difficult to discern.

A prosopography of ACTION members is nearly impossible. ACTION brought together people of many different educational and social backgrounds: It included men and women of nearly every conceivable age and many different ethnicities—white Washington University professors, a few radical labor activists, young college-educated women, young black men and women still in high school, and many others. Nevertheless, ACTION never grew to be very large: At most the group had an active membership of a little over fifty people. There were as many or more "unofficial members"—often members of Washington University's faculty or administration—who sent in regular financial contributions. ACTION consistently had more black members than white members. White members made up between 35 and 40 percent of ACTION's membership.[17]

In summing up ACTION's activities, Barbara Torrence, a white former ACTION member, asserted that the group's members "found it was relatively easy to get appointments [with the CEOs of large companies] but it was really hard to get anything beyond that. . . . You know the old joke about the elephant—first you've got to get his attention. To get his attention, you whack him where it hurts—after you've tried everything else."[18] One of the better ways ACTION found to "whack the elephant where it hurts" involved attacking something he held dear. That something was the Veiled Prophet organization's parade and ball.

In contrast to the recently founded ACTION, by 1965 the Veiled Prophet organization had been a St. Louis institution for nearly ninety years. Both the parade and the ball remained largely unchanged from the celebrations of the 1950s. In 1965 the ball was a popular event that was televised and watched by a great many St. Louisans. The parade remained a popular event. However, the parade's themes became even more escapist in nature and continued to advocate consumption. The St. Louis elite no longer felt much need to preach a capitalistic and moral gospel to their workers. The themes during this period indicate the emphasis on entertainment: The 1966 theme, "Sports"; the 1967 theme, "A Salute to the Wonderful World of Disney"; the 1972 theme, "Happiness Is . . ."; and the 1978 theme, "The Wonderful World of Children," brought with them much less moralistic cultural baggage than earlier parades.[19] Newspaper coverage of the parade was now limited to giving the time the parade would begin—no list of float titles and certainly no float descriptions.

Why did the parade during this period rapidly become just a few hours of relatively frivolous entertainment? Robert Tooley, who began working for the Veiled Prophet organization in 1969 and became Den Superintendent in 1973, argued it was the result of a conscious effort by the parade makers to change the philosophy of the organization with regard to the parade's themes. Tooley believed "a parade float is a sort of entertainment for children, should be aimed at children. That's my idea. In other words, you can't teach anyone any part of history by a parade float that just crosses by for twenty seconds." Tooley's background included working for the Scruggs, Vandervoort, and Barney department store designing animated Christmas window displays for twenty-six years. Tooley claims he sincerely wanted to please children with his parade floats.

Tooley argued that by the 1960s parade spectators were mostly parents and their children. He believed parents brought their children to the parade so they could

> watch their kids to see their reaction rather than watching the floats go by. When the little kids are happy, why, everyone's happy. Not just children as such but I mean little kids, four- and five-year-olds. That's real important as far as the parade goes, so, having a background of doing the animated Christmas windows had a tendency to make me design strictly for children and to like the children's themes and kind of steer clear of anything historical or anything that was trying to give a message of any kind.

Ultimately, the organization adopted Tooley's child-centered approach. Until Tooley's time, the Veiled Prophet for each year had set the parade's theme and a "sketch committee" then designed the parade's floats. Later, the organization allowed Tooley to set the themes. Tooley felt that some of the earlier themes had been "far-fetched" and largely unsuccessful. "So I tried to talk the organization into setting themes and titles that little kids would enjoy," Tooley said. "The average person watching the parade couldn't care less about the theme of the parade or the title of the parade. It should be something they enjoy. If they knew nothing about it, basically, they'd still enjoy it, you know. That's just my feelings on the matter."[20] The fact that these parades advocated escapism through consumption should be no surprise given Tooley's background as a designer of department-store window displays.

The parade floats changed quite a bit technologically during this period. In 1969, the floats were pulled by Chevy Blazers and later were towed by pickups or small lawn and garden tractors.[21]

Despite Tooley's contention that the Veiled Prophet parade's floats conveyed no meaning, many ACTION members were profoundly affected by the annual parade as children. "As a kid my recollections of the Veiled Prophet," said a founding member of ACTION Judge Johnson, "were that it came through the heart of the black community. I guess we were protesting even then and didn't know it. We would take our beanshooters and shoot at the VP. We thought it was time for the VP parade, let's go shoot at the VP." White ACTION members who had grown up in St. Louis had similar early memories of the Veiled Prophet. "As a child I remember being taken down to see the Queen of Love and Beauty," said Jane Sauer.

> I remember the big parade that went through the city that was sup-
> posed to be the gift given by the regal folks who inhabited the upper
> echelons of the city and it was there for us poor folks to come look. You
> could gaze at these people and they had floats to entertain you. It was
> charity. You were down lower—much lower. This is real charity—"we
> parade ourselves down Main Street in front of them and they can bring
> their lawn chairs and watch us." I still have strong feelings about that
> image. I remember watching from my childhood the Queen of Love and
> Beauty wearing a gown like a fairy princess and I can remember very
> vividly being told "Jewish girls don't do that." They don't go to this ball.
> World War II is over but Jews are not allowed in a lot of places.

The exclusive practices of the Veiled Prophet organization seemed even more obvious to a child in the black community. Judge Johnson said that the Veiled Prophet celebration "symbolized elitism and ex-clusionariness" to the African American community in St. Louis, "be-cause when you get a parade coming through and there's not one black—you had to think, 'Why is this parade coming through?'"[22]

For most members of ACTION, the Veiled Prophet celebration symbolized racism and white control of St. Louis's economy. Members of the Veiled Prophet organization held the purse strings at most of the corporations where ACTION protested. Jane Sauer believed "the VP embodied the white power structure of this city. It involved their children. It really did—the white male heads of state, heads of corpo-rations, the city fathers, the whole myth of city gentry, the whole myth of an establishment, of regalness, of blue-bloodedness. It was the figurehead of everything we were against. It was for many years a white, anglo, Episcopalian thing to do."[23]

It could be argued that ACTION's protests were yet another exam-ple of a "hidden transcript" of a subordinate group becoming public. But this time, the Veiled Prophet organization would have trouble an-swering a challenge to their authority. The seeming acquiescence of the St. Louis community since World War II had lulled many in the or-ganization into a false sense of security about the organization's pop-ularity and standing in the community. They would make a big mistake by dismissing ACTION's position as representing the feelings of only a small minority. Once ACTION had brought the hidden tran-script out into the public arena, their message would prove to be very powerful.

The Veiled Prophet represented the perfect target for ACTION—for both tactical and strategic reasons. Protests against the Veiled Prophet would draw a great deal of media attention. Sauer felt the Veiled Prophet "was like a precious child of this city. Because of that, it was something that the media wanted to defend. Of course, the editors wanted their tickets and it was a big social deal." ACTION also targeted the Veiled Prophet parade and ball because it furthered its goal of more jobs for black men. Green declared that "after we attacked all of the big industries we found out that all of the CEOs of these industries were also members of the Veiled Prophet. So we felt that attacking the Veiled Prophet was a strategic move. The CEOs of these firms were showing how racist they were because they were associating themselves with a racist organization socially. Their mental and moral fiber is tied to this." Many activists viewed the protests at the Veiled Prophet as a way to hit all of the CEOs at once. Jacqueline Bell believed that the Veiled Prophet protest represented "an opportunity to protest against twenty different corporations about their racism in their hiring practices," and "their institutional racism in all promotional and wage practices."[24]

ACTION's public statements made clear that, because the Veiled Prophet organization used Kiel Auditorium for the ball, the city's political leaders were closely linked to the white power structure. "The Veiled Prophet symbolized the power they had access to—at public expense," said Margaret Phillips. "That was a big point. For years they did it at the Kiel Auditorium—a taxpayer-supported auditorium." Many ACTION members believed one of their greatest achievements was getting people of all races to realize that, by having the ball in Kiel Auditorium, their tax dollars indirectly supported the organization. ACTION also made a public issue of the fact that the city spent a great deal of money on police protection for the ball.[25]

ACTION wanted two things from the Veiled Prophet organization. First, ACTION members wanted the CEOs in the Veiled Prophet to begin to hire more minority workers, and second, they wanted the Veiled Prophet organization to disband. They felt the money spent on this celebration, both public and private, would be better spent on something more helpful to the community as a whole.[26]

ACTION protested the Veiled Prophet celebration every year from 1965 to 1976. Most of these protests involved picketing the ball and disrupting the parade in some way. Typically, a group of ACTION members disrupted the parade by lying down in front of the parade floats while other activists passed out leaflets explaining the reasons behind the demonstration. The protest would continue until the police arrested the protesters. For instance, members acted out a scene—often as "nurses" or "doctors of social healing"—in the street in front of the floats until the police arrested them. On a few occasions members chained themselves to floats. In these protests the activists held up the parade until authorities cut their chains and arrested them. The goal was for protesters to distribute as many leaflets as possible to the crowd and, eventually, for someone to get arrested—usually for "disturbing the peace."[27]

The approach to the Veiled Prophet ball varied somewhat each year, though some things stayed consistent. Every year, ACTION picketed the ball with signs that read, for example, "VEILED PROFIT$" or "VP = KKK." ACTION's ball protests also included sending blacks to try to gain admission with legitimate or phony tickets. Police arrested some activists and charged them with "disturbing the peace" for these attempts at gaining admission.[28]

One of the more interesting protest activities of ACTION was the Black Veiled Prophet ball, a parody of the Veiled Prophet ball. In this event, members of ACTION elected a Black Veiled Prophet. Green contended that ACTION used the Black Veiled Prophet ball "to mimic the white Veiled Prophet." "We always used to say we'd like to challenge the white VP on the battlefield of justice," Green insisted. "Their queen was Love and Beauty, and our queen was called the Queen of Human Justice. We invited the white VP to the black VP and we demanded the black VP to be in their functions and be seated next to the white VP." Needless to say, the white Veiled Prophet never showed up to meet the black Veiled Prophet. The annual Black Veiled Prophet celebration became a popular festival for the African American community in St. Louis during the early 1970s. Green argued that this event was primarily intended "to make a mockery of the white Veiled Prophet, a symbol of St. Louis's racism and oppression." In no way did the Black Veiled Prophet celebration indicate that ACTION wanted blacks to become a part of the Veiled Prophet organization.[29] The Black Veiled Prophet celebration, like the 1968 Miss America Protest by radical feminist groups, was a public lampoon—an artful use of guerilla street theater.

The events of October 2, 1965—the first Veiled Prophet protest—showed the early tactics of ACTION. "There were three of us: Maryann, an Episcopal intern; and me; and a young black guy, sweet kid," said Barbara Torrence. "When the queen's float went by, we were to get in front of the float and stop the parade. We knew we were going to be arrested." The activists laid down in front of the float until the police arrested them. Then the protesters went limp. The two white women were detained by police immediately. Lost in the confusion, the young black activist was not arrested. Once apprehended, the police subjected Maryann and Torrence to the usual tactics: They were taken down to the city hospital to be checked out because they had supposedly "resisted arrest." The police employed this tactic whenever they dealt with ACTION's protesters. When Torrence heard she would be charged with resisting arrest, she remembers saying "What!—We had just gone limp. I couldn't see how going limp could be called resisting arrest!" Once the activists returned to the city jail, the police refused several bonds. As usual, ACTION had people waiting at the jail to bail out the demonstrators, but the prosecutor's office would not accept any of the bonds—including one from Torrence's husband, who had put their house up as a property bond. Torrence began to feel as if they "were in enemy territory." Finally, the prosecutor accepted a bond from a middle-class black couple who had no tangible connection with ACTION. The prosecutor tried to charge Torrence and Maryann with eight different offenses but finally settled on three, including resisting arrest. Torrence and Maryann pleaded guilty and received a year's probation. The court waived their fine.[30]

This first Veiled Prophet protest gave insight into both the early aims of ACTION and those of the police authorities who arrested them. ACTION had a simple plan: Disrupt the parade. The group used tactics that had been successful for civil rights groups throughout the country during the 1950s and 1960s. The ultimate goal was to make people stop and think, to raise people's consciousness. Members of ACTION hoped that consciousness-raising would convey their double message to the middle-class white audience: economic rights for black men and the end of the Veiled Prophet organization. In the early years of the Veiled Prophet protests, ACTION attempted to draw attention to themselves and the Veiled Prophet organization by staging protests that did not physically threaten the members of the Veiled Prophet organization. As members of ACTION wanted, the police responded by arresting the activists. The police then tried to frighten the activists by charging them with many crimes and refusing legitimate bonds. However, when the cases made their way to court, most of the charges were dropped and the fines were often waived.[31]

The Veiled Prophet organization itself did several things in reaction to ACTION's protests. First, the Veiled Prophet queen and maids ceased to take part in the parade after 1967. This move was an expression of concern on the part of the Veiled Prophet membership that the ACTION activists might do something to harm their daughters. In 1968 the parade no longer went into downtown St. Louis, staying in the relatively safe Central West End. Furthermore, the parade now avoided African American neighborhoods entirely.

In 1969 the parade moved to the daytime, and the Veiled Prophet himself did not participate between 1969 and 1973. Despite many official denials, the move to daylight hours was directly tied to ACTION's protests and the increasing animosity toward the parade among many working-class and black St. Louisans. As Tooley recalled, the parade was moved to the daytime because "we started having an awful lot of trouble at night—a lot of protests against the VP and so forth." In fact, the animosity was reaching a fever pitch by 1968 when, according to Tooley, "one of the drivers, who was driving the float [in] the last nighttime parade, said he remembered seeing something sailing through the air, and he said it looked like a pie pan, and the next thing he knew he woke up in the hospital with fourteen stitches in the side of his head." As Rusty Hager, the 1995 Veiled Prophet fair chairman admitted, "Security for any nighttime event is always a problem."[32] The 1968 parade was the last nighttime parade in the organization's history. Every Veiled Prophet parade since then has taken place in daylight. The tradition of the Veiled Prophet parade as an evening event—a tradition of ninety years—had come to an end.

The switch to a daytime parade led to several important changes regarding the personnel on the floats. Tooley recalled that at this time they began "using women on the floats. Before that, it was men dressed as women, always just members of the order riding on the floats, and the krewe were ugly enough in the nighttime, let alone in the daytime. We had to go to girls on the floats."[33] In 1969 city school students also began riding on the floats. The Veiled Prophet members thought it would be harder for ACTION's protesters to argue that the parade was exclusive with these additions to the parade's participants. Also, the addition of women and children on the floats made it less likely that anyone in the crowd would throw objects at the passing floats.

Women were also allowed into some of the organization's functions and facilities for the first time during this period. In the 1970s the organization finally lifted its rule barring all women from its "Den." Interviewed at the Den in 1995, Robert Tooley explained this rule:

> Another thing was the fact that no women were ever allowed in this building. In the old Den, either. Then, of course, the office was downtown. We eventually moved it out here. I know Ted [Satterfield, the Den superintendent from 1945 to 1973], he thought it was terrible to bring these women out here you know. And then we had a G.O. [Grand Oracle—the Veiled Prophet] who decided that—the [annual] Den party was originally all just members—and he decided that they were going to have all the members and their wives and Ted thought that was terrible. I know he said, "Some of the old G.O.s would be turning over in their graves.". . . I told the gals working here [that] when I first started here, and a member drove up for business in here and his wife was in the car, she had to wait in the car until he was finished. They could not get over that. They thought that was terrible. Even as late as 1969 women were not allowed in here—an unwritten rule.

Therefore, by the 1970s the organization had begun to rethink some of its rules regarding membership and participation in the group's activities.

The organization also made changes in the ball. Beginning in 1970 the ball was moved to the Friday night before Christmas.[34] The change in date was an attempt to disassociate the October parade, which still viewed by many people as a positive civic event, from the ball, which was becoming increasingly unpopular with many St. Louisans as a tasteless show of wealth. By having the ball during the Christmas season, it no longer seemed so closely linked with the parade. Because the ball was held on the Friday before Christmas, a large number of St. Louisans would be away or busy enjoying their Christmas holidays, thus lessening public attention and criticism. It was apparent that the organization's members thought the ball remained their private party, separate from the more civic-oriented parade.

The protest at the Veiled Prophet ball in 1972 showed major changes in ACTION's strategy. Having disrupted the parade and picketed the ball for seven straight years, members of ACTION felt they needed to step up their attack on the organization. No matter how creative the parade demonstrations, they had no direct effect on the members of the organization itself. Similarly, by ignoring the picket lines and quickly dashing inside, members of the Veiled Prophet organization arriving at the ball minimized their contact with ACTION's message. However, that did not mean that the members were oblivious to what was going on around them. As Tooley remembered, one of them came in very exasperated and asked him, "Do you know that these blacks are marching in the street here?" He replied, "Yeah, I know. They're protesting." The VP member complained: "I had to bring my fifteen-year-old daughter by them, and they were shouting 'Fuck the Veiled Prophet!' at the top of their voice, and I don't think that's right." Tooley responded, "Well, we don't think it's right, either, but that's the way it is."[35] Despite many official denials, ACTION certainly got the Veiled Prophet membership's attention—if only for short periods of time.

In 1972, members of ACTION obtained four tickets to the ball. Barbara Torrence's neighbor had given her two tickets, which she subsequently gave to ACTION. Percy Green claimed to have gotten the other two tickets from "a VP person—it was a vice president that was very, very high up in the organization." To this day, Green will not identify that person: "that was the understanding, because he would be decimated if it ever got out." ACTION's plan involved getting three white women into the ball and somehow unveiling the Veiled Prophet. Green and members of ACTION had been saying they would "unveil the Prophet" for years, but no one took them seriously.[36]

Gena Scott, Jane Sauer, and Phyllis Knight used three of the tickets to get into the balcony. "I think the idea sounds so simplified, but the symbolic goal was to unmask the VP," Scott remembered. "I did not set out personally to do it, but I knew that anyone who had the opportunity to take that thing off would have—because it was a symbolic gesture. You could write about it. . . . It was more of a class issue. I think a lot of people got a tickle out of it."[37] Unmasking the Veiled Prophet would show him to be not some "mythical figure," but merely a wealthy white male in the white male power structure. By unveiling the Prophet, ACTION wanted to show that the Veiled Prophet organization was not a kindly civic group but a supporting strut of St. Louis's ever-present white male power structure. Secondarily, ACTION wanted to embarrass the Veiled Prophet organization by conspicuously infiltrating the extensive security employed by the organization.

Scott, Sauer, and Knight's tickets were in the upper balcony in the section generally reserved for house servants or, as Sauer said, "friends of no importance." "We were told how to dress," Sauer remembers. "Not too fancy, but like it was a big night for us. And so we did it. This was theater—it was grand opera. We wore wigs. We wore— neither Gena nor I wore makeup at the time—but we wore makeup for this. We got heels and stockings and so forth. We had a whole background of who we were if we were caught. We sat away from other people—we couldn't strike up a dialogue with anyone."[38]

Although the women had been told how to get into the ball and how to be inconspicuous, they had no idea how to bring about their main objective. "The goal was to unveil the Veiled Prophet," Sauer said, "but once I got in there and saw how high that balcony was, I said no way we're going to do anything like this!" But then Gena Scott saw a three-inch electrical cable that came from the roof of the building and went down into an electrical box on the floor. "We sat there for over an hour while they just had the matrons and maids parading around," Scott said, "and each one was timed at about two minutes and thirty seconds to go around and get to the microphone and be announced as 'Mrs. August A. Busch,' etc."[39] The three women split up into different parts of the auditorium and Sauer waited for Scott to begin her move toward the cable.

As Scott neared the cable, Sauer began throwing leaflets over the balcony and shouting "Down with the VP!" The police quickly converged on Sauer and very roughly carried her out—she missed the rest of the performance. Knight's actions were not clear at this point. But Scott swiftly climbed over the balcony and grabbed the cable. As she was about halfway down, the cable broke loose from the ceiling. Fortunately, the cable, which had run diagonally from the roof to the stage, swung Scott out onto the first set of steps to the stage. "And that's where I landed," Scott said. "Later on, I learned I had three crushed ribs. I had the wind knocked out of me. I imagine I fell about fifty feet. I remember thinking: 'I didn't die, I can still go on.'"

At this point, an official came over to ask Scott what had happened. She responded that she had fallen out of the balcony and needed to get back to her seat. She moved toward the stage door, where a man met her. She told him that "Someone just fell over there" and pointed in the direction she had just come from. The man headed in that direction, allowing Scott access to the stage door. Scott made her way from the back of the stage through all of the flats. Suddenly Scott found herself behind the Bengal Lancers—the Veiled Prophet's honor guard. "There were about three rows of people all dressed up in costume like Arabian Knights or what they think Arabian Knights looked like, with swarthy skin. I thought it was so interesting that they had darkened their skin—you know, with these Aryan features." Scott nudged her way through the Lancers by saying she had an important phone call and before she knew it, she was standing next to the Veiled Prophet.

> I didn't look at him [the Veiled Prophet] directly because I was looking out front to see if anyone was going to stop me and no one was and so I just reached over and pulled off his veil. It was loosely attached. It was a very silky gossamer, like a silk stocking feeling. So I pulled it down and held it in my hand. Of course I didn't have any plans with what to do with it afterwards, which was unfortunate—what I might have done with the veil, or carried it to the front or something. But I could feel flashes—so I knew that pictures were being taken.[40]

Immediately grabbed and carried backstage by members of the Bengal Lancers, Scott now felt the pain of her broken ribs. Until then, Scott insisted the pain had been pushed back in her mind. "And the pain now was not so much because I had taken that fall," Scott said. "They then dragged me over the triangular supports of those slats and I remember thinking, 'Boy you're really angry.'" After having her ribs taped at a local hospital, police arrested Scott at around one o'clock in the morning in the halls of the hospital. At about four, the authorities released Scott from jail and gave her a court date. The Veiled Prophet organization later dropped the charges of disturbing the peace and destruction of public property (the cable) when it became obvious that, in order to prosecute Scott, they would have to reveal the name of the Veiled Prophet. Smith, although there were photographs clearly showing his face, still refuses to admit he was the Veiled Prophet in 1972. Sauer was also charged with disturbing the peace, but this charge was dropped as well.[41]

In November 1973, ACTION filed a class-action suit claiming that the city's rental of Kiel Auditorium for the Veiled Prophet ball was "tantamount to renting a public building as a private club, in violation of city law." Shortly afterward, the organization announced it was moving the ball from the Kiel Auditorium to the Chase Hotel. The last ball held in Kiel was in December of 1974. ACTION proclaimed victory.[42] Moving the ball to the Chase was more than likely a response to both ACTION's lawsuit and the unveiling in 1972. By moving to a private facility, the Veiled Prophet organization took away one of ACTION's major and most effective arguments about the annual celebration. The organization moved the ball to the Chase's much smaller Khorassan Room, which would be easier to secure against ACTION's protests.

The last two major demonstrations at the Veiled Prophet ball took place in 1975 and 1976. In 1975, Patrick Dougherty, an ACTION activist and former University of Missouri–Columbia faculty member, climbed onstage in the middle of the presentation of the maids and unfurled a banner that read "ACTION protests the racist VP." Dougherty's relatively mild form of protest was more an example of ACTION's mid-sixties nonviolent confrontational tactics than it was of the strategies of the seventies. Dougherty, whose background included several demonstrations of this type (one of which cost him his job at the university), was not interested in performing guerilla street theater. Removed roughly from the ball by two police officers, Dougherty was charged with disturbing the peace. The court later dismissed the charge when neither of the police officers appeared in court to testify against him.[43] Compared with the demonstration tactics used in the ball disruptions of 1972 and 1976, Dougherty's tactics in the 1975 demonstration appear anachronistic.

The demonstration at the 1976 Veiled Prophet ball has been called "the death rattle" of ACTION by one of its former members and "going too far" by another.[44] The plan involved a "cry-in" against racism. On December 23, 1976, ACTION activists Annette Foster and Jessie Baker climbed onstage at 8:30 P.M. shortly after the Veiled Prophet was announced. The two activists ran across the stage spraying tear gas into the air, trying carefully not to spray it directly into anyone's eyes. Jacqueline Bell, an ACTION member at the time, claimed that ACTION chose the tear gas because "basically it was a unique gesture." Although the police claimed that the tear gas "was a paralyzing gas," Green insisted it was a commercial tear gas. Bell said the gas was "very harmless" and argued that it got into the spectators' eyes when the security guards grabbed Foster and Baker, causing the spray nozzles to be pointed toward the crowd. Because the two AC-TION members lived outside of St. Louis and the police had no information on them, the police and the Veiled Prophet organization tried to make it seem as if ACTION had hired the two protesters. The Veiled Prophet organization and the police insinuated that the women were outside agitators or, at least, non–St. Louisans. Foster, found guilty nearly two years later of spraying a chemical irritant at a policeman, was sentenced to six months in prison.[45]

By 1976 ACTION had trouble garnering publicity. The "cry-in" at the ball that year had merely been an attempt to draw public attention and had skirted the edge of violence. Whereas the other protests had clearly defined goals, this protest appeared to be nothing more than a simple grab for publicity at any cost. To spray an irritant into the air and then claim that it was the security guards' fault for getting the substance into people's eyes was a dubious assertion.

Until its disbanding in 1984, ACTION continued to protest at the Veiled Prophet ball, parade, and at the fair, when it began in 1981. The 1976 tear gas incident severely damaged ACTION's credibility with the media and the public and had violated the major tenet of St. Louis public activism: Demonstrations should never be physically threatening. After 1976, ACTION was unable to garner much public attention at the Veiled Prophet protests and quietly faded away.

In 1979 the Veiled Prophet organization allowed its first black members—three doctors—to join. When asked if they were admitting black members in response to ACTION's protests, former Veiled Prophet Tom Smith—despite much evidence to the contrary—said that the Veiled Prophet organization

> hardly recognized ACTION. But we weren't aware that as much change was taking place in the community. Unfortunately, we didn't have time to keep up with the kind of changes that an institution like ACTION would like to see. We have black members now because the city began to change. There were social changes. As blacks became more active in business, they became members. We didn't think about them [ACTION]. I was too busy. Not that I wasn't interested. I just didn't have time.[46]

Ronald Henges, a longtime Veiled Prophet organization member put it even more strongly: "I don't believe the protests—I don't believe Percy Green influenced the organization any more than just having more security. That's all. . . . He got publicity and that's what he wanted and if he felt that was helpful to his cause then he accomplished that. As far as influencing any change in the VP organization, Percy Green can't take any credit for that." However, the St. Louis press certainly saw a connection between this decision and ACTION's protests. Reporters called ACTION headquarters on the day the Veiled Prophet organization announced it had admitted black members. When asked about that day, Jacqueline Bell said that "the press called us down there saying ACTION will no longer be protesting at the Veiled Prophet because they have admitted black members. I said, 'Hey, you guys have missed the point! We weren't trying to integrate the damned thing. You missed what we were trying to do.'"[47]

The Veiled Prophet organization was in fact responding to ACTION—but in an unanticipated way. In January of 1978, William H. Webster, a St. Louis native and federal judge, was nominated to become director of the Federal Bureau of Investigation. At his confirmation hearings, much was made of his membership in several exclusive all-white clubs—including the University Club, the Noonday Club, the St. Louis Country Club, and the Veiled Prophet organization. ACTION member Jacqueline Bell even testified about the nature of the Veiled Prophet organization. In a line designed to get press attention, Bell claimed the elites in the organization were "heavyweights" who "auction off their daughters among themselves, showing no respect for women" and that "we observed that there were judges and other Big Brother types in this clan."

Webster was eventually confirmed in February after assuring the Senate Judiciary Committee that he would monitor these four clubs and, if he detected any indication of racial or religious discrimination, he would resign. In September of 1979, the black members were initiated. In the article in the *Post-Dispatch* announcing the initiation (the only time in the organization's history initiates were ever publicly recognized), the spokesman for the organization admitted that the initiation committee had taken Webster's problems in getting confirmed into account and argued that "many members of the Veiled Prophet do not want to be vulnerable to the charge of racism" any longer.[48]

That the papers considered this a solution shows the way newspapers routinely distorted ACTION's pro-employment message all during that time. Both the *Globe-Democrat* and *Post-Dispatch* obscured ACTION's goals in their stories. None of the stories about the

Veiled Prophet protests mentioned ACTION's employment goals. The newspaper press depicted ACTION as a group of radical militants who advocated evil subversion of the current social order. The *Globe-Democrat* in particular published many damning editorials—many of which were written by then-editorial writer Patrick J. Buchanan—attacking ACTION as a small group of dissidents who were spoiling the annual celebration for everyone.[49]

Many ACTION members insisted that a large portion of the reporting of their protest activity had been cut by copy editors to match the newspaper owners' political and social agendas. When asked about the coverage of the Veiled Prophet demonstrations, two prominent former *Post-Dispatch* employees agreed with the ACTION members, contending that a great deal of content was cut by the editorial staff from the Veiled Prophet protest stories.[50]

One of the more telling examples of the press's bias was the coverage of the unveiling of the Prophet in 1972. In spite of the fact that everyone in the Kiel Auditorium saw Tom K. Smith and that there were probably one hundred pictures taken of his unveiled face, neither of the St. Louis newspapers ran Smith's name in its account of the unveiling. Evarts Graham, the assistant managing editor at the *Post-Dispatch* in 1972, stated that "the managing editor told me not to print it." Perhaps Tom K. Smith explains it best himself. Smith contended that "the *Post* and *Globe* appreciated the assets the Veiled Prophet organization had brought to St. Louis and the activities of the VP. So they withheld the name out of respect—telling the name would have been destructive to St. Louis." This unwillingness on the part of the newspapers to follow the dictates of journalistic practice likely stemmed from two sources: the fact that prominent members of the editorial staff at both newspapers were members of the Veiled Prophet organization and that the newspapers counted on the members of the organization for a large portion of their advertising revenue. It was not until the next month, when the *St. Louis Journalism Review* published Smith's name, that the public knew the Veiled Prophet's identity.[51]

While Smith may contend that he and other Veiled Prophet members "hardly recognized ACTION" and "didn't think about them," the experiences of some former activists suggest otherwise. A few weeks after Gena Scott unveiled the Prophet in 1972, her car was bombed in front of her apartment. In the year following the protest, Scott's apartment was also vandalized several times. Several of the former activists interviewed for this study reported receiving threatening phone calls during their time with ACTION.[52] All of their stories taken together attest to the fact that some St. Louisans not only had enough time to think about ACTION activists, they had enough time to devise ways to harass the activists as well.

Throughout the 1960s and 1970s, Percy Green was the target of much harassment. During ACTION meetings in the mid-1960s, Percy Green's wife often received phone calls telling her that her husband had been killed. After being laid off by McDonnell-Douglas in 1964, Green applied to be rehired in late 1965. The management at McDonnell-Douglas claimed that Green's participation in protests at their plant during 1965 proved he was a "disruptive person" and refused to rehire him. Over the next ten years, Green—backed by the Equal Employment Opportunity Commission—pursued a discrimination suit against McDonnell-Douglas all the way to the United States Supreme Court.[53] While the corporate executives in the Veiled Prophet organization may not have "recognized" ACTION, they clearly "recognized" Percy Green when he applied for a job. Despite thirty years of trying, Green has never been given another job at a major St. Louis corporation.

Some harassment of ACTION activists was directed by the FBI as a part of its COINTELPRO program. FBI agents—alerted by someone to the supposedly subversive nature of ACTION—frequently tormented activists. In 1970, the St. Louis office of the FBI "authorized an anonymous mailing from a soul sister" to Jane Sauer's estranged husband, Richard Simon. The letter, actually written by a male FBI agent, accused Sauer of marital infidelities with black men. Four months later, a memorandum written by the St. Louis office of the FBI to J. Edgar Hoover gloated that "while the letter sent by the St. Louis Division was probably not the sole cause of the separation, it certainly contributed very strongly."[54]

Did ACTION's Veiled Prophet protests ultimately improve employment opportunities for minorities in St. Louis? Green did not think so. He believed "these individual companies still carry on racial discriminatory practices although not to the same degree as before. The level of tokenism has gone up to some degree but not enough to say that they are fair in their employment practices." However, ACTION's protests did change employment practices at some companies—

those companies targeted for direct-action protests throughout this period. "We saw McDonnell's figures change," Jane Sauer said. "Who knows why? Maybe it was federal law. Maybe what ACTION did fed back in there somewhere."[55] Regardless, all of the former ACTION activists agreed that large-scale changes in employment practices in St. Louis did not occur as a result of any ACTION protests. The most obvious failure of ACTION's protests is the fact that the Veiled Prophet organization still exists.

Margaret Phillips senses why ACTION remained unable to achieve many tangible goals. She argues that ACTION "had no concrete plan that would help—just in effect screaming 'Ouch!' . . . Maybe the problem was we just got stuck in a rut of protest and when somebody said, 'What do you suggest?'—we'd retreat. Which isn't saying a whole lot more than just 'jobs.'" Phillips believes ACTION needed more comprehensive positions on a broad range of issues as well as possible solutions to the problems that faced St. Louis.[56]

On the other hand, ACTION did compel the Veiled Prophet organization to move the ball from the publicly funded Kiel Auditorium to the Chase Hotel. However, the move from Kiel Auditorium also stole a great deal of ACTION's thunder and may have sounded the death knell of the organization. A large number of St. Louisans seemed to have been perfectly willing to allow the Veiled Prophet organization to continue its ostentatious debutante ball as long as public facilities were not used. When asked about the achievements of the Veiled Prophet protests, Percy Green has additional victories in mind:

> The victory was that it was our staying power that encouraged the VP to do the many different things that they have done to try to discredit our claims. The victory is in that they had to discredit our charges by making these other moves: having the VP Fair, taking the ball off television. If you look at the time we started our campaign, many changes have happened. They do still get the police department to lie and say what the crowds at the fair are, they aren't as big as they claim they are. They still get the news media to cover the parade. They've tried to separate the VP from the parade to some extent (only a couple of floats are from the VP); they try to give the impression that it's a community affair. They still try to bring in the white communities from other places: St. Peter's, St. John's, Cape Girardeau, but I don't think it's working.[57]

Green and other former ACTION members see their victory in the fact that the Veiled Prophet organization had to change in response to ACTION's protests. Despite denials by current and past members, the

Veiled Prophet organization did bow to pressure and modify its ways, albeit not to the extent that most ACTION members would have liked.

Does the story of ACTION fit comfortably into the history of local black activism during this period in America? In some ways, but not in others. ACTION's employment-oriented goals were indeed similar to those of other local groups studied by scholars, such as the Coalition of United Community United Action (CUCA) in Chicago during the late 1960s. CUCA, which protested against discrimination in the Chicago building trades during 1969, favored more menacing tactics, embodied in the slogan, "You own the trades—We own the match—build or burn."[58] The membership in these groups, like the national groups, tended to be all-black; few, if any, whites participated.

Unlike other local groups studied by scholars during this "middle period," ACTION is exceptional in that its protests raised the public consciousness on some very important issues. Although large-scale changes in employment practices did not come about, ACTION's successes demonstrated that an integrated group devoted to nonviolent tactics could change some minds in a conservative midwestern city like St. Louis. While the Veiled Prophet protests did little to further ACTION's employment goals, these protests showed many St. Louisans that their tax dollars were indirectly supporting an elitist and, at the time, racist institution. ACTION's protests against corporate employers made some white St. Louisans stop and ask themselves an important question: Did minorities have equal opportunity to well-paying jobs with these major corporations? This raising of the public consciousness on a few vital issues was perhaps ACTION's most important achievement. Unfortunately, most white St. Louisans at the time seem to have rejected ACTION's employment goals.

In spite of ACTION's success in consciousness-raising, the reasons for ACTION's decline did fit the explanations offered by civil-rights scholars. Unlike other groups, ACTION's decline was slow and steady and linked to the steady rise of white backlash against civil rights groups during the late 1960s and 1970s. As James Ralph has argued, whites became "disturbed when civil rights crusaders guided the traditional quest for equality into more private realms of American life." Ralph maintains that while whites "applauded the southern black drive for basic political and civil rights," they dismissed the Chicago Freedom Movement's goal of ending housing discrimination "as an illegitimate demand that threatened their right" to make certain "basic, private decisions." Whites in St. Louis felt the controversy over the location of the Veiled Prophet ball in the early 1970s was a "legitimate" public concern about basic civil rights (involving either equal access to or proper use of public facilities). At the same time, many in the white community rejected ACTION's employment demands as a separate issue that fit into the "private decision" realm. After the ball was moved from Kiel Auditorium, the white community turned a deaf ear to ACTION's Veiled Prophet protests and to ACTION's other more employment-oriented protests as well. By the late 1970s, after a decade of increasing white backlash against civil-rights advocates, an overwhelming majority of white St. Louisans viewed ACTION's employment demands as an illegitimate infringement on their rights. Consequently, ACTION's demise was not quick and explosive like that of other civil-rights groups during this period. ACTION did not, in the words of J. Mills Thornton, die "like a fire deprived of oxygen."[59] ACTION's flame, like an abandoned campfire, slowly flickered and burned out.

Like ACTION, however, the Veiled Prophet organization was itself in dire trouble by the late 1970s. In 1978 Veiled Prophet membership was at an all-time low. Young St. Louis businessmen saw no reason to join. When asked about resignations during this period, all one "source close to the organization" would say was that "there were so many." One of these resignations was Charles Polk, an executive of the Baldwin Regalia Company. "In those days," Polk explained, "the crowds just kept diminishing. The VP wasn't perceived as a civic organization. It wasn't serving the interests of St. Louis. . . . A lot of money was being wasted on one party and a parade."[60] Public interest in the celebration itself dropped. The parade and ball were no longer covered by the media very closely. Television coverage of the ball had ended by the middle 1970s. The parade, although it was still televised, saw its attendance figures begin to drop precipitously. The organization was beginning to wither away; it seemed to be in its death throes by the late 1970s.

The Veiled Prophet celebration, once a cherished city tradition, was meeting a great deal of popular resistance and the members of the organization did not know what to do about it. In fact, some of the sons and daughters of members began to feel that the ball had outlived its usefulness. In an article that summed up the malaise of the 1970s for the Veiled Prophet organization, Curtis Wilson recounted interviews with debutantes who told him they agreed with Green that elitism was wrong and that the ball represented elitism. Wilson even spoke with one former maid who told him the ball was "a farce" and that "this kind of exhibition has got to go." Another maid described her experience with the ball as "much ado about nothing" and told him "I don't plan to have my daughter in it." The ultimate indignity for the organization was an interview with Dr. William H. Danforth, Chancellor of Washington University and a longtime Veiled Prophet organization member, who told Wilson his two daughters (aged twelve and fourteen) were already asking him if they would be presented at the ball. "I don't know what to tell them," he told Wilson frankly.[61]

ACTION, it seemed, would belatedly get its wish. As of the late 1970s, the disbanding of the Veiled Prophet organization appeared to be imminent.

"An Activity the City Could Hang Its Hat On"

THE VEILED PROPHET CELEBRATION, 1981–1995

It was a bright, sunny, and warm July afternoon in St. Louis in 1993. The crowd of around two hundred thousand underneath the Gateway Arch at the VP Fair was awaiting the McDonnell-Douglas Air Show, due to begin shortly. There was an air of anticipation in the crowd. Many in St. Louis claim that this annual air show is one of the very best in the country; the huge turnout certainly seemed to suggest as much. The crowd was remarkably diverse—bringing St. Louisans of all classes and ethnic groups together in one place for the three-day event. The air show was not the only attraction. Fair patrons could visit amusement park rides, do some bungee jumping, or go to the Family Fun Village for children's activities. By most accounts, the fair today is a hugely popular event—especially with children. Regardless of its shortcomings (and there are many), by the middle 1990s the VP Fair had become a popular civic event for St. Louisans and one of the largest events of its kind in America.

To understand the rise of the VP Fair and the rebirth of the Veiled Prophet organization, one has to go back nearly two decades to the nadir of the Veiled Prophet organization and celebration. In the middle-to-late 1970s, the organization was struggling to stay alive and, more importantly, trying to give the public a tangible reason for its existence. In a little over a decade, the celebration had gone from being viewed by most St. Louisans as a treasured local tradition to being perceived as an excessive and tasteless show of wealth by a group of wealthy "fat cats" from Ladue. The organization's fall had been meteoric and traumatic for its members.

Ronald Henges, a longtime member, argued that by the late 1970s "people just didn't like other people flaunting their wealth and their position. It's just a change in our society." He felt that as "our culture has evolved, these things are less important to people. It's just an

140

evolving situation where the in-group has gotten a little bit smaller. . . . The interest level has just waned. There's still that group. It's a smaller group and the people on the outside of that group have almost developed . . . disdain for people in that group." William Maritz, who served as Veiled Prophet during this period, explained that "a lot of members" in the late 1970s "felt uneasy with the social connotations" and that "people were saying 'Get that goddamned ball off of television, don't force that on the community.'"[1] How did the organization's members breathe life back into the dying celebration? Why did they want to?

Despite the major changes in American and St. Louis culture in the 1970s, the celebration went on as it always had. Newspaper articles at the time described the 1970s as a time of malaise and disillusionment among the organization's members. One newspaper article on the 1979 ball conjectured that "At the 96th Veiled Prophet Ball, the 1970s' final court of Love and Beauty, his Mysterious Majesty must have breathed a sigh of relief that the decade was ending."[2] Some journalists described this feeling among the organization's members as one of shock. Henges, however, disagreed.

> Do I think they were shocked? Probably not. The members of the VP have the same level of intelligence as the general public, the media, and the press. They recognized that people didn't think these were important things anymore. Particularly when we were addressing poverty and racial issues throughout the United States. This was just not as popular as it used to be. My feeling is that members of the VP knew this and didn't know what to do about it. They knew this but thought 'we're still going to have the ball. We know there's a lot of social upheaval going on but we can't do anything about it.' So I don't think it was a major issue until the late seventies, and two things occurred in the late seventies. I think the VP organization began to decline as far as membership and interest on the part of men being interested or willing to join it. And that becomes a financial problem. Then I think some enlightened members of the VP organization figured, 'Hey, we can fold this thing, or we can kind of rejuvenate it and make it a little more interesting and exciting for the greater community.' And that's where the idea of the fair was conceived.[3]

Maritz put it more succinctly: "Back in '79 I thought the city needed something—an activity the city could hang its hat on."[4] Finding such an activity would, among other things, allow the Veiled Prophet organization to justify its existence.

The founders of the VP Fair hoped to boost flagging civic pride and improve St. Louis's image—goals similar to those of the celebration's founders a century earlier. The late 1970s were an uncertain time for St. Louis. The city's economy was shaky and many recent plant closings had increased unemployment in St. Louis. The city was becoming increasingly segregated; whites now lived in the suburbs and blacks made up nearly half of the central city's inhabitants. The two communities had less contact with one another than ever before. Not surprisingly, tourism in the city dropped remarkably during the decade.[5] The founders of the VP Fair hoped they could change all that.

In 1979, Veiled Prophet members Robert R. Hermann and Maritz got approval from that year's Veiled Prophet to create the Veiled Prophet Fair. The Veiled Prophet appointed other St. Louis corporate leaders, such as Clarence Barksdale, E. R. Culver III, John R. Griesedieck, Robert Hyland Jr., Ivis Johnston, John Krey III, and Donald E. Lasater, to the executive committee of the fair. This group created a separate organization, the VP Fair Foundation, to administer the VP Fair.[6] The Fair Foundation members were also all members of the VP organization, but their names were released to the press. This was the first time since the late nineteenth century that names of individual members had been made public.

Ironically, the Veiled Prophet organization was now involved with its second fair in its century-long history. The St. Louis Agricultural and Mechanical Fair, which had died out seventy years earlier, had been the reason for creating the Veiled Prophet in the first place, as an attempt to increase interest in the fair. This time, the organizers would be creating a fair entirely by itself. As in the first fair, the Veiled Prophet parade played an integral role. However, instead of being one of many events of the week, the Veiled Prophet parade would now kick off fair weekend.

The Veiled Prophet organization did not lend its name—exactly—to the new fair. The event was to be called the "VP Fair." In fact, from about this time to the present day, the name *Veiled Prophet* is seldom used at all by the organization for any of its events. Instead, the initials *VP* are used. This move attempted to distance the organization from its recent and ignominious past in the sixties and seventies. The ploy appeared to have worked. Informal polls by newspaper reporters in the late eighties revealed that most St. Louisans did not know what

VP stood for in the name of the parade or fair. "They think it stands for Vice-President or something," Rusty Hager, the 1995 fair chairman, explained. The organization, through this very simple artifice, successfully jettisoned a great deal of the social baggage associated with it during the Civil Rights era—at least with white St. Louisans. In the early eighties, however, many in the black community of St. Louis still distrusted the organization and therefore did not attend the celebration. Activists in the black community continued to loathe anything linked to the VP organization.

Even though the VP members presented a united front of support, many members doubted the fair would be successful. As Robert Tooley recalled, "When the G.O. [the Veiled Prophet for the year 1981] who started the thing first talked about it and told the membership about it, we knew it was going to be July Fourth. Everybody that came in the year before for fittings for the parade, we asked them 'How about the fair? Are you involved in that?' And no one, not one person would admit they were even going to be in town. 'No I'm in Michigan that time of year. I can't possibly be here.'"[7] In other words, the effort to get the fair off the ground was not exactly supported by most VP members.

The celebration's change of season is significant: The VP Fair was scheduled to take place during the July Fourth holiday. Consciously rejecting autumn, the traditional season for Veiled Prophet activities, in favor of Independence Day, the organization hoped to explicitly link the celebration with patriotism. Organization members felt that all classes of St. Louisans would turn out for a civic celebration on the Fourth of July. The VP Fair programs in the 1980s touted the celebration as "America's biggest birthday party" and, like the boosters of the fair a century earlier, claimed that the celebration attracted all classes of St. Louisans and many visitors from out of town. Like the organization's founders a century earlier, VP members were attempting to create a traditional annual celebration and perpetuate it.

Because of the events of the sixties and seventies, the Veiled Prophet organization's involvement in the fair made many St. Louisans uneasy. It was one thing for the Veiled Prophet to appear once a year on his float in the parade, but it was entirely another matter for the organization to sponsor a large public event like the VP Fair. The organization's practices and symbols were suddenly a matter of public concern because the celebration involved public funds. These concerns became even more intense when the organization claimed that the event would be for the entire St. Louis community. The group had certainly not been inclusive in the past and still was not in the 1980s. Some wondered how the organization could claim to be capable of creating an all-inclusive spectacle. The challenge, in the words of Julie Berman, "would be to make that claim come true."

Many blacks and some whites were still offended by the Veiled Prophet organization's membership practices and symbolism. It had historically excluded people by race, class, gender, and religion. Many black activists were quick to point out, as Green had in the sixties and seventies, that the organization's primary symbol—a white male wearing a hood—was offensive to most African Americans. Percy Green felt the fair was a way of improving (even recasting) the organization's image with the public and reacting to the negative criticism of the 1970s. "They could not be beholden to our charges of racism, sexism and classism," Green explained. "They tried to rebuild the sense of patriotism . . . in an attempt to stop white people from knowing what the VP stands for. If you get all caught up with the glitter, you forget what the VP was about. We asked blacks not to participate and, if they did, to be part of a disruptive protest."[8] The VP Fair during the eighties had trouble attracting black St. Louisans; they stayed away in droves.

In creating public events, civic leaders try to promote their city through projecting what they think is a positive image. For example, in the nineteenth century, the parade makers presented St. Louis as a city of enlightened leadership and distinguished history. Despite their attempts to present St. Louis in the best possible light, the 1980s fair board members did not really understand that the image they were projecting was not particularly inclusive. The organization wished to promote St. Louis as the most typical of American cities—something that Walter B. Stevens had first claimed sixty years earlier.

This image came alive in the literature of the organization—fair programs and the commemorative book, *The VP Fair in Review, 1981–1990*. The image that the fair's creators ultimately projected was that of an all-white group putting on a fair that reinforced traditional patriotism. The 256-page *VP Fair in Review* book featured conventional white-bread patriotic scenes such as George Bush pledging allegiance at the first fair in 1981, a picture of the Veiled Prophet during the parade, balloons rising in front of the Arch, and children frolicking in one of the pools near the Arch. The group's literature, Berman argued, told its readers "If you're looking for authentic America, go no further. Stop here and camp beneath the Arch." The entertainment also catered to white tastes. Performers featured during the fairs in the 1980s included Bob Hope, Elton John, Roy Clark, the Beach Boys, Harry Belafonte, the Osmond Family, Charlie Daniels, Linda Ronstadt, Tom T. Hall, John Denver, Helen Reddy, Glen Campbell, Doc Severinsen, Liza Minnelli, Dolly Parton, Bernadette Peters, Tony Bennett, Loretta Lynn, and Suzanne Somers.[9] The fair offered little new to those who might have been looking for evidence of a diverse, inclusive spectacle. Furthermore, photographs of the organizers in the fair programs during the eighties demonstrated just how few blacks had roles in the fair's leadership—quite curious for a celebration that claimed to be an inclusive, citywide event.

For the first several years, the group was successful in garnering national attention, a goal that was always important for the Veiled Prophet organization. Boosters in the nineteenth century and early twentieth century often claimed that their celebration would bring St. Louis commerce, tourism, and would help to create a "bigger and better St. Louis." In the eighties, the fair's boosters argued that if they could convince more people (particularly corporate CEOs who helped sponsor the fair) that St. Louis was a great place to live, work, and do business, then all St. Louisans would profit.

In 1985 and 1987, ABC and CBS's morning television shows broadcasted live from the fairgrounds. In 1987, ABC devoted two and a half hours to the Veiled Prophet Fair on the night of July Fourth. This prerecorded show, *A Star-Spangled Celebration,* was taped the previous day and included performances by celebrities like Dwight Yoakum, Tony Bennett, Phil Driscoll, Suzanne Somers, Ben Vereen, and Loretta Lynn. The program was hosted by Robert Urich and Oprah Winfrey. According to Eric Mink, a television critic for the *Post-Dispatch,* the program was the reflection of "a white, middle-aged male mentality with middle-class tastes." Mink felt the program certainly failed to improve either St. Louis's or the organization's image with regard to diversity and demonstrated the utter lack of participation by black St. Louisans as patrons of the fair. Mink contended that "Whenever the camera left the performers, St. Louis seemed to be a sea of white faces, at best a distortion in a town where 45 percent of the people are black Americans." Mink went further to indict the production for failing to present the image of St. Louis as a diverse, progressive city:

> But the telecast gave no sense at all of St. Louis as the exciting, modern, progressive town that, with limited success so far, it is trying to become; a place that combines small-town friendliness with the cultural, social, and economic opportunities of a big city.
>
> In that respect, ABC's "A Star-Spangled Celebration" actually reinforced the stereotype of St. Louis as a nice, old-fashioned Southern-ish river town with a big July Fourth party, a long history and not much more.[10]

This observation can be extended to the entire fair during the eighties. Like the VP organization's celebration in the past, it was not inclusive and only appealed to part of the community.

Mink questioned the VP organization's very reliability in a column a week later, and in the process severely weakened the organization's credibility with the public. After a little research, he found the claims of the VP Fair communications chairperson Allyn Glaub to be highly exaggerated. For example, Glaub claimed the show cost ABC five million dollars to produce. Mink discovered that ABC had actually spent only two million on the show. Glaub claimed that 250 local dancers were used in one of the production numbers, whereas Mink found the number was actually 100. Mink argued that these unwarranted claims were typical of the organization that St. Louisans already knew better than to trust. But Mink went even further. He pointed out that the annual attendance estimates for the last several years (an estimated 3.75 million in 1982, for example) were much higher than the St. Louis metropolitan area's entire population—making them extremely suspect.[11] It did not seem likely that every person in the metropolitan area visited the fair twice or three times.

Why was such embellishment necessary? Julie Berman maintained that it was the result of a lack of self-confidence and a sense that St. Louis's image was "short of the national stature city leaders imagine it should have." Gregory Freeman, an urban columnist, told Berman that community leaders were very worried about St. Louis's image as a major city. "We're very paranoid," Freeman said. "We really are. We worry about what we look like to other cities, but then we worry that we're not being thought of at all. Particularly in the early eighties when they'd inflate the numbers—that was all part of the same thing. 'Five million people came down.' There aren't five million people in this whole area. . . . Major cities—New York, L.A., Chicago, and we're rarely on that list and we want to be on that list." By inflating the fair's attendance figures, these leaders portrayed St. Louis as a major city holding a major civic celebration. It was an attempt to say to other city boosters and to the American people, "look what we can do—our civic celebration is bigger than yours." The *Post-Dispatch*'s staff wrote other stories critical of the VP organization during the 1980s. These stories revealed the staggering cost of resodding the grounds beneath the Arch after the fair, the large salaries of some of the fair's part-time administrators, and the lack of involvement of minority musicians and vendors.[12]

The problems for the VP organization did not end there; there were many others. First among these was that the fair, despite its high attendance, had trouble becoming self-supporting during the 1980s. In 1987, the VP Fair received $650,000 from St. Louis city and county to stay afloat financially. During the late 1980s the city continued to allocate to the fair foundation large sums of money from its various convention and tourism funds. These annual appropriations were often criticized by African American activists who were having trouble getting adequate funding for city schools. During some of the celebrations in the late 1980s, inhospitable weather—several rain- and windstorms—further exacerbated the financial problems of the fair, keeping it from breaking even. "It's almost like there's a curse on this thing" Percy Green claimed in 1993. "That's what I like to think—that I put a curse on it in essence."[13] The fair was carrying a large deficit of several hundred thousand dollars in the late 1980s.

Further contradictions surfaced concerning the VP Fair's supposedly inclusive image during the 1980s—revealing the simmering racial tensions underneath. During the 1982 fair, two young white men were shot to death when they tried to stop a racially charged fight between groups of blacks and whites.[14] In 1987, the St. Louis police board, responding to pressure from the VP organization, closed the Eads Bridge, which connects St. Louis to East St. Louis (a largely African American community), to pedestrian traffic during the nighttime hours. The decision was explained as a safety matter to prevent "East Side street gangs" from "coming across the bridge to rob and mug." This decision was yet another black eye for the organization's public relations. Gregory Freeman, a columnist for the *Post-Dispatch*, maintained that "the decision to close the Eads Bridge to pedestrians for thirteen hours a day during the VP Fair will undoubtedly go down as one of the biggest tactical disasters in the history of an event that prides itself on its image."[15]

The bridge was reopened after the East St. Louis NAACP filed a complaint on July Fourth contending that the closing of the bridge "violated the right of people to travel and discriminated against them on the basis of race." Judge John F. Nangle ordered the bridge reopened, claiming they could not close the bridge on an assumption that East St. Louis was where the crime at the fair was coming from. Nangle told police officials, "You can't say the people from the East are any more dangerous than people from St. Louis."[16]

The episode was extremely embarrassing to the Veiled Prophet organization. The perception in St. Louis's black community was that the organizers did not want the participation of African Americans in the fair—especially poor African Americans. That the VP organization attempted to exclude some African Americans by closing the bridge verified the feeling among black St. Louisans that the celebration was not for them—only for whites. It told them that members of the organization believed in an old stereotype: that blacks were responsible for most of the petty crimes in the city. Despite years of supposed progress, old prejudices died hard.

In 1987 relations between the VP Fair officials and the African American community in St. Louis reached an all-time low. After the Eads Bridge debacle, the leadership of the Veiled Prophet organization realized the need to change both the nature of the celebration and the inclusiveness of their organization. Like most changes in the organization throughout its history, these would be made behind closed doors rather than in public view where community activists could monitor them. Community activists like Percy Green believed the Veiled Prophet organization would have to disband as a necessary precondition to any meaningful progress in race relations in the city. But the organization was not willing to disband; it wanted to fulfill its goal of creating an all-inclusive civic celebration—an elusive goal in the eighties.

Ron Henges, fair chairman from 1989 to 1991, felt the organization received too much criticism about minority involvement in the fair during the 1980s. "The *Post* was very critical of the fair because they felt it was an exercise by the fat cats," he explained. "They felt there weren't enough black people involved with the planning of the fair, the execution of the fair, participation in the fair. I think a lot of that was rhetoric on the part of a liberal newspaper." However, as much as he would like to dismiss the criticism, Henges's actions as chairman showed that he was listening closely to such criticism.

The first thing the organization did was expand its minority membership. The token minority membership of the early 1980s grew significantly. In fact, membership as a whole in the organization had expanded tremendously since the advent of the fair. As Robert Tooley explained: "At initiation meetings, where new members come in, at one time if we had six new members coming in at initiation that was quite a lot—if you had 10 that was unbelievable. And now there may be 50 or more at a time, two initiations a year and the age limit has been lowered. I think it was 36 or something like that. It slowly has come down. I don't know what it is now."[17] During the late eighties and early nineties, membership in the organization mushroomed. The organization's membership is now probably larger than it ever has been—which is saying a lot considering that the organization had around a thousand members during the 1910s.

Also in response to the Eads Bridge episode, the Veiled Prophet organization formed a minority relations committee. It appointed Steve Roberts, an African American businessman and city alderman, to be its chair. Under his leadership, VP members began to listen more to what the African American community was telling them. What they heard from Roberts was shocking to them. "These people were clearly civic-minded," said Roberts. "They had the best intentions but didn't understand, not just black people's, but other members of the community as well's feelings—that the city was paying for the fair, but not all groups were welcomed to it." Berman argued that the members of the VP organization in 1987 "were seemingly oblivious to the public's interpretation of the organization, focusing instead on the good they were doing the city. The problem was that in their acting for the city's well-being they were creating their own image of 'the city.' And that image, of a homogenous, white-led all-American midwestern city, wasn't sitting well with blacks and other groups."[18] The organization appointed some of these new African American members to important VP Fair committees. Therefore, the organization began making a conscious attempt to integrate both the organization and the leadership roles on the fair committees. It is unclear whether leadership roles in the VP organization, a separate organization from the VP Fair Foundation, changed at all.

The most difficult thing, according to Roberts, was getting the black community to participate in the VP Fair. There still were, as Roberts put it, the "sensitivities" from the sixties and seventies in the black community. Slowly, over the next several years, more and more African American businessmen began to participate. The increased participation of black leaders upset activists like Green, who felt that blacks who participated in the organization were forced to "succumb to the rules of the white power structure." He argued that these blacks, whom he referred to as "responsible negroes," were given their roles in the organization as "more of a PR thing to protect the integrity of the VP's name" rather than the result of a desire on the part of VP members to make meaningful changes in race relations.[19] Despite the success of the fair, many African Americans still feel this way.

Beginning with the 1988 VP Fair, the fair leadership tried hard to change the fair's image. The fair chairman from 1988 to 1990 was Ron Henges. Henges wanted the fair to perform an educational function—ironically quite similar to that of the parades of the late nineteenth century. Henges wanted to use the fair to teach cultural values and civic history and to provide "acceptable entertainment" for the masses. According to Henges, the VP Fair during his tenure as chairman was to be

> the biggest, most important, most enjoyable, most valuable contribution to the St. Louis public entertainment scene possible. Something that is internationally known, something that brings community, brings neighborhoods, together, a feeling that this is one cohesive community. We had an idea that the fair would have a very definite cultural, educational component in addition to pure entertainment. That it would showcase St. Louis companies in what they did, that it would introduce people who may not otherwise have had the opportunity to experience some of the more cultural things, the arts and things like that, and a very heavy component on education: the importance of education and the educational opportunities in St. Louis and the various not-for-profits and things like that. So that's what we wanted it to be.[20]

Henges's ideas about the role of the VP Fair as a civic event were clearly expressed in the fairs over which he presided. With his leadership, the fair gave increased free space to educational and cultural groups for exhibits and programs. The 1989 and 1990 fairs added an extra day to the traditional three-day schedule of the event for what it called Education Day. This day was devoted to educational and patriotic activities for school-aged children. Henges also moved the fair away from featuring nationally known, mostly white performers in concerts. His fairs showcased a diverse group of local performers. By using local performers, Henges was trying to drum up local interest in the fair—particularly in the black community.

As the fair entered the 1990s, the VP organization backed away from Henges's vision of the fair as a cultural and educational event. Instead, it promoted the fair simply as a diverse civic gathering. As Henges recalled,

> What it turned out to be was just a big bash—pure entertainment. The greater public did not respond significantly to the educational and cultural components. That was one of the reasons the fair spent a lot of money in its early years in those areas and didn't get a satisfactory return. What you see now is almost exclusively pure and simple entertainment. You know, the community told us what they wanted and that's what the fair did. The fair evolved. So, that's the definition of what it really is as opposed to what the originators of the fair really thought they wanted it to be.[21]

Unlike their counterparts in the sixties and seventies, the VP leaders in the eighties and nineties reacted quickly to indications of what the public really wanted.

What caused the lack of response to the VP Fair's educational and cultural activities? Perhaps St. Louisans felt they did not need to be preached to about education or "proper" cultural activities. The tone of the literature for these fairs certainly was strident as far as such themes were concerned. Furthermore, the culture of leisure and consumption that prevails in late-twentieth-century America played a role as well. Americans, stressed about their daily lives and the insecurities of today's economic developments, prefer to blow off steam for a few hours rather than listen to high-minded discourses on the plight of the world's rain forests. Most Americans now believe that civic events are meant for fun and leisure—not for commemoration or education.[22]

During the 1990s the fair became a popular civic event with most segments of the public in St. Louis. It became, in Julie Berman's words, "an event symbolic of summer in St. Louis." Black St. Louisans began to attend in greater numbers and had more important roles on the VP Fair Foundation's boards. As the fair picked up momentum, so did interest among VP members in helping with the fair. "Hell, this must have changed people's lifestyles," said Bob Tooley. "So many are involved in the fair now. I didn't think it would succeed but it certainly has. It's doing quite well now."[23]

The foundation began to bring in national performers again, but it was careful to bring in both black and white performers in order to broaden the fair's appeal. In addition to Chicago, Sawyer Brown, and the Beach Boys, the organization also brought in Aretha Franklin, James Brown, Patti LaBelle, and Gladys Knight.

As the fair's appeal broadened, the event began to make money consistently. The VP Fair Foundation reported in 1995 that the deficit—which had grown as large as $800,000 in 1991—was erased by the financial successes of the four fairs since then, especially by the very profitable fairs of 1994 and 1995. Rusty Hager, fair chairman for 1994 and 1995, felt there were other reasons for the financial success of the fair in the last few years: "What really happened was, we were carrying $800,000 worth of debt. We created a professional staff which gave the fair staff the time to work on the infrastructure of the fair to save dollars. That happened over a two-year period."[24]

In 1995 the VP Fair changed its name to something much more inclusive, Fair St. Louis. Despite the positive connotations of the change, the public and private reasons given for it are not clear. Some members cite one reason, while others cite another. Gregory Freeman, the columnist for the *Post-Dispatch,* thought that the efforts of the organization to include more members of the minority community played a role in the change.[25] In an interview with the *Post-Dispatch,* a member of the minority relations committee stated, "Now, with a name change, fair officials are trying to brush away a negative past and include everyone." Freeman Bosley Jr., St. Louis's new (and first African American) mayor, responded positively to the idea in September of 1994. "You had some folks who thought the term 'VP' and 'Veiled Prophet' had exclusive connotations," said Bosley. "This eliminates any concerns and perceptions about the VP Fair."[26] In spite of the interesting timing of the change, VP Fair officials deny that Bosley played any role in the name change.[27]

Hager, the fair chairman for the last two years, gave another reason—the need to attract corporate sponsors from outside St. Louis:

> The name of the fair was changed to Fair St. Louis and this has been contemplated over the last probably three to four years. Not that we have tapped out all of the corporate sponsors in St. Louis, but because of the size of the event, we are contacted continuously by consumer product companies outside of St. Louis that want to be a part of this event. VP Fair just does not make sense to anybody unless you live here and have been around it. . . . We decided to change the name to Fair St. Louis because it makes it all a lot simpler when we're outside of St. Louis trying to elicit corporate sponsors.

However, Hager was careful to add something about the other and more significant reason: "I'm not going to say this played any part in it but if there's any baggage with the name VP, that has now been, we think, defused."[28]

Not all VP members agree with Hager's characterization of the name change. In response to a question about why the name was changed to Fair St. Louis, Henges argued it was changed

> . . . because the black community resented the name *VP*. Totally, [the name change is] strictly a result of bad feelings within the black community. The black community has softened its position in the last few years but there is still a resentment that exists in the black community about the Veiled Prophet organization. . . . The black community attended some of the events that were particularly interesting to them, notably the black entertainers. . . . The VP organization did not begin admitting blacks until fifteen years ago, and then it was very, very token. In the last seven or eight years they have really beefed up that program, and a much greater number of blacks have been asked to join the organization. It's all kind of coming together. It's just a long process. But the name change was certainly to eliminate the reference to the Veiled Prophet organization.[29]

When presented with Hager's statements about the need to attract corporate sponsors, Henges responded rather bluntly. "That's all a bunch of bullshit. What you just heard from me is the honest truth."[30]

Regardless of these disagreements, the developments in the VP organization over the last few years suggest that the group is moving toward a very different view of what the VP Fair is all about. The fair is now to be a diverse and peaceful gathering, an all-inclusive civic event. It is no longer about gaining national attention to promote the city, nor about promoting certain cultural values and traditions. These goals have been abandoned in favor of creating a three-day, locally focused spectacle that brings the community together underneath the

Arch for food, music, and fun. The local emphasis can be seen in a number of recent developments. First, the VP organization no longer gives crowd estimates—the fairgrounds are packed anyway. The fair's administrators no longer see the need to boast about attendance for the benefit of the national media. In a related point, the organization no longer tries as it once did to get coverage from the national networks, preferring to just have local networks cover the festivities. Finally, the organization now has its program published in the Sunday edition of the *Post-Dispatch* the weekend before the fair. Fair patrons no longer have to spend two or three dollars just to find out what is going on down at the fair; they can get it from the local newspaper.

Julie Berman argued that the symbolism of the 1995 Fair St. Louis was, perhaps, more important than anything else. She described the Gladys Knight concert this way: "It was a beautiful night and all that had gathered with the purpose of hearing this entertainer who had made her debut during the tumultuous sixties and was now singing to a peaceful, racially mixed crowd in a public space (in a state that borders the nation's North and South, racial dividing lines in our national conscience)." While Berman's conclusion may be a bit optimistic, the image is powerful. The fair and the organization itself are finally becoming what they have claimed to be for the last fifteen years: inclusive and community-based. In 1996, Horace Wilkins, an African American executive at Southwestern Bell, became chairman of Fair St. Louis.[31]

For most of its history, the Veiled Prophet organization represented exclusion and elite privilege. For the first time, these elites appear to be giving something back to the citizens of St. Louis, not just to white citizens (as was the problem with the fair during the eighties) and certainly not just to white, wealthy citizens (as was the case for the first hundred years of the celebration). This new conception of the Veiled Prophet celebration represents a great change from the organization's attempts at social control and teaching cultural values in the late nineteenth and early twentieth century.

The ball, overshadowed by the more successful fair, still takes place on a night in late December. If anything, the ball may have kept the organization alive during the late 1970s. After public interest in the parade declined, the organization's members seemed to focus their attention more on the ball. The participation of one's daughter in the ball is still important for the city's social elite. Elites simply cannot let go of this symbolic crowning of themselves as the social aristocrats of St. Louis. But like the fair, the ball has become more inclusive in recent years. In the late eighties and early nineties, the first African Americans began to participate in the ball as matrons. As of the present time, no African American woman has participated as a maid of honor—the most important badge of a family's acceptance into the elite social class.

The general attitude among participants about the importance of the ball has changed. When asked if the ball is a positive event for the entire St. Louis community, Rusty Hager responded: "Well I don't know if it's a positive event for the whole community. I think what it represents is a gathering of family members and friends of the girls that are coming out after their sophomore year in college. It's kind of a uniting and a big fun party and it is no more than that." Hager was careful to caution against reading too much into the ball in its present form:

> It's just a big party and you can't take the whole process too seriously. It's a great evening. It's great to have all the kids together, to see family and friends together in one place, watching these girls. That is basically what it's given for. There's been a lot of de-emphasis of the ball probably in the last fifteen years. It was a much more prominent event years ago than it is today. It used to get a lot of news coverage, it used to be live on TV, it used to be in Kiel. . . . It was a big deal then. It went through the period of the sixties, during the war, all these tumultuous times it was downplayed. It really is at the level where it should be. There is a little bit of media there to ask a few questions but there doesn't seem to be any adversarial comments about it. It happens and it's over . . . the thing just kind of evolved into a less-focused event. It's at the Adam's Mark. It's in a ballroom. It's not in Kiel and it's not on TV.[32]

The sentiment in the organization continues that the ball is a private event whereas the fair and parade are civic events—and never the twain shall meet. The attempt to separate the two in the public's consciousness appears to have worked.

"If [the ball] was important to people years ago," Hager explained, "it's not important today." Hager posited an explanation for the Ball's drop in popularity: "Why was it important to people? People didn't have enough to do . . . I just think it happened. It was a time when that kind of thing, people just got focused on things that were a hell of a lot more important. And it just from that point forward—it is what it is. It's two thousand people watching a ball and fifteen hundred people having dinner and then at eight o'clock in the morning it's over."[33] Hager contended that American culture and the lives of St. Louisans have changed so much in the last few years that the coronation of the Queen of Love and Beauty at the Veiled Prophet ball is no longer of any importance to them. The organization has responded to this change in public interest. In the last twenty years, the queen's public appearances have dramatically decreased. Unlike earlier times, when the queen served as a celebrity at major events for an entire year, she now only presides over the VP parade and ball.

The attitudes of the debutantes themselves have also changed in a way similar to that of the organization's male members. Molly Hager, VP queen for 1995 and daughter of Rusty Hager, said that she participated because she was asked to, not because it was something important to her own life. "I don't know if it's true," Molly Hager continued,

> because I don't know a lot about the VP itself, but people say that a lot of the girls honor their fathers, so for all the girls who I've ever even talked to, I don't think it's a matter of being queen or being, you know, the last of the alphabet coming out as a debutante, everyone has just as much fun. So, all my friends were doing it and I was doing it too and they were as much a part of it as I was, I thought. . . . My best friend's a Williams and we had just as much fun together as everybody else did. It's just more of an honor for Dad and that's kind of how I looked at it.[34]

Therefore, the peculiar tradition of the VP queen and maids acting as stand-ins for their fathers in this symbolic ritual of social recognition continues to the present day.

Not surprisingly, the VP queen does still tend to be the daughter of a family that has been socially prominent in St. Louis for a long time—usually for at least one hundred years. This fact, at the very least, suggests that the VP organization helps members to maintain the social and economic status of their families. In fact, Molly Hager's selection is rather typical. As Rusty Hager recalls, "Our company's 146 years old, five generations, so, when Molly was in this thing, the family list [of invitations for the ball] was, you know, extreme."[35]

Despite their moves toward inclusion, the VP organization (a separate organization from the VP Fair Foundation) is run by a small number of men and most decisions—even those involving the fair—are made by a group of five or six people at the very top. As Ron Henges maintained, "There are other officers [than the VP] and they change routinely. They're not there forever. It's really kind of self-perpetuating from a management point of view. The officers of the VP select the new officers of the VP."[36]

This would explain why it takes so long for some changes to take place; for example, the name change from VP Fair to Fair St. Louis. "The name change was recommended by our own group five or six years ago," said Henges. "And we had a fairly extensive discussion and there were people who really felt, you know, everyone knows it's the VP, why don't we just drop it. We know it aggravates the blacks. Let's forget it and rename it. And there were diehards, so to speak [in this group of five or six leaders], who said, 'Hey, we're doing this, we're taking the risks, it's our responsibility, we're entitled to have our name associated with it.'" If one or more of these five or six people wanted to prevent a change in the celebration, they could. According to Henges, this handful of people make most of the important decisions for the organization and select the next VP and VP queen.[37]

However rosy the prospects may seem for Fair St. Louis and the VP celebration, many African American St. Louisans like Percy Green are still very leery of the elites in the VP organization.[38] Putting on a fair for three days a year does little to solve the problems faced by inner-city children in St. Louis urban schools and, more importantly, the events of the fair certainly do not help educate suburbanites about the problems of the inner city. In fact, the celebration may obscure these problems for many white St. Louisans. After all, white suburbanites may wonder, "If these folks are so bad off, what are they doing downtown whooping it up at the fair?"

Perhaps the cooperation between the leaders in both the white and African American communities in putting on the fair can lead to cooperation in the political arena. Maybe it can lead to cooperation that would reform St. Louis's schools and help the poverty-ridden inhabitants of the inner city, who are largely African Americans. Perhaps the cooperation between communities in the VP organization is merely the first step to meaningful reform for the city of St. Louis.

Unfortunately, this does not seem likely. Some of the leaders in the VP organization, when asked, do not have much sympathy for the poor of St. Louis—which makes it difficult for them to work for meaningful reform—as they tend to blame poverty solely on the poor themselves, regardless of their race. Ron Henges—the VP Fair chairman who, ironically, did the most to enhance inclusion in the VP Fair's leadership—holds such beliefs. Henges insists that a class system is just an inevitable part of American society and that poor people should understand as much and try to improve themselves through their own efforts. This view is most evident in Henges's comments about the earlier protests by ACTION in the sixties and seventies:

> Many, many [of ACTION's] protests had no foundation in fact, it's just the publicity aspect of it. To try to rip the mask off the VP or to protest the VP ball is to say, "Hey, we don't like it because they're a bunch of rich fat cats that are having this big party." That's never going to change. Rich fat cats are always going to have their big parties. If it's not public, it's going to be private. That's their prerogative. Just as the poor working-class people are welcome to have their own party too—to do their own thing. If you're protesting because I'm rich and you're poor then we've got a real big problem. Because that ain't what we're going to be doing in America.[39]

This elitist worldview makes it extremely unlikely that business leaders in the Veiled Prophet organization are minded to help the poor of St. Louis. According to these leaders, the economic and political system in St. Louis is fine; there is little need to change it. It is the poor themselves who need to change.

Despite Bosley's election as mayor, little political cooperation of a multiracial nature appears to be going on outside of the VP Den's meeting rooms. The elites in Civic Progress still play a commanding role in most of the city's important policy decisions, such as the bringing of the NFL's Rams football team to St. Louis or the building of major projects like the Trans-World Dome and the new Kiel Center. There still are no voting black members in this influential organization. There is no sign this lack of minority representation in Civic Progress will change anytime in the near future.[40]

Unfortunately, neither the leaders of the white community nor the black community are moving to capitalize on the opened lines of communication and cooperation evidenced in the recent success of Fair St. Louis. It appears that the fair may come to represent, just like the Veiled Prophet celebration has for the last century, bread and circuses for the poor and middle-class, accompanied by few if any long-term positive effects for the city at large.

Conclusion

WHITHER VP? THE VEILED PROPHET CELEBRATION AND THE HISTORIOGRAPHY OF PUBLIC CELEBRATIONS IN AMERICA

One hot and sunny July afternoon in St. Louis, I spoke with a friend at the Missouri Historical Society about the Veiled Prophet celebration. The Historical Society has been the primary depository for Veiled Prophet documents, ball gowns, crowns, gifts, invitations, and other paraphernalia since the celebration's founding in 1878. For most of this century, the society had a large permanent exhibit of ball gowns and VP queen pictures in the basement of its museum in Forest Park. In the late 1980s, a large group of professional public historians in the organization fought a bruising battle with their own executive committee to have the exhibit dismantled. They felt it was in bad taste and no longer served a historic purpose.

"You know why we have this VP celebration?" my friend said in the sweltering heat of that afternoon. "It is a form of ancestor worship. By providing this celebration and celebrating themselves in conjunction with the city's history, the elite make sure they're remembered. They make sure they'll always be remembered and appreciated by their own kids who participate in the parade and ball—and hopefully by other folks in the city as well. We are no longer in the business of helping to foster their ancestor worship. They can do that themselves." Most St. Louisans in the 1970s and 1980s seem to have agreed with this description of the celebration as the organization nearly withered away when people recognized the Veiled Prophet as an elitist symbol. Fewer and fewer St. Louisans wanted to help the elites celebrate themselves, which in turn led to major changes in the celebration. However, this study has hopefully proved there is more to this celebration than crass ancestor worship or elitism—much more.

As in most intellectual exercises, there are inevitable "so what?"

questions. What use is this study of a single public celebration in St. Louis? How does the VP celebration fit in with recent scholarship on public celebrations in America? What does the history of the Veiled Prophet celebration tell us about changes in the public sphere in America? What does it tell us about the problems of presenting history in the public sphere?

As previous chapters have demonstrated, the Veiled Prophet organization's members tried in the nineteenth century to use the parade to promote loyalty to themselves and as a way to teach spectators how to be good, moral, and virtuous citizens. From the turn of the century through the 1960s the elites went searching for other cultural vehicles for their message but continued to put on the parade. However, the civic instruction content of the annual spectacles was greatly reduced. After 1900, only major social and economic upheavals like the World Wars and the Great Depression impelled elites to reintroduce civic instruction to the celebration, but these brief periods were the exception rather than the rule. Therefore, early in the organization's history the elites had abandoned the Veiled Prophet parade as a method of public communication and the street as an arena for civic instruction. Yet, because of the parade's popularity, it continued as a local tradition.

In the sixties and seventies the Veiled Prophet parade and ball were targeted by civil rights groups who saw them as symbols of elitism and conspicuous consumption. The event, and the organization itself, lost most of its local support in a very short time. Members began leaving the organization and its demise seemed imminent. In the 1980s the Veiled Prophet celebration was reborn as a civic festival—this time as the VP Fair and later, Fair St. Louis—that included the parade as one of its many events. The ball was deemphasized and was no longer considered a part of the larger civic celebration. The VP Fair began as yet another attempt at civic instruction and local boosterism. However, by the 1990s the organization promoted the fair as a way to bring the diverse St. Louis community together. Simply bringing the community together (which had once been easily accomplished in the early years of the celebration) had become the single most important goal of the celebration.

How do this study's findings about the VP celebration fit in with recent scholarship on public celebrations in America? My findings are largely supported by historical criticism; the Veiled Prophet celebrations appear quite typical of local public celebrations in America in the nineteenth and first half of the twentieth century. Since World War II, however, the VP celebration's longevity and continued popularity have been atypical of similar public celebrations in America.

Public celebrations were used for civic instruction by elites in many large cities in the United States during the late nineteenth century. The main goal of such civic instruction was to teach immigrant working-class spectators how to be good citizens. As in other cities, this instruction involved combining local and national history, a celebration of material progress, and genteel moral messages into a single spectacular event. Elites in St. Louis and elsewhere wished to promote material and civic progress as an integral part of their community's history. Great men and great leaders had led their cities to prosperity and, with continued support from the community, would continue to do so in the future.

Social control was also an important part of public events in the nineteenth century. Scholars like Roy Rosenzweig and Francis G. Couvares have documented how industrial employers and upper-middle-class moral reformers wanted to encourage public celebrations of the Fourth of July that would promote "proper" leisure activities over the more rowdy traditional activities of the working class. Couvares argues that in these events the developing conflict between middle-class and immigrant working-class culture becomes evident. Middle-class reformers, he believes, were trying to destroy plebeian working-class culture and replace it with their own.[1] The Veiled Prophet celebrations in the nineteenth century certainly had such moralistic overtones about "proper" leisure activities. These parades promoted certain cultivated activities like reading classic literature or appreciating art. Whenever holidays or other festive occasions were depicted, it was in a restrained manner. The parades taught immigrant spectators that what they did in their leisure time mattered. Proper leisure activities, the elites believed, would lead the immigrant working class to self-improvement and, hopefully, to their eventual assimilation into the broader society.

In his work *Remaking America,* John Bodnar has argued that public celebrations in American reflect the contest between vernacular and official cultural interests. Vernacular interests are those of everyday people—in this case, the working-class and middle-class people who watched the Veiled Prophet spectacles. Everyday people tend to identify with local historical figures or symbols more than with national historic figures who seem removed from the local context of life. Official cultural interests are those of cultural leaders like the Veiled Prophet elites; local businessmen, professionals, and government officials. Official interests want to promote cultural images that encourage loyalty to the state and emphasize the average citizen's duties over their rights.[2] They wish to promote a unity of purpose for all citizens. For example, it is clear that the Veiled Prophet elites used the celebration and the historical pageant in 1914 to unify the populace behind such causes as building a prosperous city, passing a new local charter initiative, or fighting a war.

Bodnar has contended that in the nineteenth century vernacular cultural interests triumphed over official interests in shaping public events.[3] Cultural leaders mixed vernacular and official culture in these community celebrations in order to better serve their purpose of unifying the community. This triumph of vernacular over official interests is certainly reflected in the symbols used in nineteenth century Veiled Prophet parades. While Veiled Prophet members created the parades without direct guidance from the community, the symbols and historical figures they chose were largely local in origin. This shows the strength of vernacular cultural interests in St. Louis during the last two decades of the nineteenth century.

However peaceful these parades were for the most part, direct conflict between official and vernacular interests occurred in St. Louis as well—most notably when a local group of Irish immigrants succeeded in removing the Irish float from the 1882 celebration. The militant response of Slayback and other Veiled Prophet organization members showed how far apart these two groups were culturally at that point. The immigrants found the float depicting Irish stereotypes offensive; the organization felt it was just a "piece of pleasantry."

Like other civic celebrations in nineteenth-century America, the Veiled Prophet spectacle reified the social order rather than turning it upside down. There was no Bakhtinian carnival of social role-reversal in Veiled Prophet events. Part of the symbolic message of these events was that social superiors were passing on the floats in front of and *above* their social inferiors. Social inferiors did not parade on the floats. They were simply assigned the role of spectator; they could watch from down in the street.

Furthermore, Veiled Prophet elites also used female symbols in a manner similar to other elites in America during this period. Mary Ryan has argued that female symbols were used to represent "national unity and harmony" within "a male-defined cultural universe." Females were not considered political actors in the nineteenth century and therefore could stand for large ideas.[4] Many Veiled Prophet parades used female symbols to stand for abstract concepts like "industry," "wealth," and even the state of Missouri.

The Veiled Prophet symbol itself also served the St. Louis elites' local interests during the nineteenth and early twentieth century. Many St. Louisans felt that the Veiled Prophet (even if he wore strange oriental robes and a gold crown) represented the pinnacle of social success in the city. For a society that was still hierarchical by class, race, and gender, such a strange and elitist symbol evidently suited white, male, native-born, and economically mobile St. Louisans. Paintings of the Veiled Prophet always portrayed him as a kindly white male underneath the crown and veil. The Veiled Prophet organization was certainly popular with the city's social and economic elite—there was never a shortage of membership applicants during the first several decades of the organization's existence. How common working- and middle-class St. Louisans felt about the Veiled Prophet symbol is not so clear. However, the fact that the member serving as the Veiled Prophet had to wear protective eyewear during the parade demonstrates that not all St. Louisans revered the Veiled Prophet symbol. Nevertheless, historical evidence suggests that St. Louis crowds were generally well behaved during this period.

The decline of the Veiled Prophet parade as a civic event during the first few decades of the twentieth century is also supported by recent scholarship. Michael McGerr has argued that the period from 1900 to 1930 saw the widespread decline of the public parade in America—whether as a tool for civic instruction or for other purposes. The use of parades dwindled because of the decline in intimate class relations in the early twentieth century. Elites and workers no longer lived near one another, and they began to have less interest in parading down the streets together (a commonplace occurrence in the political parades of the nineteenth century). If more inclusive political parades were ruled out by workers, they would have been even less interested in watching a group of costumed elites pass by on floats.

McGerr maintains that the development of a culture of leisure further contributed to the decline of parades. There simply were more things Americans could do to entertain themselves. The turn of the century and the first three decades of the twentieth century saw the rise of many popular forms of entertainment—vaudeville, amusement parks, baseball, bicycles, movies, phonographs, automobiles, and radio. Parades and other forms of public spectacle could not compete with these alternate forms of entertainment. Moreover, as Bodnar points out, public events nationwide were increasingly devoted to entertainment rather than the serious business of civic instruction as the century advanced.[5]

The decline of local community also contributed to the dwindling of parades as public spectacle. McGerr argues that local leaders and businessmen seemed less powerful in a world where "outside trusts and corporations . . . determined the economic facts of everyday life."[6] Improved communications that linked cities also lessened the political, economic, and cultural authority of local leaders. National figures—whether they were business leaders, political leaders, or celebrities—seemed more powerful and more interesting than local elites. Therefore, watching a parade of local elites in outrageous costumes came increasingly to seem provincial and unworldly for St. Louisans of all classes.

Like other cultural leaders in America, Veiled Prophet elites began seeking other outlets for their message of civic, material, and even racial progress at the turn of the century. The parades were no longer meeting their cultural and political goals, so the elites began to look for other vehicles for civic instruction. The first of these—although its impact went far beyond the borders of St. Louis—was the World's Fair of 1904. Many of the most influential members of the Veiled Prophet organization were instrumental in planning and putting on this fair. The 1904 World's Fair promoted a message of material and racial progress similar to that of the Veiled Prophet parades of the late nineteenth century. Like the annual parades, the World's Fair's Anthropology Department and Philippine Reservation organized the peoples of the world in order from "least civilized" to "most civilized." Not surprisingly, the United States was always presented as the pinnacle of civilization and Asian peoples as the least developed in both events.[7]

Like the World's Fair, the St. Louis *Pageant and Masque* of 1914 can also be viewed as a Veiled Prophet parade writ large. The desire to reach out to common people led the city's elites to choose beloved historical figures like Pierre Laclède, Auguste Chouteau, and Thomas Hart Benton to serve as characters in the drama. They wished to encourage the audience to be loyal to their current political leaders and to vote for the upcoming charter.

The Veiled Prophet parades in the late twenties and early thirties also follow the cultural trends traced by Bodnar and other scholars. During this period, Veiled Prophet elites used the parade to promote patriotism, capitalism, and the achievements of great men in history—particularly men like George Washington. Like other public events during this time, the parade makers attempted to educate spectators about the contribution capitalism had made to St. Louis and to the nation. These elites found themselves increasingly allied with governmental interests in stressing patriotism as a way to promote unity and quell unrest during the troubling economic depression.

In fact, the 1932 Veiled Prophet parade can be viewed as part of a larger nationwide campaign by the George Washington Bicentennial Commission, headed by Congressman Sol Bloom. The commission wished to celebrate the bicentennial of Washington's birth and present him as an inspirational symbol for all Americans. In the difficult years of the Great Depression, the commission wanted to foster loyalty to the nation through the Washington symbol. The commission sought out sympathetic groups of local elites, like those in the Veiled Prophet organization, and encouraged them to prepare their own celebrations of Washington's birth. Over 4.7 million commemorative events were held during 1932.[8]

Elites in St. Louis found themselves at an important crossroads during the Great Depression. As their parades from 1928 to 1934 demonstrate, they began to see public celebrations as a way to bolster the public's flagging belief in the capitalist system and in America itself. Nevertheless, personified symbols like the Veiled Prophet, "Great Explorers," or even George Washington did not provide the kind of psychic consolation these elites hoped they would. In such trying times, elites had to search for symbols that would better resonate with everyday people. It is during this period, Bodnar argues, that cultural leaders began to promote the pioneer as a major symbol in public celebrations. The symbol of the pioneer served the needs of both ordinary people and officials. Ordinary people sought inspiration and consolation from the pioneer symbol; pioneers, too, had made it through difficult times and had prevailed.

Around the time of the 1934 parade, discussions began among business leaders in St. Louis about creating a monument to honor Thomas Jefferson and "other patriotic citizens" who had helped move the nation westward. This group of leaders began to seek federal funding for the project in December of 1934. Which is to say, at the same time the parade makers once again abandoned the Veiled Prophet parade as an instrument for civic instruction, they sought more effective avenues for their instructional message. Luther Ely Smith, a longtime member of the Veiled Prophet organization, led their efforts. Smith argued that "America was made not on the coastal plain of this country but was forged in the frontier as the pioneers went out to grapple with the conditions which confronted them. We owe [a] debt to the pioneers, to Jefferson . . . and every one of these great men who trod this great soil."[9] Smith also had other less ideological motives to celebrate Jefferson and the pioneers. He saw the project as a way to both develop the declining St. Louis riverfront and to create five thousand construction jobs during the depths of the Great Depression.

The Jefferson National Expansion Memorial—the St. Louis Arch—was completed in 1965. While the eventual monument bore little resemblance to similar monuments to pioneers and statesman from the 1930s, its origins were rooted in the insecurities of the 1930s and the desire of elites to forge a more tangible connection to the pioneer heritage of the region.[10] Despite the celebration's long history in St. Louis, Veiled Prophet elites had obviously decided the parades were no longer effective in providing St. Louisans with a cultural link to a reassuring, consoling past.

Unlike other annual celebrations in America, the Veiled Prophet parade remained a popular annual event during the first half of the twentieth century. However, given the fact that St. Louis more than doubled in population during the first three decades of the twentieth century, the consistently large crowds—which newspapers estimated at around one hundred thousand annually during this period—represented an ever smaller percentage of the St. Louis community as time went by.

The Veiled Prophet celebration's longevity is unusual. St. Louisans in the forties and fifties viewed the celebration as an eccentric local custom. Years after similar celebrations in other parts of America had disappeared from the urban landscape (with the notable exception of Mardi Gras in New Orleans, which by the 1950s was more of a national tourist event than a locally inspired celebration), the annual Veiled Prophet celebration continued to take place. White St. Louisans remained attached to the celebration and continued to attend the parade or watch it on television.

By the 1950s, however, the organization's members found themselves more attached to the ball than the parade. The ball now was the major social event for St. Louis's upper class. It was, in Allen Davis's words, "the social function in its pure form."[11] White St. Louisans also enjoyed the ball, which was televised locally during the forties and fifties. It offered the community a chance to vicariously live the lives of the wealthy elites who danced across their television screens.

While Veiled Prophet elites had come under attack in the past, nothing prepared them for the upheaval of the sixties. ACTION and other civil rights groups argued that the Veiled Prophet symbol, which at one time had represented the pinnacle of local social success to the white community, was a negative symbol of raw and unadulterated elitism—often subsidized with public money. In an era when St. Louisans were trying to ensure equality of opportunity, such elitism rapidly fell out of favor in the community. While a majority of St. Louisans were not interested in ACTION's other job-oriented goals, many St. Louisans agreed that society needed to be rid of this type of egregious elitism. The situation with ACTION and the Veiled Prophet organization in St. Louis is unique. These sorts of annual harvest celebrations no longer existed elsewhere in urban America by the sixties and seventies.

Furthermore, since the Veiled Prophet parades no longer had any overt educational message or function, the elites had no convincing arguments to offer the community for the celebration's continued existence. By transforming the VP parade into simply another entertainment event, the elites had, like the workers in 1877, abandoned the streets as an arena for civic instruction. To children and young adults of the sixties and seventies, the Veiled Prophet celebration appeared to be a strange anachronistic social custom whose time had passed. This generation felt that, in the words of a former maid, the ball and parade were a "farce" and that "this kind of exhibition ha[d] . . . to go."[12]

In response to such criticism, the Veiled Prophet organization changed the celebration drastically. The celebration, which had been founded on elitism and the flaunting of class power, now tried to mute the display of elitism and power. The ball was disassociated from the parade and moved out of the public auditorium. The organization's members invited schoolchildren and women to ride on the floats. They began using "VP" instead of "Veiled Prophet" in all public correspondence in order to distance themselves from the negative connotations of the Veiled Prophet symbol.

In its final incarnation, the celebration's transformation into an entertainment-oriented fair resembles the transformation found by Bodnar in public events elsewhere in the country since World War II. Like the Memorial Day Parade in Indianapolis, the Veiled Prophet parade and fair became dedicated to entertainment rather than civic instruction. Most St. Louisans had no idea who was behind the fair and did not seem to care. St. Louisans went to the fair for carnival rides and cotton candy, not to learn about St. Louis or American history. The organization's single attempt to use the fair for civic instructional purposes—the short-lived Education Day—was a dismal failure. Bodnar argues that elites in the late twentieth century use "commercial forms of entertainment . . . as a means of fostering unity" rather than patriotic, educational, or historical themes.[13] Evidence from the experience of the VP Fair suggests some responsibility for this change in public culture lies with the greater public, who now seem to respond much more positively to "pure entertainment" than either civic instruction or commemoration.

What does the history of the Veiled Prophet tell us about changes in the public sphere in America? According to Juergen Habermas and Mary Ryan, the public sphere is the rather vague and amorphous space between the state and the private citizen, where "the public organizes itself as the bearer of public opinion." It includes any place where public and political dialogue can take place. Habermas and Ryan argue that the public sphere became increasingly multivocal in the late nineteenth and twentieth century as more social groups were added to the electorate and political ideas were discussed more openly in public. The street in the nineteenth century was certainly a part of this increasingly democratic public sphere. Ryan contends that "public opinion was formed in the streets, in the struggles of political parties, and in the popular press."[14] Worker's parades, like those during the 1877 strike in St. Louis, were a frequent occurrence before 1880 in American cities.

However, in the last two decades of the nineteenth century the democratic nature of the street changed. Elites in government began to require parade and demonstration permits and, correspondingly, the street became a much more regulated portion of the public sphere. Spontaneous public displays were no longer allowed. In 1900, workers in St. Louis would not have been allowed to hold hastily organized parades for their cause as they had in 1877; local militia groups or the police would have stopped and arrested them. Elites wanted to reserve the street for their own performances, for educational spectacles like the Veiled Prophet celebration.

Restrictions on the use of the street—while still legally in place—began to break down in the middle twentieth century, much to the dismay of members of the Veiled Prophet organization. After all, it was in the street during the annual parade and in front of Kiel Auditorium that ACTION members made their voices heard. It is also true, however, that when ACTION members were arrested, demonstrating without a permit was usually one of the charges. The public sphere continues to be at least nominally regulated.

The street today remains a highly regulated part of the public sphere. As Susan Davis has argued, parades today "are no longer performed where people live and work, but, for reasons of traffic flow, in special, denuded spaces designated by the city." Parades in the twentieth century no longer play as much of a role in daily public life as they did in the nineteenth century. This tight regulation of the street and the increasing identification of the street only with spectacles like the Veiled Prophet celebration have, in the words of Davis, left the parade as an event that gives "only a prefabricated appearance of ties to a genuine community life."[15] The increasing regulation of street demonstrations had a major impact on how common people in the late nineteenth century expressed themselves in public—the street was no longer a place to air one's grievances on impulse. But due to this study's focus on only a few public events in St. Louis, this conclusion about the increasingly regulated nature of the street portion of the public sphere must be somewhat speculative. Further research into how the regulation of street demonstrations developed in St. Louis and other cities during the late nineteenth and early twentieth centuries is needed.

This study also raises questions about whether one can effectively teach history through public events like the Veiled Prophet parade or fair. The answer of elites to the innate problems of conducting civic instruction in a diverse twentieth-century urban society has been to give up on presenting history to the public. When faced with the cacophonous urban world of the late twentieth century, Veiled Prophet elites in the sixties, seventies, and eighties decided against using inclusive historical themes, images, or symbols in the parades in favor of more entertainment-oriented themes like "A Salute to the Wonderful World of Walt Disney," "Sports," and "Happiness Is . . ."

Their decision to abandon history leaves St. Louis with a cultural vehicle that is spent and largely meaningless. Where should the VP organization go from here? Is there a way to celebrate St. Louis's history in an inclusive public manner that would draw St. Louisans to the celebration in the same numbers as the carnival rides? Is there a way to educate Americans and St. Louisans about their history in public events that would be inclusive *and* interesting? There are no easy answers to these questions.

In the late twentieth century, history has declined as a part of public life, becoming primarily the province of academics rather than that of ordinary people. Historians should be concerned by this development. In St. Louis and cities all over the country, children are growing up ignorant of their own city's history and traditions, disconnected from their past.

For example, every semester during this project, I made it a point to tell my students at Indiana University what my work is about. I usually have several students from St. Louis approach me after the first class and ask me, "What is the Veiled Prophet celebration?" I usually tell them it now consists of the VP fair, parade, and ball. The students seldom know much about the parade and ball but have been to the fair. "Oh yeah, the big thing at the Arch with the rides" is the usual response. These students have no idea that the celebration has a long history in St. Louis.

It should concern historians that the many problems of presenting history in public have led cultural leaders to give it a smaller and smaller place in public discourse. Are there easy solutions to these problems? No. In fact, further thought just produces more questions. If the Veiled Prophet celebration vehicle and others like it are spent, are there other vehicles with which to replace them? Is there a way to publicly present a community's history that is truly inclusive? Can we as historians interest the public in this sort of celebration? These are the kinds of questions that every historian should ponder. At the very least, the history of the Veiled Prophet celebration shows us that both cultural leaders and ordinary Americans used to be much more interested in history and that history used to play a more important role in public celebrations. Unfortunately, historians may not be able to ponder these questions for very long. With the continual shrinking of history's space at the public table, it will not be long before we as historians may have lost our chance to get Americans once again interested in their own local, state, and national history.

# Notes

Introduction: The Social Meaning of Public Spectacles in the Nineteenth- and Twentieth-Century United States

1. Susan G. Davis, *Parades and Power: Street Theatre in Nineteenth-Century Philadelphia*, 5.
2. Ibid., 168.
3. David Glassberg, *American Historical Pageantry: The Uses of Tradition in the Early Twentieth Century*, 31–32. For more on "genteel intellectuals" or "urban elites," see E. Digby Baltzell, *Philadelphia Gentlemen*, and Frederic C. Jaher, "Nineteenth Century Elites in Boston and New York."

1. Power on Parade: The Origins of the Veiled Prophet Celebration

1. *Missouri Republican*, October 6, 1878.
2. The first group to suggest a negative link between the strike and the Veiled Prophet parade was the St. Louis Emergency Defense Committee. In a leaflet entitled "The Veiled Prophet: How It Began" (October 1952, Veiled Prophet Collection, Missouri Historical Society, St. Louis, Missouri [hereafter cited as VP/MHS)], they suggested a "conspiracy by Big Business and the press to hide the true origins of the VP parade." Since that time, this connection has also been mentioned by others, such as Ed Bishop and William H. Leckie in "Unveiling the Prophet: The Mysterious Origins of the Kingdom of Khorassan."
3. The invitation letter was signed by John B. Maude, John A. Scudder, George Bain, John G. Priest, and D. P. Rowland ("The Exposition Opening—Plans under Consideration for an Imposing Pageant," *St. Louis Times*, March 22, 1878, VP/MHS). Although the *Times* did not mention him as a signatory, Charles E. Slayback claimed to have "written personally, in my own hand-writing, to about twenty citizens to meet me at the Lindell Hotel on a certain evening" (Charles E. Slayback, Chicago, to Walter B. Stevens, St. Louis, July 20, 1916, from "Notes of Walter B. Stevens on the Veiled Prophet," VP/MHS).
4. Slayback to Stevens, St. Louis, July 20, 1916, VP/MHS; Walter B. Stevens, "Notes on Committee Meetings and Rules and Regulations of the Veiled Prophet Organization, 1878–1899," VP/MHS.
5. Stevens, "Notes on Committee Meetings," 41.
6. Charles Slayback is referred to as the VP's "patron saint" in "VP Order Noted for Its Anonymity," *St. Louis Globe-Democrat*, October 7, 1958.
7. Slayback to Stevens, July 20, 1916.
8. The poem in question is *Lalla Rookh: An Oriental Romance*, originally written in 1812 by the Irish poet Thomas Moore. It was a very popular romantic poem during the late nineteenth century. On the 1868 Comus float, see Arthur B. La Cour, *New Orleans Masquerade: Chronicles of Carnival*, 26.

9. The names of the founding members of this organization come from three different sources: a dedication page in the souvenir pamphlet, "His Mysterious Majesty the Veiled Prophet's Golden Jubilee: A Short History of St. Louis' Annual Civic Carnival," VP/MHS; a page listing the "originals," in "Notes of Walter B. Stevens"; and, finally, Stevens, "Notes on Committee Meetings." For names and biographical information, see tables 3–5 and appendix B in Thomas Spencer, "Knights for Revenue Only: The Origins of the Veiled Prophet Organization in St. Louis, 1877–1880." If all of these men's business partners were also members of the organization, the membership number would have been around two hundred.

10. The sixteen with upper-class backgrounds were George Bain, Daniel Catlin, Charles Chouteau, Pierre Chouteau, Frank Gaiennie, Alexander Garesche, David Gould, Henry Haarstick, William Hargadine, John Keiser, L. D. Kingsland, Leigh Knapp, Henry Paschall, Alonzo Slayback, Charles Slayback, and Julius Walsh. The twenty-one with upper-middle-class backgrounds were Shepard Barclay, Myron Buck, George Capen, John Davis, Samuel Dodd, Charles Donaldson, John Holmes, Henry Kent, Chester Krum, John Maude, George Morgan, J. C. Normile, Emil Preetorius, John Priest, David P. Rowland, William Russell, John Scudder, Frank Shapleigh, Edward Simmons, Arthur Soper, and Robert Tansey.

11. The phrase was first used by Logan Uriah Reavis as the title and as a major theme in his work, *St. Louis: The Future Great City of the World.*

12. James Neal Primm, *Lion of the Valley,* 291.

13. There is quite a bit of controversy about the causes of St. Louis's decline as a regional city in the nineteenth century. In his seminal work, *The Economic Rivalry between St. Louis and Chicago, 1850–1880,* Wyatt Belcher lays the blame for the decline at the feet of St. Louis's elite. Belcher argues they were too complacent and believed that the natural advantages of their city would lead them to wealth during the period from 1850 to 1880. More recently, Jeffrey S. Adler, in *Yankee Merchants and the Making of the Urban West: The Rise of Fall of Antebellum St. Louis,* and William Cronon, in *Nature's Metropolis: Chicago and the Great West,* have argued that the decisions by eastern investors in the 1850s to invest in railroad connections to Chicago and to eschew investment in similar railroad connections for St. Louis led to the decline. Adler further argues that these decisions were based on the rising interstate conflict between Kansans and Missourians in the "Bleeding Kansas" era. This perception of Missouri as a backward pro-slavery state led many eastern investors to send their money to Chicago. Both Adler and Cronon would agree that the victor in this rivalry had been clearly decided by the 1850s. The economic dislocations caused by the Civil War would only seal St. Louis's fate. More recently, James Neal Primm's voice has clearly been the loudest in asserting that St. Louis businessmen took a more active role in amassing their wealth. In *Lion of the Valley,* Primm also contends that Belcher's argument "underplayed Chicago's locational advantages and eastern financing and that his characterization of the St. Louisans as complacent conservatives was inaccurate and unfair" (238). Primm documents how St. Louis business leaders did attempt to build railroads before the Civil War. One suspects this controversy will not go away anytime soon. For more on the rivalry, see J. Christopher Schnell, "Chicago versus St. Louis: A Reassessment of The Great Rivalry." For a reassessment that focuses on the impact of the steel plow, see George Lipsitz, *The Sidewalks of St. Louis: Places, People, and Politics in an American City,* 93–95.

14. Primm, *Lion of the Valley,* 233.
15. The nine who were presidents of the Merchants Exchange were George Bain (1878), Jacob Ewald (1883), Frank Gaiennie (1887), Henry Haarstick (1885), David P. Rowland (1875), John Scudder (1877), Charles Slayback (1882), Alexander Smith (1880), and Robert Tansey (1872) (see the newspaper clipping entitled "Forty-seven Presidents while G. H. Morgan Served," from a 1911 issue of the *St. Louis Star,* contained in Walter B. Stevens's Scrapbook #84, 88–89, MHS). The twenty-four who were listed as members of the Merchants Exchange were Stephen Bemis, Rolla Billingsley, Myron Buck, John Crangle, Gideon Chadbourne, John Carroll, George Capen, Jacob Ewald, Moses Fraley, Jacob Goldman, Frank Gaiennie, John Gilkeson, Edward Hoppe, Henry Haarstick, Arthur Jennings, John Keiser, Henry Loudermann, John Maude, David Rowland, Alexander Smith, Charles Slayback, John Scudder, Frank Shapleigh, and Robert Tansey (see the list of members in the *Annual Report of the St. Louis Merchants Exchange, 1878,* pp. i–xviii, MHS). On Bain and the social evil ordinance, see Duane R. Sneddeker, "Regulating Vice: Prostitution and the St. Louis Social Evil Ordinance, 1870–1874."
16. Walter E. Orthwein, "Veiled Prophet Spectacle Eighty-Five Years Old," *St. Louis Globe-Democrat,* February 29, 1964; J. N. Fuglein, "The Veiled Prophet Is a Southerner, Suh," *St. Louis Globe-Democrat,* September 10, 1946.
17. Sam Kinser, *Carnival, American Style: Mardi Gras at New Orleans and Mobile,* 90.
18. Ibid.
19. Davis, *Parades and Power,* 5, 133.
20. David T. Burbank, *Reign of the Rabble: The St. Louis General Strike of 1877,* 49, 53.
21. Ibid., 73–75.
22. David R. Roediger, "America's First General Strike: The St. Louis 'Commune' of 1877," 202.
23. J. Thomas Scharf, *History of St. Louis City and County,* "The Railroad Riot of 1877," 2:1843; Roediger, "Not Only the Ruling Classes to Overcome, but Also the So-Called Mob: Class, Skill and Community in the St. Louis General Strike of 1877," 214, see also 225–26.
24. Roediger, "Not Only the Ruling Classes," 223.
25. Lucien Eaton, St. Louis, to Wife (not named), Iowa, August 1, 1877, MHS. The route given by Scharf's *History of St. Louis,* 1848–1849, of the citizen's militia parade is that it followed Twelfth from Clark to Pine, took Pine to 14th, followed 14th to Lucas Place, took Lucas Place to 18th, followed 18th to Morgan, took Morgan to 7th, 7th to Carr, Carr to Fifth, Fifth to Clark, and Clark to the Four Courts building, where, like the worker's parade, it disbanded.
26. Roediger, "America's First General Strike," 203. The "Originals" who founded the Veiled Prophet were George Bain, Henry T. Kent, Leigh O. Knapp, John B. Maude, George Morgan, J. C. Normile, Henry Paschall, Emil Preetorius, John G. Priest, D. P. Rowland, W. H. H. Russell, John A. Scudder, Alonzo Slayback, and Charles Slayback. This list is from a leaked report of their secret meeting contained in "Exposition Opening," *St. Louis Times,* March 22, 1878. Charles Slayback stated later, in his letter of July 20, 1916, to Walter B. Stevens, that "the paper had no authority for publishing this article," which leads one to believe that it was probably very accurate.
27. *St. Louis Evening Post,* October 9, 1878, 5.
28. Priest's name appears prominently in the pages of the October 9, 1878 *St. Louis Globe-Democrat.*

29. *St. Louis Missouri Republican,* March 17, 21, and 23, 1878.
30. Kinser, *Carnival, American Style,* 74; see also Scharf's *History of St. Louis;* and William Hyde and Howard L. Conard, *Encyclopedia of St. Louis History;* the quote is from Scharf, 2:1118.
31. Hyde and Conard, *Encyclopedia,* 991.
32. Bertram Wyatt-Brown, *Southern Honor: Ethics and Behavior in the Old South,* 35, 63, and 355. These page numbers denote passages that suggest the concept of a paternalistic system in which "proper deference" needed to be paid to "city fathers." In his 1882 dealings with Cockerill, Slayback—an ex-Confederate officer himself—was clearly following some of the dictates of the old Southern code of honor described by Wyatt-Brown in his work.
33. "Alonzo W. Slayback Shot and Killed by John A. Cockerill," *St. Louis Missouri Republican,* October 14, 1882. Orrick Johns, whose father was a longtime friend of Cockerill and later an editor of the *Post-Dispatch,* makes it clear that Cockerill was baiting Slayback in his version of the events in *Time of Our Lives: The Story of My Father and Myself,* 58–60.
34. Johns, *Time of Our Lives,* 110.
35. Ibid.
36. Mary Ann Clawson, *Constructing Brotherhood: Class, Gender, and Fraternalism,* 95–98.
37. The one known Jewish member was Moses Fraley. The other three non-Protestant members were very prominent Catholics: Charles Chouteau, Pierre Chouteau, and Alexander Garesche.
38. Clawson, *Constructing Brotherhood,* 95–98.
39. Peter Pencilstubs [pseud.], *The Veiled Prophets Unveiled.*
40. Slayback to Stevens, July 20, 1916.
41. Clawson, *Constructing Brotherhood,* 239–40.
42. Clawson's analysis in *Constructing Brotherhood* does not address this sort of motivation at all. Although Clawson's work does include a chapter on "The Business of Brotherhood," this section is more concerned with examining the men who made money from the marketing of fraternal organizations (especially the traveling agents for these groups who made a commission every time a new lodge was founded). In fact, Clawson misses a possible double meaning in the quote she cites at the end of the chapter, in which she recounts that some of the prominent members of the Knights of Pythias bemoaned the fact that many of their fellow members were becoming "Knights for Revenue only." It is likely that the reference was not just to the traveling "fraternal salesmen," as Clawson believes, but to fellow lodge members who joined the organization primarily for personal gain and business contacts. The idea of business contacts as a primary motivation for fraternal membership is addressed very briefly in one sentence of the prologue to Mark C. Carnes's *Secret Ritual and Manhood in Victorian America,* 2. Carnes never returns to this idea throughout the remainder of the work. For more on nineteenth-century fraternalism, see Lynn Dumenil, *Freemasonry and American Culture, 1880–1930.*

2. A "Panorama of Progress": The Veiled Prophet Celebration, 1878–1899

1. Alonzo W. Slayback, "Personal Diary of A. W. Slayback," October 5, 1878, VP/MHS.
2. T. J. Jackson Lears, "From Salvation to Self-Realization: Advertising and the Therapeutic Roots of the Consumer Culture, 1880–1930," in Richard Wightman Fox and T. J. Jackson Lears, eds., *The Culture of Consumption: Critical Essays in American History, 1880–1980*, 4–5. For more on cultural hegemony, see T. J. Jackson Lears, "The Concept of Cultural Hegemony: Problems and Possibilities."
3. See Mikhail Bakhtin, *Rabelais and His World;* William H. Beezley, "The Porfirian Smart Set Anticipates Thorstein Veblen in Guadalajara," 177; this sort of idea is also expressed in Kinser's *Carnival, American Style.*
4. "Over Thirty Responses Describe Thrills of First Veiled Prophet Parade Here," *St. Louis Globe-Democrat,* September 13, 1953; "St. Louisan Has Seen All but First V.P. Parade," *St. Louis Globe-Democrat,* October 5, 1953.
5. *St. Louis Missouri Republican,* October 1 and 6, 1878.
6. *St. Louis Missouri Republican,* September 29, 1878.
7. Ibid., October 1 and 4, 1878,
8. See pages 6–8. *Missouri Republican,* October 6, 1878.
9. *Missouri Republican,* October 9, 1878.
10. Ibid., October 11, 1878.
11. *St. Louis Evening Post,* October 9, 1878.
12. The seventeen tableaux in the 1878 parade were as follows: The Glacial Period (of Winter); Helios, the Sun-God (Chariot of the Sun); Primitive Life; Fiends of Darkness; Genius of Humanity (the Centaur); Flora; Persephone and Pluto in Hades; The Golden Globe; Demeter; Triptolemus; The Husbandman (Plowing); Fruits; Silenus; Bacchus; Industry; Wealth; and The Grand Oracle (The Veiled Prophet) (listed in the *Missouri Republican,* October 9, 1878; the same floats are listed in the *Globe-Democrat* and the *Evening Post* of October 9, 1878, as well).
13. *Missouri Republican,* October 9, 1878; *St. Louis Globe-Democrat,* October 9, 1878. The *Globe-Democrat* article identified many others on the floats as well, including John Bonnet, George Bain, J. C. Normile, John Finn, Erastus Wells, Alexander Garesche, Gus Priest, Bill Belt, John Finney, Myer Rosenblatt, Frank Capitain, William Hyde, Charles Slayback, Mayor Overstoltz, Edward Adreon, George A. Madill, E. T. Farish, David Nicholson, George Knapp, Ellis Wainright, John Grady, Charles Vogel, and Chauncey F. Schultz.
14. *Missouri Republican,* October 9, 1878.
15. Ibid.
16. *St. Louis Evening Post,* October 9, 1878; *Republican,* October 9, 1878.
17. *Republican,* October 8, 1878.
18. *Republican,* October 10, 1878. This "natural advantages" argument made by St. Louis boosters is dealt with extensively in Belcher, *Economic Rivalry,* and more recently in Cronon, *Nature's Metropolis.*
19. Mary Ryan, "The American Parade: Representations of the Nineteenth-Century Social Order," 148.
20. The three papers are the *St. Louis Globe-Democrat, Missouri Republican,* and *Post-Dispatch.* The *Evening Post* became the *Post-Dispatch* in December 1878 (*History of St. Louis,* 1:936).

21. *Republican,* October 6, 1880, 10; October 7, 1884.
22. *St. Louis Missouri Republican,* October 5, 1887.
23. *St. Louis Post-Dispatch,* October 2, 1893.
24. *Post-Dispatch,* October 5, 1892.
25. *St. Louis Missouri Republican,* October 6, 1880, and October 5, 1881.
26. The first column of Table 4 summarizes data from Table 3. The remaining columns are compiled from the lengthy lists printed in the *Missouri Republican/St. Louis Republic* of the invitation and reception committees for the years 1890 (October 5, 1890) and 1899 (October 2, 1899) (the *St. Louis Missouri Republican* became the *St. Louis Republic* in 1892). I have used the same occupational categories for the years 1890 and 1899, with the exception of the additional category of "financial services." The 1899 list of 373 members of the reception and invitation committees is more than likely the entire membership of the organization, which was supposed to be around 400 at that time ("Notes of Walter B. Stevens"). I compiled these tables as I did in Table 3, based on members' occupations as listed in David B. Gould, *Gould's City Directory of St. Louis* of that year.
27. However, the business elites who served as the Veiled Prophet during this entire period were usually involved in agricultural commerce—and all were members of the original seventy-three that founded the organization. This group remained in control of the organization until the turn of the century. The businessmen who served as Veiled Prophet during this era were John G. Priest (1878–1879, 1885–1886), Charles E. Slayback (1880), John T. Davis (1881), E. C. Simmons (1882–1883), George Bain (1884), Frank Gaiennie (1887–1893), and L. D. Kingsland (1894–1902) ("Notes of Walter B. Stevens," 40).
28. The two parades that best fit this description took place in 1890 and 1897. The 1890 parade theme, "Nonsensical Alphabet," seemingly had no coherent theme at all. Each float depicted some random topic associated with one or more letters of the alphabet. The 1897 parade, "Old Time Songs," was composed of tableaux upon which members performed several traditional songs (*Republican,* October 5, 1890, 30; *Post-Dispatch,* October 5, 1890, 28; and *Post-Dispatch,* October 3, 1897, 10).
29. On 1881, see *St. Louis Missouri Republican,* October 5, 1881, 9–10, and *St. Louis Post-Dispatch,* October 4, 1881, 4. On 1883, see *Republican,* October 3, 1883, 3, and *Post-Dispatch,* October 3, 1883, 12. On 1899, see *Republic,* October 4, 1899, 7, and *Post-Dispatch,* October 2, 1899, 4. On 1888, see *Republican,* October 2, 1888, 2, and *Post-Dispatch,* September 30, 1888, 17–18.
30. *Republican,* October 7, 1884, 12; *Post-Dispatch,* October 7, 1884, 9–14; and Ted Satterfield, comp., "Royfax Copies of Veiled Prophet Information," 1884, VP/MHS (hereafter referred to as "Royfax Copies").
31. *Globe-Democrat,* October 3, 1885, 10–11; *Post-Dispatch,* October 7, 1885, 2; *Republican,* October 5, 1885, 2–6; "Royfax Copies," 1885.
32. *Post-Dispatch,* October 4, 1891, 25–26. The other authors whose stories were presented were Jules Verne, Charles King, George Eliot, Alexander Dumas, Sir Walter Scott, Lew Wallace, and H. Rider Haggard.
33. *Post-Dispatch,* October 4, 1896, 30.
34. *Post-Dispatch,* October 1, 1893, 26.
35. Herbert G. Gutman, *Work, Culture, and Society in Industrializing America: Essays in American Working-Class and Social History,* 23–25.
36. Beezley, "Porfirian Smart Set," 178, 181.

37. *Republican,* October 9, 1879, 9.
38. Ibid. The twenty-two tableaux in the 1879 parade were The Volcano, Cave of the Cyclops, Pottery, Wood Carving, Sculpture, Music, Weaving, Painting, Architecture, The Wheel, Ship Building, Engines of War, Glass, Implements of Artificial Light, Instruments for Measuring Time, Astronomy, Printing, Steam, Electricity, Caldron of the Veiled Prophet, Their Dinner Service, and The Veiled Prophet (ibid.; see also "Royfax Copies," 1879).
39. *Globe-Democrat,* October 9, 1879, 6.
40. *Post-Dispatch,* October 3, 1882.
41. Ibid., October 3, 1882; Robert Tooley, VP Den superintendent, interview by author, St. Louis, August 4, 6, and 11, 1995; Ronald Henges, VP Fair chairman, 1983–1987, interview by author, tape recording, St. Louis, September 8, 1995.
42. *Post-Dispatch,* October 3, 1882; October 4, 1882.
43. *Post-Dispatch,* October 4, 1882.
44. Ibid.
45. Ibid.
46. *Post-Dispatch,* October 3, 1882.
47. The "great men" tableaux in the parade depicted (in order): The Discovery of America by Norsemen, Landing of Columbus, Columbus Received by Ferdinand and Isabella, Ponce de Leon, Meeting of Cortes and Montezuma, King Nezhualcoyotl at Tezcoco, DeSoto Discovering the Mississippi, Pocahontas and John Smith, Henry Hudson, Burning of the Dutch Village by Indians, Landing of the Pilgrims, Washington Crossing the Delaware, The Heroes of '76, Daniel Boone, Hunting the Buffalo, Statue of Jackson, Westward Ho, Cotton Field, Missouri, and The Veiled Prophet (*Post-Dispatch,* October 6, 1886, 9; *Republican,* October 6, 1886, 9; "Royfax Copies," 1886).
48. *Globe-Democrat,* October 2, 1892, 27.
49. Tableaux 8 through 22 in the 1892 parade were (in order): Missouri, The Veiled Prophet, Father of Waters, Death of DeSoto, Arrival of Pontiac, Reception of Marquette and Joliet, La Salle Taking Possession of Louisiana Territory, Founding the City of St. Louis, Lieutenant Governors of Upper Louisiana, Purchase of Territory of Louisiana, Incorporators of St. Louis, Governors of Louisiana, First Missouri State Officials, Visit of Lafayette to St. Louis, and Native Missourian Inaugurated President (Ibid., 27; "Royfax Copies," 1892).
50. Interestingly, the *Republic*'s writer was only off by three years in guessing the date when the first Missourian would be inaugurated as president (in the writer's eagerness to predict the future, he forgot to check his dates—1942 was not a presidential election year). It seems unlikely that the parade makers envisioned a machine politician like Harry Truman becoming Missouri's first president. Plus, the native Missourian was supposed to be tall and (presumably) elected president in a general election. The parade makers probably also assumed the individual would be a St. Louisan, not a man from Independence (*Republic,* October 2, 1892, 14). For criticism of St. Louis's leaders, see Belcher, *Economic Rivalry,* and Cronon, *Nature's Metropolis.*
51. *Republic,* September 30, 1894, 26.
52. Beezley, "Porfirian Smart Set," 178, 179.
53. Identical sets of rules can be found on the day of the celebration in the *Missouri Republican/St. Louis Republic, Post-Dispatch,* and *Globe-Democrat* during the period from 1878 to 1899.

54. Walter B. Stevens, *History of St. Louis, the Fourth City,* 2:662.
55. Kinser, *Carnival, American Style,* 120–22.
56. Ibid., 122.
57. This idea, while fairly elemental, must be attributed to Allen Y. Davis's "The Veiled Prophet's Order: A Study of a Contemporary Social Organization," prepared for the Harvard University Anthropology Department, December 1946–January 1947, VP/MHS.
58. Steven M. Stowe, *Intimacy and Power in the Old South: Ritual in the Lives of the Planters,* 71 and 73. While Gilded Age St. Louis certainly was not the Old South, the debutantes from these families probably were told similar things by their families—many of whom had southern roots. Stowe's musing on this subject, in addition to some from Kinser's *Carnival, American Style* seem applicable to the meaning of the Veiled Prophet ball to those debutantes who participated.
59. There is a suggestion of this idea in Stowe's *Intimacy and Power,* 84. However, Stowe does not make any explicit statement about how elite balls and parties provided parental control of courtship. Of course, the idea of parents trying to control courtship is not new, as Beth L. Bailey's study of twentieth-century courtship, *From Front Porch to Back Seat: Courtship in Twentieth-Century America,* would certainly attest.
60. Helen Dudar, "VP: Virgin Cult in St. Louis," 24.
61. Mrs. Wellington Adams (Susie Slayback), Washington, D.C., to Mrs. G. R. Bartling (daughter), St. Louis, September 1934, VP/MHS.
62. Ibid. (my italics); Dudar, *VP,* 24.
63. Karen McCloskey Goering, "Pageantry in St. Louis: The History of the Veiled Prophet Organization," 4; Marguerite Martyn, "The Veiled Prophet's Early Visits to His City," *St. Louis Post-Dispatch,* October 7, 1931, 2D.
64. "Notes of Walter B. Stevens."
65. Goering, "Pageantry in St. Louis," 5. For more specifically about souvenirs and invitations, see John L. Drew III, *The Veiled Prophet's Gifts: A Saint Louis Legacy: The Official Collector's Guide, 1878–1984.*
66. "Notes of Walter B. Stevens."

3. "His Mysterious Majesty": The Veiled Prophet Celebration, 1900–1942

1. "His Mysterious Majesty the Veiled Prophet's Golden Jubilee: A Short History of St. Louis' Annual Civic Carnival," VP/MHS.
2. For comparison to other cities, see Kinser, *Carnival, American Style,* 76.
3. A few of the more interesting parade themes during this period were "Pageant of Nations" in 1900, "Pageant of the Louisiana Purchase" in 1901, "Art and Architecture" in 1904, and "Drama and History" in 1907 ("Royfax Copies," 1900, 1901, 1904, and 1907).
4. "Royfax Copies," 1902.
5. "Notes of Walter B. Stevens," 41; Tooley interview.
6. "Big Thursday: Gala Days of the Old St. Louis Agricultural and Mechanical Association Fairs," 45–52. The phrase "Fair Week" was used by all three papers during this period. The phrase "Gala Week" was used to describe this week in the *Globe-Democrat* of October 6, 1889.

7. *St. Louis Post-Dispatch,* October 5, 1915.
8. Column 1 in Table 5 is the occupational data presented in Table 4 for the year 1899, the last year that the Veiled Prophet organization published a nearly complete membership list in the annual paper. Thus, to get a sense of the Veiled Prophet organization's membership, I was forced to use the yearly lists of matrons of honor—for example, "Mrs. Harry Wuertenbaecher"—to compile an occupational breakdown of the group's membership. Whatever the drawbacks to this method, it probably provides a fair representation of the organization's membership. In fact, if anything, these lists may tell us more about who the truly "powerful" were in St. Louis during this period, for these matrons were more than likely chosen to please those members with whom the organization's leadership wished to curry favor. The remaining occupational data was compiled from the annual lists of matrons that appeared in the *Post-Dispatch* for the years 1914, 1919, 1930, 1935, and 1940. Members' occupations are from the *City Directory* (formerly *Gould's City Directory*) for the respective years.
9. Scott McConachie, "The Big Cinch: A Business Elite in the Life of a City, St. Louis, 1895–1915," 295. Several examples of the organization's role in the cross-generational success of families are recounted in McConachie's work.
10. The generalization about the continuity of power and social status holds up when occupational data from the matrons of honor lists that appear in the *Post-Dispatch* in 1899, 1914, 1919, 1930, 1935, and 1940. McConachie, "Big Cinch," 139–89. McConachie chronicles the development of the popular idea of the Big Cinch in the St. Louis press during the period from 1905–1915. *Big Cinch* was first used by William Marion Reedy in the early 1900s to denote a small group of wealthy men who, by controlling capital and politics in the city, were holding St. Louis back. McConachie, who is never quite sure the Big Cinch conspiracy existed, does find significant evidence of collusion between downtown businessmen and politicians during this pivotal era in St. Louis's history. The Big Cinch theory certainly gave middle-class and working-class St. Louisans someone to blame for St. Louis's growing problems in the early twentieth century. It is plausible that the Veiled Prophet organization provided an important meeting place for members of the supposed Big Cinch. For the ultimate presentation of this conspiracy theory in a novel, see Leo Landau, *The Big Cinch: A Society and Financial Novel;* for more on Reedy and his literary magazine, *The Mirror,* see Max Putzel, *The Man in the Mirror: William Marion Reedy and His Magazine.*
11. *World's Fair Bulletin,* volume 2 (8); a detailed account of the celebrations from 1909 is contained in Walter B. Stevens's *St. Louis: One Hundred Years in a Week: Celebration of the Centennial of Incorporation, October 3–9, 1909.*
12. "One Thing Looked Good to Taft at Ball—A Chair," *St. Louis Post-Dispatch,* October 7, 1908, 9.
13. David Thelen, *Paths of Resistance: Tradition and Democracy in Industrializing Missouri,* 24. While Thelen's treatment of the Veiled Prophet organization in this work is rather impressionistic, his generalizations about the political outlook and vision of St. Louis elites for the future seem accurate. "Minutes of the St. Louis Commercial Club," February 1, 1881, Constitution, Box 1, MHS. This group existed from 1881 to 1943, and many Veiled Prophet members played important roles in the club throughout its history.
14. Elizabeth Noel Schmidt, "Civic Pride and Prejudice: St. Louis Progressive Reform, 1900–1916," 36–37; McConachie, "Big Cinch," 190–207.

15. Schmidt, "Civic Pride," 34–91.
16. Ibid., vi, 107–9.
17. The *Pageant and Masque of St. Louis,* Bulletin No. 1, February 1914, 8. The two best sources for discussion of the St. Louis *Pageant and Masque* are Donald Bright Oster, "Nights of Fantasy: The St. Louis *Pageant and Masque* of 1914"; and Glassberg, *American Historical Pageantry.*
18. McConachie, "Big Cinch," 244–55; Schmidt, "Civic Pride," 105–10.
19. *St. Louis Post-Dispatch,* June 2, 1914; quoted in Schmidt, "Civic Pride," 105.
20. Schmidt, "Civic Pride," 105; Glassberg, *American Historical Pageantry,* 193.
21. *St. Louis Labor,* July 4, 1914, 1; Schmidt, "Civic Pride," iv–vii. For more on the segregation ordinance, see Daniel T. Kelleher, "St. Louis' 1916 Residential Segregation Ordinance."
22. *St. Louis Post-Dispatch,* October 2, 1900, 1; October 7, 1902, 1; October 2, 1904, 1B.
23. *St. Louis Post-Dispatch,* October 2, 1906, 13; October 4, 1909, 4; and October 1, 1911, 1B.
24. This information comes from a biographical sketch in the *World's Fair Bulletin,* 9; and "Hats Off to Former Globe Editor," *St. Louis Globe-Democrat,* October 7, 1958, 17X. Later, Stevens served as secretary of the St. Louis City Planning Commission from 1912 to 1917. His interest in history led him to write several books on Missouri and to serve as president of the State Historical Society of Missouri at Columbia from 1916 to 1925.
25. Walter B. Stevens, *History of St. Louis,* 2:661–62.
26. Ibid., 2:663.
27. James C. Scott, *Domination and the Arts of Resistance: Hidden Transcripts,* 17–20. See also Robin D. G. Kelley, *Race Rebels: Culture, Politics, and the Black Working Class,* 6–7.
28. Stevens, *History of St. Louis,* 2:664.
29. Tom K. Smith, 1972 Veiled Prophet, and Harry E. Wuertenbaecher Jr., executive director of the Veiled Prophet organization, interview by author, St. Louis, October 12, 1993. This detail was mentioned during a guided tour of the Veiled Prophet organization's Den that followed the interview.
30. Stevens, *History of St. Louis,* 2:664.
31. *St. Louis Argus,* October 6, 1916, 5; on the African American Veiled Prophet balls, see *St. Louis Argus,* September 3 and October 3, 1919; September 24 and October 8, 1920; October 7, 1921; and September 28, 1928.
32. Curtis Wilson, "Aura of Veiled Prophet Fades, with an Assist from Percy Green," *St. Louis Post-Dispatch,* March 8, 1972.
33. Tooley interview; the Veiled Prophet "Den" was the old warehouse where the parade floats were constructed and important meetings were held.
34. Kelley, *Race Rebels,* 8.
35. Dina M. Young, "Broadway and Washington: 'Washington Avenue Massacre' and the 1900 Streetcar Strike," 5–7. For more on the Streetcar Strike, see Dina M. Young, "The Streetcar Strike of 1900: Pivotal Politics at the Century's Dawn," 4–17; and Steven L. Piott, "Modernization and the Anti-Monopoly Issue: The St. Louis Transit Strike of 1900," 3–16.
36. "Russian Cossack Horrors in St. Louis," *St. Louis Labor,* September 30, 1905.
37. *St. Louis Labor,* October 14, 1893, and October 13, 1906.
38. *St. Louis Labor,* October 12, 1907, 5.
39. *St. Louis Labor,* October 11, 1913, 4.
40. *St. Louis Labor,* September 17, 1910, and October 14, 1911.

41. *St. Louis Labor,* October 10, 1925, 4.
42. Martin A. Dillmon, "Hot Slugs," *St. Louis Labor,* October 25, 1930, 3.
43. "Proclamation of the Veiled Prophet," *St. Louis Globe-Democrat,* August 17, 1917.
44. Gary M. Fink, *Labor's Search for Political Order: The Political Behavior of the Missouri Labor Movement, 1890–1940,* 76–81.
45. "Royfax Copies," 1919.
46. "His Mysterious Majesty"; even though it is thirty or so pages long, the pamphlet has no page numbers.
47. "The Veiled Prophet's 'Golden Book' Tells of His Fifty-Year Reign," *St. Louis Globe-Democrat,* September 30, 1928.
48. "His Mysterious Majesty"; the next number of quotations are also to this pamphlet.
49. "Description of the St. Louis Merchants Exchange Collection."
50. This information comes from the cover of the Veiled Prophet Ball Invitation for 1986. It lists the five venues for the ball during its history: the Merchants Exchange, 1876–1908; the Coliseum, 1909–1935; Kiel Auditorium, 1936–1973; Chase Park Plaza, 1974–1985, and the Adam's Mark Hotel, 1986–present.
51. This observation comes from examining the large number of programs and invitations that are kept in the Veiled Prophet Collection of the MHS. This collection includes nearly every invitation and program issued between 1878 and the mid-1970s.
52. Shirley Althoff, "The Veiled Prophet's Bengal Lancers: Membership in Guard a Coveted Honor in V.P. Organization," *St. Louis Globe-Democrat,* October 3, 1951, B–1.
53. "His Mysterious Majesty."
54. "Where Are the V.P. Queens of the Past?" *St. Louis Globe-Democrat,* October 14, 1914; "Four Special Maids of Honor Members of First Families: Young Ladies Descendants from Pioneer St. Louisans," *St. Louis Globe-Democrat,* October 6, 1932; and Marguerite Shepard, "Miss Koehler Third in Family to be V.P. Queen," *St. Louis Globe-Democrat,* October 4, 1950.
55. "V.P. Appeared in 1878: Mystic Ruler's Parade Becomes More Elaborate Every Year," *St. Louis Globe-Democrat,* October 6, 1915.
56. "Royfax Copies," 1928.
57. "V.P. Queen a Regal Figure in Gold and Moire Fabric: Costume, Set Off by Sparkling Glass Spangles and Crystal, Outdoes Those of Four Maids," *St. Louis Post-Dispatch,* October 4, 1928.
58. "Married Queen of V.P. Abdicates Her Throne," *St. Louis Post-Dispatch,* October 23, 1928.
59. "A Queen Who Lost Her Crown," *St. Louis Times,* January 8–9, 1979, 4.
60. Ibid.
61. Scott, *Domination,* 202–27.
62. Rosemary Feuer, "City Hall and the Unemployed Protests of the 1930s," in *The St. Louis Labor History Tour,* 21–23. See also "Police Drive Three Thousand Led by Communists from City Hall with Tear Gas," *St. Louis Post-Dispatch,* July 11, 1932; and Rosemary Feuer, "The Nutpickers' Union, 1933–34: Crossing the Boundaries of Community and Workplace."
63. "Traditions of St. Louis: Description of the Gorgeous Veiled Prophet Pageant on Tuesday, October 8th, Also Announcing Contest for School Children," pamphlet produced by the Veiled Prophet organization, 1929, VP/MHS.
64. Ibid.

65. Ibid.

66. "The Making of a Great Nation: Description of the Gorgeous Veiled Prophet Pageant on Tuesday, October 7th," VP/MHS.

67. Unfortunately, the descriptive pamphlet for 1931 has been lost. However, the newspaper accounts in the *Globe-Democrat* and *Post-Dispatch* were detailed enough to make a rudimentary analysis of the parade.

68. "Twenty Floats Depicting Life of Washington to Be Seen in Veiled Prophet's Parade," *St. Louis Post-Dispatch,* October 2, 1932.

69. "Veiled Prophet to Bring 'Great Adventurers' from Noah to Beebe Here October 2," *St. Louis Post-Dispatch,* September 16, 1934.

70. "Royfax Copies," 1935–1941. The *Globe-Democrat* and *Post-Dispatch* for this period provide the same lists that were reprinted in "Royfax Copies."

71. "Enlarging the Prophet's Court," editorial, *St. Louis Globe-Democrat,* September 18, 1937.

72. "V.P. Parade to Depict War and Plight of the Conquered," *St. Louis Globe-Democrat,* October 11, 1942.

73. "Twelve Thousand Hear V.P. Plea at Auditorium Show," *St. Louis Globe-Democrat,* October 23, 1942, 1–6A.

4. "More and More a Social Phenomenon": The Veiled Prophet Celebration, 1946–1965

1. Davis, "Veiled Prophet's Order," 13.

2. Ibid., 7.

3. Ibid., 15–16.

4. "Royfax Copies," 1946–1964.

5. Lears, "Salvation to Self-Realization," in Fox and Lears, *Culture of Consumption;* see also Lizabeth Cohen, *Making a New Deal: Industrial Workers in Chicago, 1919–1939,* 99–158.

6. "Royfax Copies," 1946; Tooley interview; "Royfax Copies," 1954.

7. This brief portrait of Civic Progress is culled from several different sources: Robert K. Sanford, "City Aided by Group of Executives," *St. Louis Post-Dispatch,* October 30, 1966; "Civic Progress, Inc., Members Contribute in Team Pattern" *St. Louis Post-Dispatch,* November 1, 1966; "Put Up or Shut Up Challenge Helped Start Jobs Project Here," *St. Louis Post-Dispatch,* November 3, 1966; "Behind the Scenes of Civic Progress"; and a three-part series, "Movers and Shakers in Civic Progress," *St. Louis Post-Dispatch,* August 4–6, 1991.

8. St. Louis Emergency Defense Committee, "Veiled Prophet: How It Began."

9. Ibid.

10. William Sentner, "Origin of the Veiled Prophet," press release, William Sentner Collection, Series 5, Box 6, Folder 4, Washington University Archives, St. Louis, Missouri.

11. Vincent H. Sanders and Theodore D. Drury Jr., *The Story of the Veiled Prophet.*

12. A few of the more prominent stories about the Veiled Prophet celebration during this period include Fuglein, "Veiled Prophet Is a Southerner, Suh"; Foster Eaton, "The Veiled Prophet Comes to St. Louis Again!" *St. Louis Star-Times,* October 4, 1946; Foster Eaton, "The First Veiled Prophet Parade," *St. Louis Star-Times,* October 3, 1949; Francis A. Klein, "First Veiled Prophet

Celebration in 1878 Was Show of a Lifetime," *St. Louis Globe-Democrat,* October 4, 1949; Foster Eaton, "First VP Parade: Humor, Near Tragedy," *St. Louis Star-Times,* October 2, 1950; and Orthwein, "Veiled Prophet Spectacle Eighty-Five Years Old." The last referred to is "VP: Special Section," *St. Louis Globe-Democrat,* October 7, 1958, section X, 1–20; this section is quite a collection of newspaper stories written by several authors for the *Globe-Democrat* about the celebration. Many of the stories from this special section appear in several newspaper clipping collections about the Veiled Prophet organization in St. Louis.

13. Davis, "Veiled Prophet's Order," 14.
14. Helen Dudar, *VP,* 22.
15. Ibid., 24.
16. Ibid.
17. "Royfax Copies," 1950.
18. Ibid.
19. *St. Louis Post-Dispatch,* October 5, 1950, and October 3, 1951; Tooley interview.
20. Dudar, *VP,* 24.

5. "Whacking the Elephant Where It Hurts": The Veiled Prophet Organization, ACTION, and Economic Justice in St. Louis, 1965–1980

1. Bishop and Leckie, "Unveiling the Prophet"; Tommy Robertson, "Rope Trick by ACTION Unveils the Prophet," *St. Louis Post-Dispatch,* December 23, 1972; Gary Ronberg, "How They Unveiled the Prophet," *St. Louis Post-Dispatch,* December 31, 1972; "Veiled Prophet Unveiled by *Review: Post* and *Globe* Withhold Identity"; Jane Sauer, member of ACTION, 1969–1974, interview by author, tape recording, St. Louis, September 30, 1993; and Gena Scott, member of ACTION, 1970–1974, interview by author, tape recording, St. Louis, October 7, 1993.
2. Smith and Wuertenbaecher interview; Henges interview.
3. Jack M. Bloom, *Class, Race, and the Civil Rights Movement,* 208–9; Herbert H. Haines, *Black Radicals and the Civil Rights Mainstream, 1954–1970,* 57–63; and Manning Marable, *Race, Reform, and Rebellion: The Second Reconstruction in Black America, 1945–1982,* 106–8.
4. James Ralph, *Northern Protest: Martin Luther King, Jr., Chicago, and the Civil Rights Movement,* 185; it must pointed out that King ultimately decided against this sort of economic target—the Chicago Freedom Movement centered on attacking discrimination in the Chicago housing market.
5. Percy Green, chairman of ACTION, 1965–1984, interview by author, tape recording, St. Louis, September 14, 1993.
6. August Meier and Elliott Rudwick, *CORE: A Study in the Civil Rights Movement, 1942–1968,* 312–13.
7. Gerald J. Meyer, "Percy Green's Tactic: Stir Public Outrage," *St. Louis Post-Dispatch,* July 12, 1970.
8. Sauer interview.
9. Green interview; Sauer interview.

10. Sauer interview.
11. Jacqueline Bell, member of ACTION, 1975–1984, telephone interview by author, tape recording, St. Louis, October 14, 1993; Green interview.
12. Green interview.
13. Margaret Phillips, member of ACTION, 1968–1971, interview by author, tape recording, St. Louis, September 30, 1993.
14. ACTION, *Why You Must Raise Hell—A Seven-Year Public Document Featuring ACTION's Scientific-Struggle against St. Louis' Institutional Elitism and Racism (1970 thru 1976)*, sections 1–2; Scott interview; Phillips interview. *Why You Must Raise Hell* is a compilation of newspaper clippings that chronicle ACTION protest activities from 1969 to 1976. On May 24, 1971, two ACTION protesters at McDonnell-Douglas actually reached the top secret F-15 department—and were promptly arrested. These protesters, Gena Scott and Margaret Phillips, were sentenced in Circuit Judge John Rickhoff's court to seven-month jail terms for "criminal trespassing" on June 14, 1972. After several appeals failed, Scott and Phillips began serving their terms in May of 1974. According to an editorial that appeared in the *Post-Dispatch* on May 9, 1974, the usual penalty for this offense was ten days in jail and a "nominal fine." Once in jail, Scott and Phillips reported about unhealthy conditions in the women's jail by writing a letter to the editor of the *Post-Dispatch,* and, in at least one instance, by speaking with television reporters. In response to public pressure concerning the very stern sentence (according to Scott, hundreds of letters were written to Judge Rickhoff) and stinging editorials on some editorial pages, Rickhoff paroled Scott and Phillips after only two weeks in jail. Their parole also came only two days after their letter appeared in the *Post-Dispatch.*
15. Sauer interview; Phillips interview.
16. Alice Echols, *Daring to Be Bad: Radical Feminism in America, 1967–1975,* 92; Phillips interview.
17. Phillips interview; Barbara Torrence, member of ACTION, 1965–1970, interview by author, tape recording, St. Louis, September 21, 1993.
18. Torrence interview.
19. Thomas Spencer, "Knights for Revenue Only: The Origins of the Veiled Prophet Organization in St. Louis, 1877–1880," 5–24; Thomas Spencer, "Power on Parade: The Origins of the Veiled Prophet Organization"; the parade themes come from "Royfax Copies," 1960–1993.
20. Tooley interview.
21. "Royfax Copies," 1969–1980.
22. Judge (George) Johnson, co-chairman of ACTION, 1967–1975, interview by author, tape recording, St. Louis, September 27, 1993; Sauer interview.
23. Sauer interview.
24. Ibid.; Green interview; Bell interview.
25. Phillips interview; Sauer interview.
26. Green interview; Bell interview.
27. Phillips interview; Scott interview.
28. Johnson interview; "Two Found Guilty, Fined for VP Ball Disturbance," *St. Louis Globe-Democrat,* May 28, 1970.
29. ACTION, *Why You Must Raise Hell,* section 6; Green interview.
30. Torrence interview.
31. Ibid.

32. Tooley interview; Rusty Hager, VP Fair chairman, and Molly Hager, VP queen, 1995, interview by author, tape recording, St. Louis, August 18 and 23, 1995.
33. Tooley interview.
34. "Royfax Copies," 1960–1993.
35. Tooley interview.
36. Green interview; Torrence interview.
37. Scott interview.
38. Ibid.; Sauer interview.
39. Sauer interview; Scott interview.
40. Scott interview.
41. Scott interview; Smith and Wuertenbaecher interview; Sauer interview.
42. "ACTION Files Suit to Prohibit Use of Kiel for Veiled Prophet Ball," *St. Louis Post-Dispatch*, November 15, 1973; "Veiled Prophet Looking for New Home," *St. Louis Post-Dispatch*, December 7, 1973; and "Decision Announced in Court: ACTION Calls Exodus of Veiled Prophet Ball from Kiel a Victory," *St. Louis American*, December 13, 1973.
43. Bishop and Leckie, "Unveiling the Prophet"; Ted Gest, "Ousted Professor Wins Pay, but Wants to Teach," *St. Louis Post-Dispatch*, October 9, 1973; "Veiled Prophet Ball Disrupted," *St. Louis Globe-Democrat*, December 24, 1975; and "VP Ball Charge is Dismissed," *St. Louis Post-Dispatch*, March 2, 1976, 3A.
44. Phillips interview; Sauer interview.
45. Bell interview; Edward L. Cook, "VP Demonstrators Hired to Disrupt Ball, Police Say," *St. Louis Globe-Democrat*, December 25–26, 1976; and "Two Seized in Spraying of Gas at Veiled Prophet Ball," *St. Louis Post-Dispatch*, December 24, 1976; "Convicted In Veiled Prophet Ball Incident," *St. Louis Post-Dispatch*, June 1, 1978.
46. Smith and Wuertenbaecher interview.
47. Henges interview; Bell interview.
48. Richard Dudman, "Webster to Watch His Clubs' Policies," *St. Louis Post-Dispatch*, January 29, 1978, 1A, and "Judge Webster Lists Assets of $898,296," *St. Louis Post-Dispatch*, January 30, 1978, 1A; Sally Bixby Defty, "Prophet Lifting His Veil to Blacks after 101 Years," *St. Louis Post-Dispatch*, September 7, 1979, 1A.
49. For example, see "Why Not Just a Night of Fun?" *St. Louis Globe-Democrat*, September 17, 1968; "A Community Thrill," *St. Louis Globe-Democrat*, October 7, 1972; and "VP Shows a White Feather," *St. Louis Globe-Democrat*, December 8, 1973.
50. Evarts Graham, former managing editor of the *St. Louis Post-Dispatch*, telephone interview by author, tape recording, St. Louis, October 14, 1993; Jake McCarthy, columnist for the *St. Louis Post-Dispatch*, 1971–1982, telephone interview by author, tape recording, St. Louis, November 2, 1993.
51. Graham interview; Smith and Wuertenbaecher interview; "Veiled Prophet Unveiled by *Review*."
52. Green interview; Sauer interview; Scott interview; Torrence interview.
53. Green interview; Carter Stith, "Judge Meredith Dismisses Suit by Percy Green," *St. Louis Post-Dispatch*, February 27, 1975.
54. FBI, Memorandum, SAC, St. Louis to Director, FBI, June 19, 1970. This memorandum is from the contents of Jane Sauer's FBI file.
55. Sauer interview.

56. Phillips interview.
57. Green interview.
58. Ralph, *Northern Protest,* 229.
59. Ibid., 234; J. Mills Thornton, "Comment," 151 (as quoted in Ralph's *Northern Protest,* 235).
60. Bishop and Leckie, "Unveiling the Prophet," 13a.
61. Wilson, "Aura of Veiled Prophet Fades."

6. "An Activity the City Could Hang Its Hat On": The Veiled Prophet Celebration, 1981–1995

1. Henges interview; Maritz quoted in Bishop and Leckie, "Unveiling the Prophet," 13a.
2. Anita Buie Lamont, "Veiled Prophet Ball: The Prophet Must Be Relieved That the 1970s Have Finally Ended," *St. Louis Globe-Democrat,* December 25, 1979, 1H.
3. Henges interview.
4. Bishop and Leckie, "Unveiling the Prophet," 13a.
5. Julie E. Berman, "From Veiled Prophet Fair to Fair St. Louis: The Remaking of a Culturally Contested Event," 6. Berman, a longtime volunteer at the VP Fair and then a graduate student in communications at St. Louis University, writes persuasively that the Veiled Prophet Fair (and later Fair St. Louis) is a cultural text "upon which changes in the city have been written and continue to be etched" (22). She traces some of these changes in her paper.
6. *St. Louis Globe-Democrat Magazine,* July 20, 1981, 6.
7. Tooley interview.
8. Berman, "Veiled Prophet Fair," 7–10.
9. Ibid., 10; "VP Fair, 1981–1990: America's Biggest Birthday Party," 72–88.
10. Eric Mink, "Stars' Performances Save ABC-TV Show," *St. Louis Post-Dispatch,* July 6, 1987, 5A.
11. Eric Mink, "HBO Special on Cute, Clever Kids," *St. Louis Post-Dispatch,* July 13, 1987, 7F.
12. Quoted from Berman, "Veiled Prophet Fair," 17; Bill McClellan, "VP Fair Is at Forefront in Age of Part-Timers," *St. Louis Post-Dispatch,* May 30, 1988; Bill McClellan, "Daughter of a Knave May Never Be Queen," *St. Louis Post-Dispatch,* July 8, 1987; Terry J. Hughes, "Fair's Damage to Grounds Could Exceed $100,000," *St. Louis Post-Dispatch,* July 12, 1987, 1A.
13. Bishop and Leckie, "Unveiling the Prophet," 13A; and J. A. Lobbia, "What's $650,000 among Friends?"; Green interview.
14. Lisha Gayle, "VP Fair Foundation Not Liable for Damages in Shooting Death," *St. Louis Post-Dispatch,* March 6, 1987, 8A.
15. Quoted in Berman, "Veiled Prophet Fair," 11.
16. Cynthia Todd, "Judge Orders Eads Bridge Opened to Pedestrians," *St. Louis Post-Dispatch,* July 5, 1987, 1A, 5A.
17. Tooley interview.
18. Berman, "Veiled Prophet Fair," 15–17.
19. Ibid.
20. Henges interview.
21. Ibid.

22. The conclusion reached in this paragraph is based loosely on two works by John E. Bodnar, "Commemorative Activity in Twentieth-Century Indianapolis: The Invention of Civic Traditions," and "Commemoration in the City: Indianapolis and Cleveland," in Bodnar's *Remaking America: Public Memory, Commemoration, and Patriotism in the Twentieth Century.*
23. Berman, "Veiled Prophet Fair," 18; Tooley interview.
24. Rusty Hager interview.
25. Berman, "Veiled Prophet Fair," 18.
26. Jo Mannies, "Profits of Change: VP Fair Revises Name to Broaden Appeal—Riverfront Extravaganza Will Be Known as 'Fair St. Louis,'" *St. Louis Post-Dispatch,* September 24, 1994.
27. Rusty Hager interview; Henges interview.
28. Rusty Hager interview.
29. Henges interview.
30. Henges interview.
31. Berman, "Veiled Prophet Fair," 20.
32. Rusty Hager interview.
33. Ibid.
34. Molly Hager interview.
35. Rusty Hager interview.
36. Henges interview.
37. Ibid.
38. Green interview.
39. Henges interview.
40. "Crossroads: Group's Role under Scrutiny," *St. Louis Post-Dispatch,* August 4, 1991, 1, 14–15.

Conclusion: Whither VP? The Veiled Prophet Celebration and the Historiography of Public Celebrations in America

1. Roy Rosenzweig, *Eight Hours For What We Will: Workers and Leisure in an Industrial City,* 153–57, 171–72; and Francis G. Couvares, *The Remaking of Pittsburgh: Class and Culture in an Industrializing City, 1877–1920,* 65–73.
2. Bodnar, *Remaking America,* 13–20.
3. Ibid., 21–38.
4. Ryan, "American Parade," 149–50.
5. Michael E. McGerr, *The Decline of Popular Politics: The American North, 1865–1928,* 146–48; Bodnar, *Remaking America,* 92, 108–9.
6. McGerr, *Decline of Popular Politics,* 149.
7. For more on the St. Louis World's Fair, see Robert W. Rydell, *All the World's a Fair: Visions of Empire at American International Expositions, 1876–1916,* 154–83.
8. Bodnar, *Remaking America,* 174–75; see also Karal Ann Marling, *George Washington Slept Here: Colonial Revivals and American Culture, 1876–1986,* 325–64.
9. Bodnar, *Remaking America,* 126–37; "Minutes of the United States Territorial Expansion Memorial Commission," May 1, 1935, quoted in Bodnar, 189.
10. For more on the motives behind the Jefferson National Expansion Memorial, see Bodnar, *Remaking America,* 186–90.

11. Davis, "Veiled Prophet's Order," 16.
12. Wilson, "Aura of Veiled Prophet Fades."
13. Bodnar, *Remaking America,* 91–92, 108–9.
14. Mary Ryan, *Women in Public: Between Banners and Ballots, 1825–1880,* 11–12, 130–32, 175–76; see also Juergen Habermas, *The Structural Transformation of the Public Sphere: An Inquiry into a Category of Bourgeois Society,* 215–16.
15. Davis, *Parades and Power,* 166–73.

Bibliography

Archival Materials

Adams, Mrs. Wellington (Susie Slayback), Washington, D.C., to Mrs. G. R. Bartling (daughter), St. Louis, September 1934. VP/MHS.

Annual Report of the Saint Louis Merchants Exchange, 1878. MHS.

"Carnival of the Veiled Prophets." Reproduction of the carnival program from the first VP parade, [1878]. VP/MHS.

Davis, Allen Y. "The Veiled Prophet's Order: A Study of a Contemporary Social Organization." Study prepared for the Harvard University Anthropology Department, December 1946–January 1947. VP/MHS.

Eaton, Lucien, St. Louis, to Wife (not named), Iowa. Daily Letters of July 22–August 1, 1877. MHS.

"The Exposition Opening—Plans under Consideration for an Imposing Pageant." *St. Louis Times,* March 22, 1878. VP/MHS.

FBI, Memorandum, SAC, St. Louis to Director, FBI, June 19, 1970.

"Forty-seven Presidents while G. H. Morgan Served." *St. Louis Star,* 1911. In Walter B. Stevens scrapbook #84, pp. 88–89. MHS.

"His Mysterious Majesty the Veiled Prophet's Golden Jubilee: A Short History of St. Louis' Annual Civic Carnival." Pamphlet produced by the Veiled Prophet organization, in celebration of the fiftieth anniversary of the Veiled Prophet fair, 1928. VP/MHS.

"The Making of a Great Nation: Descriptive of the Gorgeous Veiled Prophet Pageant on Tuesday, October 7th." Pamphlet produced by the Veiled Prophet organization, 1930. VP/MHS.

"Minutes of the St. Louis Commercial Club." February 1, 1881, Constitution, Box 1, MHS.

Missouri Historical Society *Necrologies.* Volume and page number follow name: M. C. Humphrey (IV, 102), George M. Wright (C, 39), J. G. Butler (C, 1–4), Moses Fraley (X, 67, 68A), William Duncan (IX, 97), John Robb Holmes (XIII, 134; XI, 119), G. W. Chadbourne (I, 77), Charles D. Greene, Jr. (IIp, 29), Wallace Delafield (IIp, 73), Henry T. Kent (IIc, 245), Martin Collins (IIc, 226), Henry G. Paschall (IIc, 216), Joseph Franklin (IIc, 190), Rolla Billingsley (IIc, 63), John H. Reifsnyder (2b, 74), H. B. Loudermann (D, 42), and John Crangle (IIc, 63). MHS.

Satterfield, Ted, comp. "Royfax Copies of VP Information." 1879–1993. VP/MHS.

Sentner, William. "Origin of the Veiled Prophet." Press release. William Sentner Collection, Series 5, Box 6, Folder 4, Washington University Archives, St. Louis, Missouri.

Slayback, Alonzo W. Personal Diary of A. W. Slayback. Entries: October 25, 1879; October 1879; and December 1 and 9, 1879. VP/MHS.

Slayback, Charles E., Chicago, to Walter B. Stevens, St. Louis, July 20, 1916. VP/MHS.

Stevens, Walter B. "Notes of Walter B. Stevens on the Veiled Prophet." VP/MHS.

———. "Notes on Committee Meetings and Rules and Regulations of the Veiled Prophet Organization, 1878–1899." VP/MHS.

———. "Walter B. Stevens's Scrapbook." #84. MHS.

St. Louis Emergency Defense Committee. "The Veiled Prophet: How It Began." Leaflet printed by VP committee, October 1952. VP/MHS.

"Traditions of St. Louis: Description of the Gorgeous Veiled Prophet Pageant on Tuesday, October 8th, Also Announcing Contest for School Children." Pamphlet produced by the Veiled Prophet organization, 1929. VP/MHS.

VP Ball Invitation Collection. VP/MHS.

References

ACTION. *Why You Must Raise Hell—A Seven-Year Public Document Featuring ACTION's Scientific-Struggle against St. Louis' Institutional Elitism and Racism (1970 thru 1976).* St. Louis: ACTION, 1977.

Adler, Jeffrey S. *Yankee Merchants and the Making of the Urban West: The Rise and Fall of Antebellum St. Louis.* Cambridge: Cambridge University Press, 1991.

Bailey, Beth L. *From Front Porch to Back Seat: Courtship in Twentieth-Century America.* Baltimore: Johns Hopkins University Press, 1989.

Bakhtin, Mikhail. *Rabelais and His World.* Bloomington: Indiana University Press, 1984.

Baltzell, E. Digby. *Philadelphia Gentlemen: The Making of a National Upper Class.* Glencoe, Ill.: Free Press, 1958.

Barclay, Thomas S. *The St. Louis Home Rule Charter of 1876: Its Framing and Adoption.* Columbia: University of Missouri Press, 1962.

Beckner, Jeffrey. "Are the Rich Really Different from You and Me?" *St. Louis Magazine,* December 1985, 62–66.

Beezley, William H. "The Porfirian Smart Set Anticipates Thorstein Veblen in Guadalajara." In *Rituals of Rule, Rituals of Resistance: Public Celebrations and Popular Culture in Mexico.* Wilmington, Del.: Scholarly Resources, 1994.

"Behind the Scenes of Civic Progress." *St. Louis Commerce,* March 1990, 7–9.

Belcher, Wyatt. *The Economic Rivalry between St. Louis and Chicago, 1850–1880.* New York: Columbia Press, 1947.

Berman, Julie E. "From Veiled Prophet Fair to Fair St. Louis: The Remaking of a Culturally Contested Event." Paper presented at the Mid-America American Studies Association Conference, St. Louis, April 19, 1996.

Bernstein, Iver. *New York City Draft Riots.* New York: Oxford University Press, 1990.

"Big Thursday: Gala Days of the Old St. Louis Agricultural and Mechanical Association Fairs." *Missouri Historical Society Bulletin* 12, no. 1 (October 1955–1956): 45–52.

Bishop, Ed, and William H. Leckie. "Unveiling the Prophet: The Mysterious Origins of the Kingdom of Khorassan." *Riverfront Times,* June 17–23, 1987.

Bloom, Jack M. *Class, Race, and the Civil Rights Movement.* Bloomington: Indiana University Press, 1987.

Blumin, Stuart. *The Emergence of the Middle Class: Social Experience in the American City, 1760–1900.* Cambridge: Cambridge University Press, 1989.

Bodnar, John E. *Remaking America: Public Memory, Commemoration, and Patriotism in the Twentieth Century.* Princeton: Princeton University Press, 1992.

Burbank, David T. *Reign of the Rabble: The St. Louis General Strike of 1877.* New York: Sentry Press, 1966.

Campbell, R. A. "Campbell's Guide Map of St. Louis." St. Louis: Campbell Publishing, 1880.

Carnes, Mark C. *Secret Ritual and Manhood in Victorian America.* New Haven, Conn.: Yale University Press, 1989.

Chudacoff, Howard P. *The Evolution of Urban Society.* Englewood Cliffs, N.J.: Prentice-Hall, 1975.

Clawson, Mary Ann. *Constructing Brotherhood: Class, Gender, and Fraternalism.* Princeton, N.J.: Princeton University Press, 1989.

Cohen, Lizabeth. *Making a New Deal: Industrial Workers in Chicago, 1919–1939.* Cambridge: Cambridge University Press, 1990.

Compton, Richard J. *Veiled Prophet 6th Annual Autumn Festival Week Program.* St. Louis: Woodman and Tiernan Press, 1883.

Couvares, Francis G. *The Remaking of Pittsburgh: Class and Culture in an Industrializing City, 1877–1920.* Albany: SUNY Press, 1983.

Cronon, William. *Nature's Metropolis: Chicago and the Great West.* New York: Norton, 1991.

Dacus, John A. *Annals of the Great Strikes.* 1877. Reprint, New York: Arno Press, 1969.

Darst, Katherine. "The Prophet's Pearls." *St. Louis Magazine,* September 1963, 32.

Davis, Susan G. *Parades and Power: Street Theatre in Nineteenth-Century Philadelphia.* Philadelphia: Temple University Press, 1986.

"Description of the St. Louis Merchants Exchange Collection." *Missouri Historical Society Bulletin* 6, no. 1 (October 1949): 53–56.

Destler, Chester McArthur. *American Radicalism, 1865–1901: Essays and Documents.* New York: Octagon Books, 1965.

Dreiser, Theodore. *Journalism.* Vol. 1, *Newspaper Writing, 1892–1895.* Philadelphia: University of Pennsylvania Press, 1988.

Drew, John L., III. *The Veiled Prophet's Gifts: A Saint Louis Legacy: The Official Collector's Guide, 1878–1984.* St. Louis: Khorassan Press, 1985.

Dry, Camille, and Richard J. Compton. *Pictorial St. Louis—1875: A Topographical Survey Drawn in Perspective.* 1875. Reprint, St. Louis: Knight Publishing, 1971.

Dudar, Helen. "VP: Virgin Cult in Saint Louis." *Focus Midwest* 1 (June 1962): 22–24.

Dumenil, Lynn. *Freemasonry and American Culture, 1880–1930.* Princeton, N.J.: Princeton University Press, 1984.

Echols, Alice. *Daring to Be Bad: Radical Feminism in America, 1967–1975.* Minneapolis: University of Minnesota Press, 1989.

Feuer, Rosemary. "City Hall and the Unemployed Protests of the 1930s." In *The St. Louis Labor History Tour,* St. Louis: Bread and Roses, 1994.

———. "The Nutpickers' Union, 1933–34: Crossing the Boundaries of Community and Workplace." In *"We Are All Leaders": The*

Alternative Unionism of the Early 1930s, ed. Staughton Lynd. Chicago: University of Illinois Press, 1996.

Fink, Gary M. *Labor's Search for Political Order: The Political Behavior of the Missouri Labor Movement, 1890–1940.* Columbia: University of Missouri Press, 1973.

Foner, Philip S. *The Great Labor Uprising of 1877.* New York: Monad Press, 1977.

Fox, Richard Wightman, and T. J. Jackson Lears, eds. *The Culture of Consumption: Critical Essays in American History, 1880–1980.* New York: Pantheon Books, 1983.

Glassberg, David. *American Historical Pageantry: The Uses of Tradition in the Early Twentieth Century.* Chapel Hill: University of North Carolina Press, 1990.

Goering, Karen McCoskey. "Pageantry in St. Louis: The History of the Veiled Prophet Organization." *Gateway Heritage: Quarterly Journal of the Missouri Historical Society* 4 (spring 1984): 2–16.

Gould, David B. *Gould's City Directory of St. Louis.* 1878, 1890, 1899, 1914, 1919, 1930, 1935, 1940.

Griffith, Robert. *The Politics of Fear: Joseph R. McCarthy and the Senate.* Lexington: University Press of Kentucky, 1970.

Gutman, Herbert G. *Work, Culture, and Society in Industrializing America: Essays in American Working-Class and Social History.* New York: Knopf, 1976.

Guttman, Allen, and Benjamin Munn Ziegler, eds. *Communism, the Courts, and the Constitution.* Boston: D. C. Heath, 1964.

Habermas, Juergen. *The Structural Transformation of the Public Sphere: An Inquiry into a Category of Bourgeois Society.* Cambridge: MIT Press, 1989.

Haines, Herbert H. *Black Radicals and the Civil Rights Mainstream, 1954–1970.* Knoxville: University of Tennessee Press, 1988.

Hart, Jim Allee. *A History of the St. Louis Globe-Democrat.* Columbia: University of Missouri Press, 1961.

Hyde, William, and Howard L. Conard. *Encyclopedia of St. Louis History.* New York, Louisville: The Southern History Company, 1899.

Jaher, Frederic C. "Nineteenth Century Elites in Boston and New York." *Journal of Social History* 6 (fall 1972): 32–77.

Johns, Orrick. *Time of Our Lives: The Story of My Father and Myself.* New York: Stackpole and Sons, 1937.

Kargau, E. D. *Mercantile, Industrial, and Professional St. Louis.* St. Louis: Nixon-Jones Printing, 1902.

Kelleher, Daniel T. "St. Louis' 1916 Residential Segregation Ordinance." *Missouri Historical Society Bulletin* 26:239–248.

Kelley, Robin D. G. *Race Rebels: Culture, Politics, and the Black Working Class.* New York: Free Press, 1996.

Kinser, Sam. *Carnival, American Style: Mardi Gras at New Orleans and Mobile.* Chicago: University of Chicago Press, 1990.

Kirschten, Ernest. *Catfish and Crystal.* Garden City, N.Y.: Doubleday and Company, 1960.

La Cour, Arthur B. *New Orleans Masquerade: Chronicles of Carnival.* New Orleans: Pelican Publishing Company, 1952.

Landau, Leo. *The Big Cinch: A Society and Financial Novel.* St. Louis: Franklin, 1910.

Lears, T. J. Jackson. "The Concept of Cultural Hegemony: Problems and Possibilities." *American Historical Review* 90 (June 1985), 567–93.

Lionsberger, L. H. *The Annals of St. Louis, 1764–1928.* St. Louis: Missouri Historical Society, 1929.

Lipsitz, George. *A Life in the Struggle: Ivory Perry and the Culture of Opposition.* Philadelphia: Temple University Press, 1988.

———. *The Sidewalks of St. Louis: Places, People, and Politics in an American City.* Columbia: University of Missouri Press, 1991.

Lobbia, J. A. "What's $650,000 among Friends?" *Riverfront Times,* June 17–23, 1987, 1A and 6A.

Marable, Manning. *Race, Reform, and Rebellion: The Second Reconstruction in Black America, 1945–1982.* Jackson: University Press of Mississippi, 1984.

Marling, Karal Ann. *George Washington Slept Here: Colonial Revivals and American Culture, 1876–1986.* Cambridge: Harvard University Press, 1988.

McConachie, Scott. "The Big Cinch: A Business Elite in the Life of a City, St. Louis, 1895–1915." Ph.D. diss., Washington University, 1976.

McGerr, Michael E. *The Decline of Popular Politics: The American North, 1865–1928.* New York: Oxford University Press, 1986.

McIntyre, Stephen L. "Hegelian Reformers and Labor Radicals: The St. Louis Workingmen's Party and the School Board Election of 1877." Master's thesis, University of Missouri–Columbia, 1989.

Meier, August, and Elliott Rudwick. *CORE: A Study in the Civil Rights Movement, 1942–1968.* New York: Oxford University Press, 1973.

The Mirror, ed. William Marion Reedy, 1895–1920.

Moore, Thomas. *Lalla Rookh: An Oriental Romance.* 1816. Reprint, New York: Frederick A. Stokes and Brother, 1890.

Oster, Donald Bright. "Community Image in the History of St. Louis and Kansas City." Ph.D. diss., University of Missouri–Columbia, 1969.

———. "Nights of Fantasy: The St. Louis *Pageant and Masque* of 1914." *Missouri Historical Society Bulletin* 21:175–205.

The Pageant and Masque of St. Louis. Bulletin no. 1 of the St. Louis Pageant Drama Association, February 1914.

Pencilstubs, Peter [pseud.]. *The Veiled Prophets Unveiled.* St. Louis: John J. Jennings, 1881.

Piott, Steven L. "Modernization and the Anti-Monopoly Issue: The St. Louis Transit Strike of 1900." *Missouri History Society Bulletin* 35 (1): 3–16.

Primm, James Neal. *Lion of the Valley.* Boulder, Colo.: Pruett Publishing Company, 1981.

Putzel, Max. *The Man in the Mirror: William Marion Reedy and His Magazine.* Cambridge: Harvard University Press, 1963. Reprint, Columbia: University of Missouri Press, 1998.

Ralph, James. *Northern Protest: Martin Luther King, Jr., Chicago, and the Civil Rights Movement.* Cambridge: Harvard University Press, 1993.

Rammelkamp, Julian S. *Pulitzer's Post-Dispatch, 1878–1883.* Princeton: Princeton University Press, 1967.

Reavis, Logan Uriah. *Saint Louis: The Future Great City of the World.* St. Louis: Gray, Baker and Company, 1875; reprint, 1882.

Reedy, William Marion, ed. *The Makers of St. Louis.* St. Louis: Mirror, 1906.

Roediger, David R. "America's First General Strike: The St. Louis 'Commune' of 1877." *Midwest Quarterly* 21 (winter 1980): 196–206.

———. "Not Only the Ruling Classes to Overcome, but Also the So-called Mob: Class, Skill, and Community in the St. Louis General Strike of 1877." *Journal of Social History* 19 (winter 1985): 213–39.

Rosenzweig, Roy. *Eight Hours for What We Will: Workers and Leisure in an Industrial City.* Cambridge: Cambridge University Press, 1983.

Rowan, Steven, and James Neal Primm. *Germans for a Free Missouri:*

Translations from the St. Louis Radical Press, 1857–1862. Columbia: University of Missouri Press, 1983.

Ryan, Mary. "The American Parade: Representations of the Nineteenth-Century Social Order." In *The New Cultural History: Essays,* ed. Lynn Hunt. Berkeley and Los Angeles: University of California Press, 1989.

———. *Women in Public: Between Banners and Ballots, 1825–1880.* Baltimore: Johns Hopkins University Press, 1990.

Rydell, Robert W. *All the World's a Fair: Visions of Empire at American International Expositions, 1876–1916.* Chicago: University of Chicago Press, 1984.

Said, Edward. *Orientalism.* New York: Pantheon Books, 1978.

Sanders, Vincent H., and Theodore D. Drury Jr. *The Story of the Veiled Prophet.* St. Louis: Sanders and Drury, 1956.

Scharf, J. Thomas. *History of Saint Louis City and County.* 2 vols. Philadelphia: Louis H. Everts and Co., 1883.

Schmidt, Elizabeth Noel. "Civic Pride and Prejudice: St. Louis Progressive Reform, 1900–1916." Master's thesis, Washington University, 1986.

Schnell, J. Christopher. "Chicago versus St. Louis: A Reassessment of the Great Rivalry." *Missouri Historical Review* (April 1977): 245–65.

Scott, James C. *Domination and the Arts of Resistance: Hidden Transcripts.* New Haven: Yale University Press, 1990.

Smith, Charlotte. "Charles E. Slayback." *The Inland Monthly,* 3 (March 1873): 125–27.

Sneddeker, Duane R. "Regulating Vice: Prostitution and the St. Louis Social Evil Ordinance, 1870–1874" *Gateway Heritage* 10 (fall 1990): 20–47.

Spencer, Thomas. "Knights for Revenue Only: The Origins of the Veiled Prophet Organization in St. Louis, 1877–1880." Master's thesis, University of Missouri–Columbia, 1992.

———. "Power on Parade: The Origins of the Veiled Prophet Organization in St. Louis, 1877–1878" *Gateway Heritage: The Quarterly Journal of the Missouri Historical Society in St. Louis,* December 1993, 38–53.

Stevens, Walter B. *St. Louis, the Fourth City, 1764–1911.* Vol. 2. St. Louis: S. J. Clarke Publishing Company, 1911.

———. *St. Louis, the Fourth City, 1764–1909.* Vol. 3. Chicago: S. J. Clarke Publishing Company, 1909.

————. *St. Louis: One Hundred Years in a Week: Celebration of the Centennial of Incorporation, October 3-9, 1909.* St. Louis: Woodward and Tiernan Printing Company, 1910.

————. "The Veiled Prophet Appeared in St. Louis in 1878." *American Woman's Review,* September 1909, 21–31.

St. Louis American, December 13, 1973.

St. Louis Argus, 1914–1966.

St. Louis Evening Post [became *St. Louis Post-Dispatch* in December 1878], October 7, 8, and 9, 1878.

St. Louis Globe-Democrat, 1878–1979.

St. Louis Globe-Democrat Magazine, July 20, 1981.

St. Louis Jewish Light, vols. 1–26, 1947–1973.

St. Louis Labor [became *St. Louis Progressive News* in 1930], 1893–1930.

St. Louis Missouri Republican [became *St. Louis Republic* after 1892], 1878–1899.

St. Louis Post-Dispatch [formerly *St. Louis Evening Post*], 1882–1994.

St. Louis Progressive News [formerly *St. Louis Labor*], 1930–1932.

St. Louis Star-Times, October 6, 1932; October 3, 1949; October 2, 1950.

St. Louis Times, January 8–9, 1979.

Stowe, Steven M. *Intimacy and Power in the Old South: Ritual in the Lives of the Planters.* Baltimore: Johns Hopkins Press, 1987.

Thelen, David. *Paths of Resistance: Tradition and Democracy in Industrializing Missouri.* Columbia: University of Missouri Press, 1991.

Thornton, J. Mills. "Comment." In *The Civil Rights Movement in America,* ed. Charles Eagles. Jackson: University of Mississippi Press, 1986.

Tracy, Walter P. *Men Who Make St. Louis the City of Opportunity.* St. Louis: Con P. Curran Printing Co., [1915].

————. *St. Louis Leadership.* St. Louis: Con P. Curran Printing Co., 1944.

United States Biographical Dictionary and Portrait Gallery of Eminent and Self-Made Men, Missouri Volume. New York: U.S. Biographical Publishing Co., 1878.

Veblen, Thorstein. *The Theory of the Leisure Class: An Economic Study of Institutions.* New York: Random House, 1934 (original publication date: 1899).

"Veiled Prophet Unveiled by *Review: Post* and *Globe* Withhold Identity." *St. Louis Journalism Review,* January 1973.

"VP Fair, 1981–1990: America's Biggest Birthday Party." Souvenir Program and Magazine for 1990 VP Fair. St. Louis: VP Fair Foundation, 1990.

Wilensky, Harry. *The Story of the Post-Dispatch.* St. Louis: St. Louis Post-Dispatch, n.d.

World's Fair Bulletin, vol. 2 no. 8. St. Louis: World's Fair Publishing Company, 1901.

Wyatt-Brown, Bertram. *Southern Honor: Ethics and Behavior in the Old South.* New York: Oxford University Press, 1982.

Yeakle, Mahlon M. *St. Louis of Today.* St. Louis: J. Osmun Yeakle and Company, 1889.

Young, Dina M. "Broadway and Washington: 'Washington Avenue Massacre' and the 1900 Streetcar Strike." In *The St. Louis Labor History Tour.* St. Louis: Bread and Roses, 1994.

———. "The Streetcar Strike of 1900: Pivotal Politics at the Century's Dawn." *Gateway Heritage* 12 (summer 1991): 4–17.

Zunz, Olivier. *Making America Corporate, 1870–1920.* Chicago: University of Chicago Press, 1990.

Index